CALVIN'S DOCTRINE
OF THE
WORD AND SACRAMENT

TO MY WIFE

CALVIN'S DOCTRINE
OF THE
WORD AND SACRAMENT

RONALD S. WALLACE

SCOTTISH ACADEMIC PRESS
EDINBURGH

Published by
Scottish Academic Press Ltd.
56 Hanover Street
Edinburgh EH2 2DX

© 1995 Ronald S. Wallace

First published UK 1953
First published USA 1955
Book Club Edition 1957
Paperback Edition 1983
This Edition 1995

ISBN 0 7073 0747 3

British Library Cataloguing in Publication data

A catalogue record of this book is available from the British Library

Printed by Martins The Printers, Berwick upon Tweed.

PREFACE

This book is the result of some years of study begun when I was asked to prepare two separate papers for the *Scottish Church Theology Society*, one on Calvin's doctrine of Scripture and the other on his doctrine of the Lord's Supper. In the course of study it became clear that these doctrines can be properly understood only when each is viewed in close connection with the other and in the context of Calvin's whole conception of the nature of Biblical revelation as given through word and sign. Account had also to be taken of Calvin's Christology and his teaching on the nature of our union with Christ, since these latter doctrines are also decisive in the formation of his thought on everything that relates to the Word and Sacrament. All these considerations have determined the scope of this work.

Since Calvin is above all a Biblical scholar, his thought can very profitably be studied by reference to his *Commentaries*, where it is often given most interesting and varied expression. Therefore it has been the aim of this work to show how the particular doctrines under review arise for Calvin out of his exposition of the Bible, and though the *Institutes, Tracts* and *Sermons* have not been neglected, the main source from which quotations have been taken has been his *Commentaries*.

No attempt has been made to trace in detail the historical development of Calvin's thought in the midst of the various sacramental controversies in which he was involved. These controversies, though they coloured and moulded his thought to some extent, and determined the theological language he was bound to use, served only to drive him back to the Bible for confirmation and inspiration. It is hoped, therefore, that this book will be of value not only to those who wish to study Calvin's sacramental doctrines, but also to those whose main interest is Bible study. Accordingly, references have been given in the footnotes not only to the volume and page of the *Corpus Reformatorum*, but also, where possible, to the Biblical passages which gave rise to Calvin's comments.

Many of the English quotations have been taken from the various older translations of Calvin's works, especially those of the *Calvin*

Translation Society (Edinburgh, 1843–55). Constant reference has been made to the *Ioannis Calvini Opera* in the *Corpus Reformatorum* (edited by G. Baum, E. Cunitz and E. Reuss, Brunswick, 1863–1900), and A. Tholuck's edition of the *Institutio Christianae Religionis* (Berlin, 1846). The *Opera Selecta*, edited by P. Barth and W. Niesel (Münich, 1926–36), has also been used. Expressions in the English translations have been altered when necessary, to make them either less archaic or more accurate. The Latin and French of the original work have been cited whenever this might add interest, or clarify the meaning for the student, or serve those who wish to compare Calvin's use of similar terms in different contexts.

I have been greatly encouraged by the cordial reception of my book, *Calvin, Geneva and the Reformation* (1985), and I have recently received several requests that I should make this book on *The Word and Sacrament*, which is at present being translated into Korean, again available to English readers. I have to thank the Hope Trust for their generous help to do this.

R. S. Wallace
Edinburgh 1995

CONTENTS

Chapter I

Revelation under the Old Covenant

1. The impossibility of direct revelation

ACCORDING to Calvin, the great barrier to the possibility of revelation taking place between God and man is the intervening gulf created on the one hand by the holiness and majesty of God and on the other hand by the sinfulness and feebleness of man.[1] There can be no "direct communication" between God and man. "The divine nature is infinitely exalted above the comprehension of our understanding."[2] So great is God's majesty that for man to be faced with the task of comprehending God as He is in Himself "this would be to measure with the palm of his hands a hundred thousand heavens and earths and worlds. For God is infinite; and when the heaven of heavens cannot contain Him, how can our minds comprehend Him?"[3] Moreover, so destructive of all that is evil is the holiness of God that sinful man in direct contact with Him would be "brought to nothing by the incomprehensible brightness".[4] The glory of God, contemplated alone by man, could only fill the beholder with despair.[5] "If the angels are majestic in their appearance to men, how will it be when God appears in His glory? For the light of the majesty of the glory of God is not only as the brightness of the sun, but is greater than ten thousand suns."[6] Therefore "should God institute no medium of intercourse, and call us to a direct communication with heaven, the great distance at which we stand from Him would strike us with

---

[1]Cf. Inst. 2 : 16 : 3. *Atqui si perpetuum et irreconciliabile dissiduum est inter iustitiam et iniquitatem.*

[2]Comm. on Ps. 86 : 8, C.R. 31 : 749.

[3]Comm. on Ezek. 1 : 28, C.R. 40 : 60.

[4]Comm. on Exod. 33 : 20, C.R. 25 : 111. *Ille incomprehensibilis fulgor in nihilum nos redigat.* Cf. Comm. on 1 Pet. 1 : 20, C.R. 55 : 226–7. *Quod si appropinquamus iustitia eius instar ignis est, qui nos penitus consumat.*

[5]Comm. on Heb. 4 : 16, C.R. 55 : 55.

[6]Serm. on Acts 1 : 9–11, C.R. 48 : 615.

dismay and paralyse invocation".[1] How then, asks Calvin, can
man come to know God? "If the angels tremble at God's glory,
if they vail themselves with their wings, what should we do
who creep upon this earth?"[2] "For if the mountains melt at the
sight of Him, what must needs happen to mortal man, than
whom there is nothing more frail and feeble?"[3]

It is to be noted that, in his exposition of the Old Testament,
when Calvin comes to the discussion of those passages which
speak of man as having "seen God", he almost invariably points
out that such phrases should not be interpreted to mean that
they saw God "as He really is", but only "as far as He can be
beheld by mortal man".[4] "Thus in ancient times God appeared
to the Holy fathers, not as He is in Himself but so far as they
could endure the rays of His infinite brightness."[5] "When God
exhibited Himself to the view of the fathers, He never appeared
such as He actually is, but such as the capacity of men could
perceive."[6] God, in revealing Himself to man, has to transform
Himself by covering over that in Himself which man by reason
of his sinfulness cannot bear to see, and by modifying that in
Himself which man's mind is too small to grasp.

2. God, in revealing Himself, adapts Himself
to the capacity of man

The gulf between God and man can be bridged.   In this
impossible situation in which man cannot bear that God as He

---

[1]Comm. on Ps. 132 : 8, C.R. 32 : 346. *Nam si Deus nullo medio interposito,
recta nos in coelum vocet, quia nobis horrorem incutit longa distantia, friget
invocationis tudium.* Cf. Serm. on 1 Tim. 2 : 5–6, C.R. 53 : 163–4. *Venons-
nous donc devant Dieu? Si nous ne contemplons que ceste haute maiesté et incomprehensible qui est en luy, c'est pour nous espovanter, il faut que nous soyons confus,
et qu'un chacun recule : et mesmes que plustost nous desirions que les montagnes
nous couvrent, et nous accablent, que de sentir la presence de Dieu.*

[2]Comm. on Ezek. 1 : 28, C.R. 40 : 60.

[3]Comm. on Exod. 24 : 11, C.R. 25 : 77; cf. on Ezek. 11 : 4, and Inst. 1 : 1 : 3.

[4]Comm. on Ezek. 1 : 28, C.R. 40 : 60.

[5]Comm. on Matt. 17 : 2, C.R. 45 : 485. *Sic olim Deus sanctis patribus
apparuit, non qualis in se erat, sed quatenus immensi eius splendoris radios ferre
poterant.*

[6]Comm. on Isa. 6 : 1, C.R. 36 : 126. *Quoties se patribus spectandum praebuit
Deus, nunquam apparuisse qualis est, sed qualis hominum sensu capi poterat.*
Cf. Serm. on Deut. 4 : 32–5, C.R. 26 : 206. *Il est dit, que les montagnes
decoulent devant son regard. Il est dit que si seulement il iette l'oeil sur toute la
terre qu'elle tremblera : car la maieste de Dieu en soy est si espouvantable, que ce
seroit pour abysmer tout le monde.*

is in Himself should confront him, there is a true revelation of the nature of the holy and incomprehensible God given to men, through a miracle of grace—God's "incomparable lenity whereby in manifesting Himself to His elect, He does not altogether absorb and reduce them to nothing".[1] God *can* reveal Himself so that man, without being annihilated or brought to despair, can come really to know and enter communion with Him. Moreover, so full and satisfying is the revelation thus given that man can indeed be said to see God "face to face".

This miracle of "incomparable lenity" takes place in an act through which God belittles Himself, and takes upon Himself such a lowly form or disguise as can appeal to the capacity of man and give indication to the dull human mind of the glory and mystery of Him who has come in this form. God, says Calvin frequently, "assumes a form we are able to bear".[2] "As we cannot attain to that infinite height to which He is exalted, in descending among us by the exercise of His power and grace, He appears as near as is needful, and as our limited capacity will bear."[3] He, as it were, veils Himself in earthly symbols, placing before the vision of men certain signs which can indicate to the humble and believing mind that He is present. Such symbols and signs at the same time indirectly represent His hidden being and convey what He has to say to man at that moment of revelation. The Old Testament fathers saw the God of Israel "not in all His reality and greatness, but in accordance with the dispensation which He thought best, and which He

---

[1]Comm. on Exod. 24 : 11, C.R. 25 : 77. *In eo igitur se prodit incomparabilis Dei clementia, dum se electis suis manifestans, non prorsus eos absorbet, ac in nihilum redigit.*

Cf. Serm. on Deut. 4 : 32–5, C.R. 26 : 206. *Quand il parle il faut que sa voix non seulement espouvante toutes creatures, mais qu'elle les rend confuses du tout, iusques à les aneantir. C'est donc un grand miracle, quand les hommes mortels qui sont tant fragiles et caduques, qui ne sont rien du tout qu'un ombrage, qu'ils peuvent ouir la voix de Dieu, et que cependant ils n'en soyent point consommez.*

[2]Cf. Serm. on John 1 : 1–5, C.R. 47 : 469. "If we heard God speaking to us in His majesty, it would be useless to us, for we would understand nothing. Therefore, since we are carnal, He has to stutter or otherwise He would not be understood by us."

Cf. Serm. on Deut. 4 : 36–8, C.R. 26 : 212. *Dieu s'abbaisse a nostre infirmité . . . il condescend a nostre petitesse . . . Dieu s'accommode a nostre rudesse.* Cf. also Serm. on Job 1 : 6–8, C.R. 33 : 62–3. *Il se conforme a nous . . . il se rend familier, il est comme transfiguré.*

[3]Comm. on Ps. 78 : 60, C.R. 31 : 741.

accommodated to the capacity of man."[1] God never gave them a sight of Himself "except according to their capacity. He always had respect to their faculties."[2] "Under symbols which were adapted to the capacity of the flesh, He enabled them to taste in part what could not be fully apprehended."[3] Speaking, in particular, of the revelation given to Moses at the burning bush, Calvin writes, "I indeed allow, that Moses was strengthened in his faith by that vision . . . but I do not admit that it was such a view of God, as divested him of his bodily senses, and transferred him beyond the trials of this world. God at that time only shewed him a certain symbol of His presence; but he was far from seeing God as He is."[4]

This symbolic form which God takes upon Himself in the act of revealing Himself can be thought of as a veil through the putting on of which the light of the glory of God is obscured yet nevertheless transmitted to the beholder. In coming to commune with men behind such symbolic forms, God covers over that in Himself which would bring the human subject to nothing. Calvin can speak of Christ as showing Himself "under coverings (*sub involucris*)" in the "obscure revelation" of the Law.[5] He can speak of God as "attempering the amount of light to our capacity".[6] He can also liken revelation to an oblique, in contrast to a direct, illumination. "As one who is shut up in a deep and obscure place, may receive some advantage from the light, yet never see the sun itself nor enjoy its brightness, thus we imprisoned as it were in our bodies, cannot behold God's glory

---

[1]Comm. on Exod. 24 : 9, C.R. 25 : 76–7. *Non qualis et quantus est, sed pro modo dispensationis, quem ipse optimum statuit, et quem attemperavit ad captum hominum.*

[2]Comm. on Ezek. 1 : 28, C.R. 40 : 60. . . . *nisi pro ipsorum modulo. Semper enim respexit qualis esset eorum facultas.*

[3]Comm. on Matt. 17 : 2, C.R. 45 : 485–6. *Symbolis, quae carnis modulo congruerent, ex parte gustandum praebuit, quod in totum percipi nondum poterat.*
Cf. Serm. on Job 1 : 6–8, C.R. 33 : 57. *Il faut donc que Dieu descende pour estre comprins de nous, c'est a dire, qu'l ne se monstre point selon sa gloire, qui est infinie, mais selon qu'il voit quel est nostre sens, qu'il s'y accommode.*

[4]Comm. on Heb. 11 : 27, C.R. 55 : 163. . . . *Nego talem fuisse Dei conspectum, qui eum exueret sensu carnis, et extra mundi pericula educeret. Signum duntaxat quoddam praesentiae suae tunc illi Deus ostendit : sed multum abfuit quin Deum, qualis est, videret.*

[5]Comm. on Heb. 2 : 1, C.R. 55 : 21.

[6]Comm. on Exod. 33 : 20, C.R. 25 : 111. *Imo lucis mensuram nostro modulo attemperans.*

freely and directly. He illuminates us obliquely, so that at least we see Him from behind."[1]

3. Revelation as mediated through signs and symbols

It is for this reason, then, that whenever we read of God as appearing to men or being present with men in the Old Testament we always find that it is really something other than God that appears, as a sign that God is there. This sign or symbol of God's presence holds the attention of the worshipper and obscures the glory of the One who is seeking to reveal Himself by means of it. Calvin calls the Ark and the Burning Bush "symbols of the presence of God",[2] but this term can also be applied to the cloud and smoke and flame and other accompanying phenomena of Old Testament revelation.[3] These too are regarded as "symbols of celestial glory" and as veils behind which God stands in communicating Himself to men. The ceremonies ordained for the temple, too, are forms in which God wraps Himself up in order that He may reveal Himself. Referring to the ancient fathers, Calvin says in one place, "They did not see God in any other way than wrapped up in many folds."[4]

The symbol by which God signifies His presence need not be a concrete earthly object. God can symbolise His presence equally well by means of a vision or a dream. In his commentary on Isaiah's vision in the temple Calvin refers to the forms seen there by the prophet as a "token of God's presence".[5] "The word vision," he says elsewhere, "signifies a certain symbol which was set before the eyes to testify God's presence."[6] The opening of the heavens in Matthew 3 : 16 is referred to as a

[1]Comm. on Exod. 33 : 21, C.R. 25 : 111. . . . . *Nos oblique irradiat, ut eum saltem quasi a tergo videamus.*
[2]Cf. e.g. comm. on Ps. 84 : 7, C.R. 31 : 783; on Ps. 132 : 8, C.R. 32 : 346.
[3]Cf. Inst. 1 : 11 : 3, comm. on Ps. 99 : 6 f., C.R. 32 : 53. In comm. on Ps. 81 : 7, C.R. 31 : 762, Calvin calls the thunder "an evident indication of God's secret presence".
[4]Comm. on John 1 : 8, C.R. 47 : 19. *Deum non videbant nisi multis involucris obtectum.* Cf. on Ps. 74 : 4, C.R. 31 : 693.
[5]Comm. on Isa. 6 : 1, C.R. 36 : 126.
[6]Comm. on Acts 9 : 10, C.R. 48 : 205. *Visio hic significat symbolum aliquod oculis obiectum ad testandam Dei praesentiam.*

"symbol of the divine presence". God can also with equal effect use the forms seen in dreams in order to reveal Himself to men.[1] All these phenomena are for Calvin the forms in which God veils Himself in order to reveal Himself. They are the shapes He assumes in order to convey H's life and His word to men who cannot grasp the mystery of His being or bear His presence in any other form. To the men of the Old Testament God is described as speaking in "various and manifold modes".[2] The symbolic form which God most frequently assumes throughout the course of Old Testament revelation is, however, the form of the angel of the Lord who appears as the one to convey God's message and to represent His person at certain critical moments in the history of the patriarchs, prophets and people. Of the appearance of this angel to Moses Calvin writes, "It was necessary that He should assume a visible form, that He might be seen by Moses, not as He was in His essence but as the infirmity of the human mind could comprehend Him. For thus we must believe that God, as often as He appeared of old to the holy patriarchs, descended in some way from His majesty, that He might reveal Himself as far as was useful and as far as their comprehension would admit."[3]

---

[1]Cf. comm. on Gen. 28 : 12, C.R. 23 : 390. "When mention is made of a dream no doubt that mode of revelation is signified, which the Lord formerly was wont to adopt towards His servants" (Num. 12 : 6). Dreams through which revelation took place were "impressed with a divine seal" to give the minds of the subject a certainty which ordinary dreams did not have. Cf. comm. on Gen. 28 : 12, on Matt. 1 : 20, on Acts 10 : 3.

[2]Comm. on Heb. 1 : 1, C.R. 55 : 9.

[3]Comm. on Exod. 3 : 2, C.R. 24 : 35. . . . *descendisse quodammodo ex sua altitudine, ut illis se patefaceret quatenus utile erat, et ferebat eorum captus.*

Calvin shows a fascinating realism, and goes into rather daring speculation, in his comments on the appearances of angels to men in the Bible. They are sometimes called men, but "we ought not to believe them to be really men. Christ indeed was really man. . . . But as regards angels, God clothes them for a day or short period in bodies for a distinct purpose and special use" (comm. on Dan. 10 : 5–6, C.R. 41 : 198). After discussing the eating of fish by the risen Jesus, Calvin comments: "Thus the angels at the table of Abraham (Gen. 18 : 1), having been clothed with real bodies, did actually, I have no doubt, eat and drink, but yet I do not admit that the meat and drink yielded them . . . refreshment. If we acknowledge that the bodies which they assumed for a time were reduced to nothing after they had discharged their embassy who will deny that the same thing happened as to the food?" (comm. on Luke 24 : 43, C.R. 45 : 815). Calvin does not insist that they were always clothed with real bodies, however. "To me it is enough that the Lord gave them a human shape so that the women might see them" (comm. on John 20 : 12, C.R. 47 : 431). This is all done "on account of the ignorance of men" (ibid).

4. Revelation as veiling and unveiling

To sum up Calvin's teaching on this matter we can say that there takes place when God reveals Himself a veiling and an unveiling. In all revelation there is a veiling. Calvin is never weary of repeating that God covers over His face when He reveals Himself. The Scripture speaks loosely and comparatively when it says that men saw God *face to face*. Even Moses, though his vision of God was vastly superior to that of Jacob, "did not so perfectly see God such as He is in Himself, but so far as the human mind is capable of bearing"[1]—and according to Calvin the capacity of the human mind in this respect, even assisted by grace, is small. Even although the angels "see God's face in a more excellent manner than men, still they do not apprehend the immense perfection of His glory, whereby they would be absorbed".[2] But in this very act of veiling Himself God unveils Himself. What is known through such a veiled revelation, when man is thus confronted by God, really corresponds to what is there to be known, had man only the capacity to see it "more directly". It is no exaggeration to say that Isaiah in the temple saw the glory of God. "Though men may be said to creep on the ground, or at least dwell far below the heavens, there is no absurdity in supposing that God comes down to them in such a manner as to cause some kind of mirror to reflect the rays of His glory. There was, therefore, exhibited to Isaiah such a form as enabled him, according to his capacity, to perceive the inconceivable majesty of God. . . . Hence we learn the profitable doctrine that whenever God grants any token of His presence, He is undoubtedly present with us, for He does not amuse us by unmeaning shapes. . . . Since, therefore, the exhibition was no deceitful representation of the presence of God, Isaiah justly declares that he *saw Him*. . . . In the representation there is no deception."[3] Calvin admits that his state-

---

[1]Comm. on Exod. 33 : 20, C.R. 25 : 111.
[2]Comm. on Exod. 33 : 20, C.R. 25 : 111.
[3]Comm. on Isa. 6 : 1, C.R. 36 : 126. *Quia ergo species minime fallax Dei praesentis symbolum fuit, eum se vidisse merito affirmat Isaias. . . . In repraesentatione nulla erat fallacia.*
Cf. serm. on Deut. 4 : 11–14, C.R. 26 : 140. *Cognoissons donc que Dieu ne veut point estre incogneu des hommes : mais il se veut manifester en sorte, que nous sachions discerner entre luy et les idoles qui ont este forgees, que nous le tenions pour*

ments on this subject seem paradoxical. There seems to be a contradiction between these two things, that the beauty of God should be shown to Moses, and still that the sight of Him should be refused, but he is never weary of emphasising both sides of the paradox. "Although God has never appeared in His immeasurable glory and has never manifested Himself as He really exists, yet we must nevertheless hold that He has so appeared as to leave no doubt in the minds of His servants as to their knowing that they have seen God."[1]

5. Christ as the Mediator of all revelation

The Mediator of all revelation between God and man in the Old Testament is the Word of God, the second Person of the Trinity, the same Christ who became incarnate in Jesus of Nazareth. Throughout the whole national history of Israel, it was always He, the Son of God, who dealt with His people in judgement and mercy, bringing them, with His Presence in their midst, light and life and salvation. Calvin asserts positively that Christ, the Word of God, who "remains with God perpetually one and the same and who is God Himself",[2] was "always the bond of connection between God and man",[3] and "the source of all revelations",[4] being "always present in all the oracles".[5] He is equally emphatic in the frequent negative assertion, "Never did God reveal Himself outside of Christ".[6] "Nor indeed, had any of the saints ever any communication with God except through the promised Mediator."[7] "God formerly manifested Himself in no other way than through

nostre pere, que nous sachions que nous avons este appellez à la cognoissance de sa verite, et comme nous pouvons venir a luy en pleine hardiesse pour l'invoquer, et avoir nostre refuge à luy.
[1]Comm. on Ezek. 1 : 28, C.R. 40 : 60. . . . Tenendum nihilominus sic apparuisse, ut nihil dubitationis relinqueret servis suis, quin scirent se Deum vidisse.
[2]Inst. 1 : 13 : 7.
[3]Comm. on Gen. 48 : 15, C.R. 23 : 584. Semper vinculum fuit coniunctionis hominum cum Deo.
[4]Inst. 1 : 13 : 7. Oraculorum omnium scaturiginem.
[5]Comm. on Gen. 16 : 10, C.R. 23 : 228. Christum mediatorem semper omnibus oraculis praefuisse.
[6]Comm. on John 5 : 23, C.R. 47 : 115. Nunquam tamen citra Christum se patefecit Deus.
[7]Comm. on Exod. 3 : 2, C.R. 24 ; 35–6.

Him."[1] God never otherwise revealed Himself to the Fathers "but in His eternal Word and only begotten Son".[2] The whole story of the Old Testament is thus the story of how Christ, the Word of God, breaks in upon the life of those whom He has chosen to make His people, and confronts them in these veiled forms through which they can come to know His nature and have communion with Him. "When God, therefore, delivered His people from the hand of Pharaoh, when He made a way for them to pass through the Red Sea, when He redeemed them by doing wonders, when He subdued before them the most powerful nations, when He changed the laws of nature on their behalf —all these things He did through the Mediator. For God could not have been propitious either to Abraham himself or to his posterity, had it not been for the intervention of a Mediator."[3]

The frequent appearance of the "Angel of the Lord" as the representative of God to the Old Testament Fathers, and as a guide of the people throughout their history is a sign that Christ is always fulfilling His Mediatoral office of saviour and revealer, and uniting even then the members of His Church to Himself as the Head through whom they are joined to God Himself. Calvin, following the "orthodox doctors"[4] on this point, identifies the "chief angel" who appears among the other angelic visitors to earth with "God's only begotten Son who was afterwards manifest in the flesh".[5] Even then He performed in a preliminary fashion "some services introductory to His execution of the office of Mediator".[6] "There is then no wonder," says Calvin, "that the Prophet should indiscriminately call Him Angel and Jehovah, He being the Mediator of the Church and also God. He is God, being of the same essence with the Father; and Mediator, having already undertaken His Mediatoral office, though not then clothed in our flesh so as to become our brother; for the Church could not exist nor be united to God without a Head."[7] "The angel who appeared at first to Moses, and was

---

[1]Comm. on Gen. 48 : 15, C.R. 23 : 584.
[2]Comm. on Isa. 6 : 1, C.R. 36 : 126; cf. Inst. 2 : 6 : 2.
[3]Comm. on Hab. 3 : 13, C.R. 43 : 581.
[4]Inst. 1 : 13 : 10.
[5]Comm. on Exod. 14 : 19, C.R. 24 : 153.
[6]Inst. 1 : 13 : 10. *Qui iam tunc praeludio quodam fungi coepit mediatoris officio.*
[7]Comm. on Zech. 1 : 18–21, C.R. 44 : 152.

always present with the people during their journeying, is frequently called Jehovah. Let us then regard it as a settled point that the angel was Son of God, and was even then the Guide of the Church of which He was the Head."[1]

[1]Comm. on 1 Cor. 10 : 9, C.R. 49 : 459. . . . *Statuamus ergo, angelum illum, filium Dei fuisse, et iam tunc fuisse ecclesiae directorem, cuius erat caput.*
It is only of certain angelic appearances that all this can be said. When groups of angels appear to men Calvin finds that usually one is more prominent than the rest, the chief of angels who commands others. This is the angel of the Lord (cf. Inst. 1 : 13 : 10, comm. on Zech. 1 : 8, C.R. 44 : 137; on Exod. 3 : 2, C.R. 24 : 35–6; on Joshua 5 : 13). This Angel is "undoubtedly the only begotten Son of God" (on Joshua 5 : 13, C.R. 25 : 463; on Exod. 14 : 19) and is "truly and essentially God" (cf. comm. on Hos. 12 : 3–5, C.R. 42 : 455; on Exod. 33 : 2), though sharing the subordination of the Mediator (comm. on Joshua 5 : 13). He is thus both angel and God at the same time (cf. comm. on Hos. 12 : 3–5, C.R. 42 : 455). But though Angels have bodily form, and sometimes indeed put on real bodies (see note on p. 6), we must beware of imagining that, in appearing as this angel, Christ put on our flesh. "Though Christ appeared in the form of an Angel we must remember (Heb. 2 : 16) that *He took not on Him the nature of angels* so as to become one of them, in the manner in which He truly became man" (comm. on Gen. 48 : 16, C.R. 23 : 585). "I willingly receive what ancient writers teach on this subject—that when Christ anciently appeared in bodily form it was a prelude to the mystery which was afterwards exhibited when God was manifested in the flesh. We must beware, however, of imagining that Christ at that time became incarnate. . . . It was only a likeness of man" (comm. on Joshua 5 : 14, C R. 25 : 464). Of this Angel Calvin has no hesitation in saying, "The body was not created as to substance, but the form was created for the time" (comm. on Ezek. 1 : 26, C.R. 40 : 55). It was a "bare vision" (comm. on Ezek. 8 : 2, C.R. 40 : 178).

Chapter II

Revelation under the New Covenant

1. Revelation in Jesus Christ as the self-humiliation of God

WE have seen that revelation in the Old Testament is an event in which God, by a miracle of grace and power, overcomes all the impossibilities of the gulf which separates His sinful creature from Himself. In revealing Himself, God assumes such veiled and symbolic forms as enable Him to invite men into communion with Himself without their being destroyed and as enable man with all the limitations of his mind to apprehend all that he needs to know of the mystery of the divine being. It is, however, only when we turn to the New Testament and face the revelation of God given in Jesus Christ that we begin to realise how great is this impossible gulf between the holy God and sinful men, and how great is the condescension of God in the act in which He bridges the gulf in order to make Himself apprehensible by men.

Revelation in the New Testament means the Cross. It involves the coming of God in Christ in an act of self-humiliation that can have its origin only in the sheer undeserved mercy revealed there. The form which God assumed in Jesus in order to reveal Himself was not a form of glory and divinity. The humanity of Jesus was not a form that could be called a worthy medium for revealing God's true nature, but a form that was, for God, a form of deep abasement. Calvin speaks in several passages of "the mean condition of Christ in the flesh". When the Scripture says that the *Word was made flesh*, or rather *was made man*, this point is being emphasised. "The word *flesh* expresses the meaning of the evangelist more forcibly than if he had said that *He was made man*. He intended to show to what a mean and despicable condition (*vilem et abiectam conditionem*) the Son of God on our account descended from the height of His heavenly glory. When Scripture speaks of man contemptuously, it calls him *flesh*. Now though there be so wide a distance between the spiritual glory of the *Speech*[1] of God and the abominable filth of our flesh (*putidas carnis nostrae sordes*), yet the Son of God stooped so low as to take upon Himself that *flesh* subject to so many miseries. The word *flesh* is not taken here for corrupt nature (though it is often used thus by St. Paul), but for mortal man. It marks disdainfully his frail and perishing nature."[2] "There is also great emphasis in the contrast of the two words, *God in flesh*. How wide the difference between God and man! And yet in Christ we behold the infinite glory of God united to our polluted flesh in such a manner that they become one."[3] "Instead of being resplendent with divine glory, the human form only appeared in a mean and abject condition."[4] His purpose in thus humiliating Himself to become "a poor worm of the earth stripped of all good" was "in order that we might have easy access to Him and that we might have no uncertainty of being received".[5]

2. The humanity of Jesus as the veil of God's glory and majesty

In the New Testament, then, the humanity of Jesus is like a veil behind which God conceals His majesty in order to reveal

[1]Calvin sometimes prefers the translation λoyos=Lat. *sermo* (i.e. speech) rather than *verbum* (word); cf. comm. on John 1 : 1, C.R. 47 : 1–3. The fact that Christ is not only the source and inspiration but also the substance of all revelation should be kept in mind in all subsequent discussion. In using the phrase "the Word of God" we are apt to think of the Word merely as a "fleeting and evanescent voice" (*fluxam et evanidam vocem*) which is sent into the air, and comes forth beyond God Himself (*prodeat extra ipsum Deum* Inst. 1 : 13 : 7), whereas, for Calvin, "the reference is rather to the wisdom (*sapientia*) ever dwelling with God, and by which all oracles and prophecies were inspired" (ibid). We in our thinking can abstract a man's word from his person, and indeed from the thought which it expresses. Calvin, however, warns us against such a habit. *Quand S Jehan appelle Jesus Christ la Parolle, c'est comme s'il disoit, Le conseil eternel de Dieu, ou la sagesse qui reside en luy. Toutesfois il nous faut noter que Dieu n'est point semblable aux hommes. Quand nous avons un conseil : il pourra changer, mais il n'est pas ainsi de Dieu : car ce qui est en Dieu, est immuable. Apres, le conseil que nous avons n'est point nostre essence mesme : mais le conseil qui est en Dieu, il est vrayment Dieu : car Dieu n'est point comme un voile, où il y a des ombrages. . . . Il faut tousiours regarder la longue distance qui estre entre nous et Dieu.* Serm. de la Divinité de Christ. C.R. 47 : 470–1.

[2]Comm. on John 1 : 14, C.R. 47 : 13–14.

[3]Comm. on 1 Tim. 3 : 16, C.R. 52 : 290. . . . *Quantum enim interest inter Deum et hominem? Et tamen immensam Dei gloriam sic videmus in Christo coniunctam cum hac nostra carnis putredine, ut unum efficiant.*

[4]Inst. 2 : 13 : 2.

[5]Serm. on Luke 2 : 1–14, C.R. 46 : 957. *Comme un povre ver de terre, desnué de tout bien.* Cf. serm. on 1 Cor. 10 : 8–9, C.R. 49 : 634.

Himself. "The abasement of the flesh was like a veil by which His divine majesty was concealed."[1] It is the "humble clothing" which hides the true identity of the King who has laid aside all His insignia.[2] "When as God He might have displayed to the world the brightness of His glory, He gave up His right, and voluntarily emptied Himself. . . . He assumed the form of a servant, and, contented with that humble condition, suffered His divinity to be concealed under a veil of flesh."[3] "He says, however, that the treasures are *hidden*, because they are not seen glittering with great splendour, but do rather, as it were, lie hid under the contemptible abasement and simplicity of the Cross."[4] Calvin admits that there is ingenuity in the application of the verse Isaiah 45 : 15, *Thou art a God that hidest thyself*, to the incarnation.   Therefore, if we are to be able to grasp the revelation of God in Jesus, we must be able to look beyond His human nature to the divine nature so graciously veiled therein.   "We must not content ourselves by looking at the bodily presence of Jesus Christ, which was visible, but we must look higher. . . . It is not enough for us to behold Him with our natural eyes; for in this case we should rise no higher than man."[5]

So thick was this veil formed by the humanity of Jesus during His life on earth, that the ordinary observer, watching Jesus as He moved about, saw nothing divine about Him and was very naturally offended when He spoke as if He were any more than a mere man.   On the verse, *The Jews murmured concerning Him*, Calvin comments, "The Jews were offended at the mean condition of Christ's human nature, and did not perceive in Him anything divine or heavenly."[6]   "These wretched men," he goes on to say in his comment on John 7 : 27, "when they perceived in Christ nothing but what is liable to contempt, draw the absurd conclusion that He is not the person who has been

[1]Comm. on Phil. 2 : 7, C.R. 52 : 26. *Carnis humilitatem nihilominus fuisse instar veli, quo divina maiestas tegebatur.*
[2]Inst. 2 : 14 : 3. Cf. serm. on Matt. 2 : 16–22, C.R. 46 : 449. *Iesus Christ est nay en povrete : et quant à sa vie, il a este tenu là comme caché.* This humiliating obscurity was part of the cross which He bore all the days of His life. *Il n'a point falu qu'il fust seulement crucifié une fois, mais qu'il commençast dès son enfance* (serm. on Matt. 2 : 23, C.R. 46 : 451–2).
[3]Inst. 2 : 13 : 2. . . . *Carnis velamine suam divinitatem abscondi passus est.*
[4]Comm. on Col. 2 : 3, C.R. 52 : 100.
[5]Serm. on 1 Tim. 3 : 16, C.R. 53 : 327.
[6]Comm. on John 6 : 41, C.R. 47 : 148.

promised."[1] Nevertheless, in drawing this absurd conclusion the Jews were merely following the dictates of human reason, which is bound to be offended at the claim that God could become so abject. "Nothing is more absurd in the view of human reason than to hear that God has become mortal—that life has been subjected to death—that righteousness has been veiled under the appearance of sin—that the source of blessing has been made subject to the curse, that by this means men might be redeemed from death, and become partakers of a blessed immortality—that they might obtain life—that sin being destroyed, righteousness might reign—and that death and the curse might be swallowed up."[2] In a passage in which he shows that Isaiah foretold not only the deep humiliation that the Son of God must enter but also the rejection which He must suffer under such a humble guise, Calvin sums up his teaching on this point. "He says that Christ will be such that all men will be shocked at Him. He came into the world so as to be everywhere despised; His glory lay hid under the humble form of the flesh; for though a majesty worthy of *the only begotten Son of God* shone forth in Him, yet the greater part of men did not see it, but, on the contrary, they despised that deep abasement which was the veil or covering of His glory."[3]

In spite of all he writes about the humble form of the Son of Man, however, Calvin emphatically asserts that God was there in Jesus in all His glory and majesty, so that men who were confronted by Jesus as He walked on earth were really being confronted by God in His fullness. God the Son did not deprive Himself of any of His divine attributes even in becoming incarnate. "Even during the time that He emptied Himself, He continued to retain His divinity entire though it was concealed under the veil of His flesh."[4] "The majesty of God was not

[1] See comm. *in loc.*

[2] Comm. on 1 Cor. 1 : 21, C.R. 49 : 326. *Et sane alioqui humanae rationi absurdius nihil est quam audire Deum mortalem, vitam morti obnoxiam, iustitiam peccati similitudine obtectam, benedictionem subiectam maledictioni. . . .*

[3] Comm. on Isa. 52 : 14, C.R. 37 : 252. *. . . Illa exinanitio, quae velum fuit vel integumentum gloriae eius.*

[4] Comm. on Matt. 17 : 9, C.R. 45 : 490. *Ut certo constaret, etiam quo tempore exinanitus fuit, deitatem tamen suam illi integram stetisse, licet abscondita esset carnis velo.* Cf. on Phil. 2 : 7, C.R. 52 : 26. *Non potuit quidem Christus abdicare se divinitate : sed eam ad tempus occultam tenuit, ne appareret sub carnis infirmitate. Itaque gloriam suam non minuendo, sed supprimendo, in conspectu hominum deposuit.*

annihilated, though it was surrounded by *flesh*: it was indeed concealed under the low condition of the flesh, but so as to cause its splendour to be seen."[1] The transfiguration is for Calvin a proof that "so long as Christ remained in the world, bearing the form of a servant . . . nothing had been taken from Him".[2] The transfiguration is thus the breaking through the veil of the flesh of a glory that was always there.[3]

This view is consistent with Calvin's teaching that in the act of the incarnation the Word of God did not abandon His heavenly throne. Though really dwelling in the flesh in all His fullness so that it may be said that the whole of God is in Jesus Christ, nevertheless the Word at the same time continued to fulfil all His heavenly functions unimpaired, so that it may be said that the whole Godhead also was outside of Christ. "Another absurdity . . . viz. that if the Word of God became incarnate, it must have been enclosed in the narrow tenement of an earthly body, is sheer petulence. For although the boundless essence of the Word was united with human nature in one person, we have no idea of any enclosing. The Son of God descended miraculously from heaven, yet without abandoning heaven; was pleased to be conceived miraculously in the virgin's womb, to live upon the earth, and hang upon the cross, and yet always filled the world as from the beginning."[4] "His being a servant was not owing to His nature, but to a voluntary humility, as Paul testifies; and at the same time His sovereignty remained to Him entire. . . . Christ is a minister in such a way that though He is in our flesh, nothing is diminished from the majesty of His dominion."[5]

---

[1]Comm. on John 1 : 14, C.R. 47 : 15. *Unde sequitur dei maiestatem non fuisse exinanitam, quamvis carne circumdata esset.*

[2]Comm. on Matt. 17 : 1, C.R. 45 : 485.

[3]This veiling of the divinity of Jesus is a gracious necessity in His work of revealing the Father. Cf. comm. on Luke 19 : 41, C.R. 45 : 576. "On all occasions when it was necessary that He should perform the office of teacher, His divinity rested (*quievit*) and was in a manner concealed (*abscondit*) that it might not hinder what belonged to Him as Mediator."

[4]Inst. 2 : 13 : 4. *Quod etiam pro absurdo nobis obtrudunt, si Sermo Dei carnem induit, fuisse igitur angusto terreni corporis ergastulo inclusum, mera est procacitas : quia etsi in unam personam coaluit immensa verbi essentia cum natura hominis, nullam tamen inclusionem fingimus. Mirabiliter enim e coelo descendit Filius Dei, ut coelum tamen non relinqueret ; mirabiliter in utero virginis gestari, in terris versari, et in cruce pendere voluit, ut semper mundum impleret, sicut ab initio.*

[5]Comm. on Heb. 1 : 14, C.R. 55 : 20.

For Calvin the "kenosis" referred to in Philippians 2 : 7 cannot mean a self deprivation on the part of the Word of any of His divine attributes, but should be applied to the self-concealment of the Word, in the gracious act of uniting Himself with flesh, and to the humiliation experienced throughout His human life.[1] "Christ indeed could not divest Himself of His Godhead; but He kept it concealed for a time, that it might not be seen, under the weakness of the flesh. Hence He laid aside His glory in the view of men, not by lessening it, but by concealing it. . . . This emptying is applicable exclusively to His humanity."[2] In taking upon Himself our condition, He always retained His divine majesty.[3] Calvin strongly repudiates any suggestion that the union of the divine and human altered either nature in any way. "There have been heretics who have endeavoured to maintain that the majesty and Godhead of Jesus Christ, His heavenly essence, was forthwith changed into flesh and manhood. Thus did some say, with many other cursed blasphemies, that Jesus Christ was made man. What will follow hereupon? God must forego His nature and His spiritual essence must be turned into flesh. They go on further and say Jesus Christ is no more man, but His flesh has become God. These are marvellous alchemists to make so many new natures of Jesus Christ."[4]

3. God revealed in Jesus

The question must now arise, how, though thus concealed, did the glory and majesty of God in Jesus actually come to be

[1] Cf. Serm. on Isa. 53 : 11, C.R. 35 : 664. *Et encores qu'il ne se soit point despouillé de sa Maieste Divine, si est-ce qu'elle a este cachee pour un temps, et on ne l'a point aperceuë entre les hommes.* Cf. serm. on 1 Cor. 11 : 2–3, C.R. 49 : 716–7.

[2] Comm. on Phil. 2 : 7, C.R. 52 : 26. *. . . Hanc tamen inanitionem non convenire nisi soli humanitati.*

[3] Cf. serm. on Luke 2 : 1–14, C.R. 46 : 957. *Mesmes que ce qu'il avoit prins de nostre condition n'estoit pas qu'il ne peust maintenir sa maiesté celeste. Tous les deux donc nous sont yci monstrez : car nostre Seigneur Jesus Christ est là en une creche et il est comme reietté du monde . . . toutesfois il est magnifié des anges de Paradis, lesquels luy font hommage.* And ibid p. 959. *Le fils de Dieu ne perd rien de sa maiesté et de sa gloire, et qu'il n'est pas amoindri en ce qu'il s'est humilié pour nostre salut.*

[4] Serm. on 1 Tim. 3 : 16, C.R. 53 : 325.

"seen" and believed in by His disciples? To this question a study of Calvin's commentaries enables us to give several answers.

(i) *In certain aspects of His humanity*

In apparent contradiction to what has already been said, Calvin admits that there were features of the humanity[1] of Jesus that shone with divine glory. Though some men did not see it, "a majesty worthy of *the only begotten Son of God* shone forth in Him".[2] "Christ is not only the image of God in so far as He is the eternal Word of God, but even in His human nature, which He has in common with us, the likeness of the glory of the Father has been engraved so as to form His members to the resemblance of it."[3] These divine features about Jesus are to be seen not in any striking physical or psychological characteristics which Jesus might be supposed to have possessed, but rather in the gentler characteristics of a gracious and beautiful character. "Christ is called *the perfection of beauty*, not that there was any striking display of it in His countenance, as some men grossly imagine, but because He was distinguished by the possession of singular gifts and graces, in which He far excelled all others."[4] "When Christ receives us under His patronage, He covers with His goodness the majesty of God, which would otherwise be terrible to us, so that nothing appears there but grace and paternal favour."[5] There are thus features in the humanity of Jesus which really represent God. The Father "exhibits Himself to us by His Son, and makes Himself in a manner visible".[6]

[1]Serm. on Isa. 53 : 9–10, C.R. 35 : 653. *Non pas que tousiours il n'ait eu certaines marques pour estre honoré comme le Fils unique de Dieu, mais cela a este obscurci en telle sorte par ce qu'il a enduré.*
[2]Comm. on Isa. 52 : 14, C.R. 37 : 252.
[3]Comm. on John 17 : 22, C.R. 47 : 388. *Christus non tántum, quatenus est aeternus Dei sermo, viva est imago ipsius, sed humanae quoque naturae, quam nobiscum habet communem, insculpta fuit paternae gloriae effigies, ut membra sua in eam transfiguret.*
[4]Comm. on Ps. 45 7 f., C.R. 31 : 453. *Eodem sensu sciamus Christum vocari speciosum forma, non quod oris pulcritudine spectabilis fuerit, sicuti crassi homines somniant : sed quia eximiis dotibus ornatus fuerit, quibus alios omnes supereminet.* Cf. ibid v. 2. "A noble disposition of mind often shines forth in the very countenance of a man . . . as this excellence was displayed in Solomon, so also did it shine forth more fully afterwards in Christ." (C.R. 31 : 450.)
[5]Comm. on Heb. 4 : 16, C.R. 55 : 56.
[6]Comm. on 2 Cor. 4 : 4, C.R. 50 : 51. Cf. on Luke 19 : 41, C.R. 45 : 576

(ii) *In His miracles*

The miracles of Jesus gave indication, to those who could properly interpret them, of His divine glory.[1] "He was not known as the Son of God by the external form of His body, but because He gave illustrious proofs of His divine power, so that in Him shone forth the majesty of the Father as in a distinct and living image."[2] "When we see that by miracles and mighty works, He shows Himself to be the Son of God, it is a seal and proof, that in abasing Himself, He did not leave off His heavenly majesty."[3]

(iii) *In His resurrection glory*

The divine glory, concealed as by a veil throughout the earthly life of Jesus, nevertheless from time to time shone through the obscurity of the flesh in such a way that it could be recognised by His disciples. It was in the resurrection of Jesus that the divine glory finally shone through the flesh which had concealed it throughout His earthly life, and indeed transfigured the flesh so that His humanity was now a translucent medium for revealing His divinity.   But even before the resurrection there were occasions when the rays of divine glory shone through the human nature of Jesus. "The divine majesty of Christ was not so concealed under the mean and contemptible appearance of the flesh as not to give out the rays of His brightness in a variety of ways."[4] As has already been mentioned, the incident of the transfiguration is for Calvin the supreme occasion on which this shining forth beforehand of the glory of the resurrection took place during His earthly life. In his comments on the transfiguration Calvin calls it "a temporary exhibition of His glory".[5]

(on Jesus' weeping over Jerusalem). "By this weeping He proved not only that He loved like a brother those for whose sake He became man, but also that God made to flow into human nature (*transfusum*) the Spirit of fatherly love."
[1]Cf. comm. on Matt. 21 : 23, C.R. 45 : 587.
[2]Comm. on 1 John 1 : 1, C.R. 55 : 300. *Neque enim ab externa corporis figura agnitus fuit Dei filius, sed ex eo, quod illustria divinae suae potentiae documenta edidit, ita ut in eo, tanquam viva et expressa imagine, refulserit patris maiestas.*
[3]Serm. on 1 Tim. 3 : 16, C.R. 53 : 328. *Voila une signature, voila une approbation telle qu'il ne faut plus douter ;* cf. C.R. 35 : 617.
[4]Comm. on John 6 : 41, C.R. 47 : 148. *Deinde non sic latebat divina Christi maiestas sub contemptibili et abiecta carnis specie, quin multiplicis fulgoris sui radios emitteret.*
[5]Comm. on Matt. 17 : 9, C.R. 45 : 490. Calvin suggests that at certain times

The story of the transfiguration, however, would have gained no credence except among those who had witnessed His resurrection, therefore the three witnesses were warned to keep the vision secret till Christ was risen.

Ultimately it is only in the resurrection of Jesus that we have a "clear proof" of His divinity formerly hidden and unknown, and for this reason Jesus in answer to the challenge to prove His divinity could only refer His challengers to the future glory of His resurrection.[1] "We must note, then, that when St. Luke says that Jesus Christ showed Himself alive he speaks of something necessary for the assurance of our salvation. Wherefore, if we want to have the main thing in Christianity, we must grasp this resurrection, by which He has acquired life and salvation for us, and by which He has shown Himself to be the true Son of God."[2] No man can become convinced of Christ's divinity merely by studying His humanity, which was so full of weakness and in which He suffered such a shameful death. It was only when He was raised by the power of the Spirit that "He displayed at last a glory under which we all, both great and small, ought to tremble".[3]

(iv) *His glory discernible only through faith*

Whatever signs of His divinity Jesus gave during His earthly life, and whatever rays of divine glory shone through·the veil of

in the life of Jesus there was a clearer manifestation of His glory than at other. Cf. comm. on John 6 : 62, C.R. 47 : 158. *What if you shall see the Son of Man ascend where He was before?* "The mean and despicable condition of Christ . . . prevented them from submitting to His divine power; but now—by withdrawing, as it were, the veil (*quasi subducto velo*)—He calls them to behold His heavenly glory."

[1]Comm. on John 8 : 14, C.R. 47 : 193. *Revocat eos ad futuram resurrectionis suae gloriam, quae divinitatis prius occultae et incognitae illustre specimen fuit.* Cf. serm. on Isa. 53 : 1, C.R. 35 : 601.

[2]Serm. on Acts 1 : 1–4, C.R. 48 : 587.

[3]Serm. on 2 Thess. 1 : 6–10, C.R. 52 : 232.

Cf. comm. on John 6 : 62, C.R. 47 : 159, and serm. on Isa. 53 : 7–8, C.R. 35 : 639. *Il a este declaré Fils de Dieu en sa resurrection. Car si nous ne regardons Jesus Christ qu'en sa vie, selon qu'il a conversé yci bas au milieu des hommes, et puis en sa mort, nous ne trouverons pas en luy ce qui est requis a nostre salut. Il est vray que les miracles qu'il a faits, la doctrine qu'il a preschee, les autres signes qu'il a montrez, estoyent bien pour le declarer Fils de Dieu : voire si nous n'estions pas trop debiles de foy. Mais encores nous demeurerions tousiours confus en perplexite, quand Jesus Christ se presenteroit comme un homme commun et mesmes mesprisé . . . mais quand de la mort nous passons a la resurrection, voyla comme nous scavons que nostre Seigneur Jesus nous a acquis victoire.*

His flesh, His divine nature could be discerned only by those who had faith. Those who were offended in Him "wanted eyes to see His conspicuous glory". The glory of Christ is discerned not "by human view" but by faith, for human sense "cannot comprehend that lofty greatness".[1] It was the folly of the contemporaries of Jesus that they refused to seek the vision of the glory of God that could have come to them had they been willing to give their humble adoration to the humiliated Christ. Because they despised His Cross they could not see His glory, for there is no other way to the divinity save through the humanity of Christ. Calvin appeals frequently to his readers not to follow them in the fatal error of seeking to know the risen Christ apart from the Jesus who was crucified. "On the mean condition of Christ in the flesh let us therefore learn to look in such a manner, that this state of humiliation which is despised by wicked men, may raise us to His heavenly glory. Thus *Bethlehem*, where the man was to be born, will be to us a door by which we may enter into the presence of the eternal God."[2] "As the veil covered the recesses of the sanctuary and yet afforded an entrance there, so the divinity, though hid in the flesh of Christ, yet leads us even to heaven; nor can anyone find God except he to whom the man Christ becomes the door and the way. Thus we are reminded that Christ's glory is not to be estimated according to the external appearance of His flesh; nor is the flesh to be despised, because it conceals as a veil the majesty of God, while it also conducts us to the enjoyment of all the good things of God."[3] "In order to know His glory we must proceed from His death to His resurrection . . . if anyone chooses to begin with the resurrection, he will not . . . comprehend the Lord's strength and power."[4] "True, indeed, God in Christ appears in the first

[1]Comm. on Isa. 53 : 2, C.R. 37 : 256.
[2]Comm. on John 7 : 27, C.R. 47 : 175.
[3]Comm. on Heb. 10 : 20, C.R. 55 : 129. . . . *Ita admonemur, non aestimandam esse Christi gloriam ab externo carnis adspectu, nec despiciendam esse carnem, quia Dei maiestatem quasi velum occultet : quum eadem nobis ad fruenda omnia Dei bona sit directrix.*
[4]Comm. on Isa. 53 : 3, C.R. 37 : 256. *Ut cognoscatur eius gloria, a morte ipsius ad resurrectionem progrediendum est. . . .*
Cf. serm. on Isa. 53 : 7–8, C.R. 35 : 640. *Car s'il fust seulement apparu en sa maieste, comment aujourd'huy pourrions nous estre asseurez que nos pechez nous sont remis? Nous verrions le Fils de Dieu qui est la fontaine de vie, mais il seroit comme separé de nous, et nous n'aurions rien de commun avec luy, nous n'en pourrions approcher.*

instance to be mean, but He appears at length to be glorious in view of those who hold on, so as to come from the cross to the resurrection."[1]

(v) *His full glory known only hereafter*

The glory seen by the disciples when they witnessed the resurrection of Jesus was not the full glory of God. Even then they were far from seeing God "as He is". "We shall not see God as He is," says Calvin, "until we shall be like Him."[2] "When the Apostle says that we shall see Him as He is, he intimates a new and ineffable manner of seeing Him, which we enjoy not now; . . . hence the majesty of God, now hid, will then only be in itself seen, when the veil of this mortal and corruptible nature shall be removed."[3] Calvin, in a rather speculative mood, seems to teach that even Christ's glorified humanity is a veil which refracts and thus obscures for us the full glory of God, but that ultimately even this will be changed and we shall indeed see God face to face. "Nor will He in this way resign the Kingdom, but will transfer it in a manner from His humanity to His glorious divinity, because a way of approach will then be opened up, from which our infirmity now keeps us back. Thus then, Christ will be *subjected to the Father*, because the veil being then removed (*remoto velo*), we shall openly behold God reigning in His majesty, and Christ's humanity will then no longer be interposed to keep us back from a closer view of God."[4]

4. The Word and Sacraments as means of revelation

The foregoing discussion may enable us to understand the place which Calvin gives to the Word and Sacraments as means

[1]Comm. on 2 Cor. 4 : 6, C.R. 50 : 53. *Humilis quidem initio apparet in Christo Deus : sed gloriosus tandem iis, qui a cruce ad resurrectionem pervenire sustinent.*

[2]Comm. on Exod. 33 : 20, C.R. 25 : 111. *Non ante ipsum videbimus sicuti est, quam similes ei erimus.*

[3]Comm. on 1 John 3 : 2, C.R. 55 : 332. . . . *Ubi ablatum fuerit mortalis huius et corruptibilis naturae velum.*

[4]Comm. on 1 Cor. 15 : 27, C.R. 49 : 549.
Calvin has other qualifications to make: "The perfection of glory will not be so great in us, that our seeing will enable us to comprehend all that God is;

of revelation. The Word and Sacraments are the forms of abasement which Christ the Mediator to-day assumes in confronting us with His grace and challenge. They are the symbols by which He to-day accommodates Himself to our limited capacity for apprehending the divine and veils that in Himself with which we cannot bear to be directly confronted. The same self-revealing Lord who showed Himself to the people of Israel in many and varied forms, ceremonies, dreams and visions, confronts us to-day when the Word is preached and the Sacraments administered, and it is to the Word and Sacraments that we must turn if we wish to enter into communion with Him. "As men are made known by countenance and speech, so God utters His voice to us by the voice of the prophets, and in the sacraments takes, as it were, a visible form, from which He may be known by us according to our feeble capacity."[1] We need no longer expect to have revelation mediated to us by means of angels and visions. A new "perpetual order"[2] has been established in the Church whereby, instead of sending angels from heaven to be the bearers of His Word, God puts in His place a man like ourselves[3]—a minister of the Gospel—thus addressing us and exhorting us "that He may more gently draw us to Himself". The significance that the Ark and Temple had for the ancient people of God has in our present case been transferred to Word and Sacraments. "Mount Sion, it is true, is not at this day the place appointed for the sanctuary, and the ark of the covenant is no longer the image or representation of God dwelling between the cherubim, but as we have this privilege in common with the fathers, that, by the preaching of the Word

for the distance between us and Him will be even then very great" (comm. on 1 John 3 : 2, C.R. 55 : 331–2). "Although full vision will be deferred until the day of Christ, a nearer view of God will begin to be enjoyed immediately after death" (comm. on 1 Cor. 13 : 12, C.R. 49 : 515).

[1] Comm. on John 5 : 37, C.R. 47 : 124. *Nam sicuti vultu et sermone homines se patefaciunt, ita Deus vocem ad nos suam prophetarum voce emittit, et in sacramentis quasi visibilem formam induit, unde cognosci pro modulo nostro queat.*

[2] C.R. 8 : 414. *Vray est que la grace de Dieu n'est point attachée, et la vertu de son Esprit n'est point enclose ni aux Sacremens, ni à toutes choses externes, qu'il ne puisse besongner, quand il luy plaira, sans nul moyen : mais ici nous traictons de l'ordre perpetuel qu'il a mis en son Eglise, et non pas de ce qu'il faict extraordinairement comme miracle.* Cf. serm. on Deut. 5 : 23–7, C.R. 26 : 405. *Voila donc un ordre inviolable, et qui procede de Dieu, qu'il y ait des pasteurs en l'Eglise, qui annoncent sa doctrine.* Cf. comm. on Isa. 59 : 21, C.R. 37 : 351 f.

[3] Comm. on Acts 9 : 6, C.R. 48 : 203–4.

and the Sacraments, we may be united to God, it becomes us to use these helps with reverence."[1] Word and Sacrament can have for us all the tremendous significance that Jacob's vision at Bethel had for him when, assured that he had been confronted and pardoned by the God of His Fathers, he called the place of his vision the *gate of heaven.* "The preaching of the gospel is called the Kingdom of Heaven and the sacraments may be called the gate of Heaven, because they admit us into the presence of God."[2]

Word and Sacrament, therefore, do not merely take for us the place that visions and oracles and the elaborate temple ceremonies took in the Old Testament; more particularly, they are to us what Jesus and His Word and works were to those who received His grace during the days of His flesh. They are for us the "flesh" of Jesus Christ, the lowly humble form He takes in revealing Himself and apart from which we cannot come to know His glory or experience the power of His resurrection. The Word and Sacraments are thus the chief treasure of the Church. They are the signs of the presence of Jesus in the midst, the "form" in which He "appears" before men, and the veil through which the rays of His glory are refracted so that men can come to know Him as One who, when He comes, does not come to destroy those who have sinned against Him, but gently to stretch out His hands to invite them to Himself. "We have in the Word (in so far as is expedient for us) a naked and open revelation of God."[3] "There God shows Himself, as much as is expedient for us."[4] "Although the voice of God has not sounded in our ears, yet the experience of His ancient people ought to be sufficient to persuade us assuredly that, when God sets teachers over us, He makes the best provision for our

---

[1]Comm. on Ps. 24 : 7, C.R. 31 : 248.
[2]Comm. on Gen. 28 : 17, C.R. 23 : 394.
  Cf. serm. on Deut. 4 : 11–14, C.R. 26 : 143. *Voila quel est le vray but de tous fideles : c'est que quand ils s'assemblent au nom de Dieu, qu'ils ayent sa voix qui leur soit comme un tesmoignage de sa maieste presente. Et de faict comme l'aureille a este cause de faire aliener de Dieu le premier homme, ainsi faut-il qu'elle nous y attire aujourd'huy.*
[3]Comm. on 1 Cor. 13 : 12, C.R. 49 : 514. *Est enim aperta et nuda Dei revelatio in verbo (quantum nobis expedit).*
[4]Serm. on Eph. 4 : 20–24, C.R. 51 : 607. Cf. serm. on Matt. 3 : 9–10, C.R. 46 : 544. *Auiourd'huy quand l'Evangile se presche, il est vray que Dieu nous apparoist là comme Pere, et tasche de nous gaigner par douceur et humanite.*

salvation; because if He Himself should thunder from heaven His majesty would be intolerable to us."[1] "God the more evidently manifests His fatherly care in calling men to Himself by His Word. And it is a very significant and forcible kind of speech, when He thus stretches out His hand, because in procuring and furthering our salvation by the ministers of His Word, He reaches forth His hands to us, as if a father, being ready to take His son into His lap, should extend His arms."[2] "As if he had said . . . 'There is no happiness which will be of greater importance to thee or which thou oughtest to desire more earnestly, than to feel that I am present by the *Word* and the *Spirit*.' Hence we infer that this is a most valuable treasure of the Church, that He has chosen for Himself a habitation in it to dwell in the hearts of believers by His Spirit, and next to preserve among them the doctrine of His Gospel."[3] "By Baptism and the Lord's Supper, God appears to us in His only begotten Son."[4]

5. The Word and Sacraments as the mirror of the glory of God

The figure which Calvin frequently uses in describing the function of the Word and Sacrament in revelation is that of the mirror into which men can look to see the image of God. In the use of this figure emphasis is laid on the fact that the image of Christ is thus presented in a refracted manner and to a degree that is obscure when compared with direct vision, i.e. the Word and Sacraments veil the One who is revealing Himself by their means. In the Word men can view the secrets of Heaven, which otherwise seen would dazzle their eyes, astonish their ears and amaze their minds.[5] "The ministry of the Word, I say, is like a *looking glass*. For the angels have no need of preaching, or other inferior helps, nor of Sacraments, for they enjoy a

[1]Comm. on Deut. 5 : 24, C.R. 24 : 206.
[2]Comm. on Rom. 10 : 21, C.R. 49 : 210. Cf. serm. on 2 Tim. 1 : 9–10, C.R. 54 : 62–3.
[3]Comm. on Isa. 59 : 21, C.R. 37 : 352.
[4]Comm. on Lev. 16 : 16, C.R. 24 : 503–4.
[5]Comm. on Rom. 10 : 8, C.R. 49 : 200. *Perinde enim est ac si moneret in hoc speculo contemplanda esse coelorum arcana.*

vision of God of another kind. . . . We, who have not as yet reached that great height, behold the image of God as it is presented before us in the Word, in the Sacraments, and in fine in the whole service of the Church. This vision Paul here speaks of as partaking of obscurity—not as though it were doubtful or delusive, but because it is not so distinct as that which will be afforded on the final day; cf. 2 Corinthians 5 : 7, *so long as we dwell in the body we are absent from the Lord ; for we walk by faith, not by sight.* Our faith, therefore, at present beholds God as absent. How so? Because it sees not His face but rests satisfied with the image in the mirror."[1] But, though he admits that the image of Christ given in Word and Sacrament is comparatively obscure, Calvin insists that it is nevertheless vivid and real and satisfying. There is nothing about it that is "confused or perplexed, or dark". "In this glass," writes Calvin, referring to the Word, "the secrets of Heaven are to be seen," and he assures his readers that "they may as safely rest therein as in the most present beholding of things, or as in anything that is present and in hand".[2] Even the Apostles when confronted by the glory of God shining through the Risen Jesus were not privileged any more than the ordinary Christian of to-day who hears the Word and is invited to the Lord's table. "Does Christ now give less light to the world than when He was in the presence of men and conversed with them?" asks Calvin. "I reply, when Christ had finished His course of office He laboured not less powerfully by His ministers than He had laboured by Himself when He lived in the world." "After the death of Christ the power of God shone more illustriously both in the fruit of the doctrine and in miracles."[3] Calvin actually refers the text John 12 : 23, *The hour is come when the Son of man should be glorified,* not to the death and resurrection of Jesus but to the hour when the preaching of the gospel over all the earth would begin, for it is through hearing the Word that men behold His glory.[4] In the Gospel, Christ the "living image of God is evidently set before our eyes".[5] "Let the proud boasters of this

[1]Comm. on 1 Cor. 13 : 12, C.R. 49 : 514.
[2]Comm. on Rom. 10 : 8, C.R. 49 : 200.
[3]Comm. on John 9 : 5, C.R. 47 : 219.
[4]See comm. *in loc,* C.R. 47 : 288.
[5]Comm. on Gen. 32 : 30, C.R. 23 : 447.

world jeer as much as they please since God has graciously condescended to stoop down to us; let us not be ashamed to give this honour to His Word and Sacraments—to behold Him there is face to face."[1]   "Therefore, though He (Christ) be absent from us in the body, and is not conversant with us here on earth, it is not that He hath withdrawn Himself as though we could not find Him; for the sun that shineth doth no more enlighten the world than Jesus Christ showeth Himself openly to those who have the eyes of faith to look upon Him, when the Gospel is preached."[2]

[1]C.R. 8 : 427.
[2]Serm. on 2 Tim. 1 : 9–10, C.R. 54 : 61.

Chapter III

Unity of Revelation—Unity of Substance

ALVIN, in opposition to the views both of the Anabaptists and of the Schoolmen, seeks constantly to prove that the revelation given under the Old Testament and that given under the New have the most substantial identity. "The covenant made with all the fathers is so far from differing from ours in substance and reality (*substantia et re*) that it is altogether one and the same."[1] "The Jews as well as ourselves were enjoined to yield a spiritual worship to God. . . . *God is Spirit* (John 4 : 24). He was no less Spirit, however, under the period of the legal ceremonies than after they were abolished; and must therefore have demanded then the same mode of worship which He now enjoins. . . . In every essential respect the worship was the same. The distinction was one entirely of outward form."[2]

1. All Old Testament revelation a participation
in Christ

For Calvin, all revelation in the Bible is revelation of Christ the Mediator. All the Old Testament stories of God's appearing to men, if they are to be rightly understood and interpreted, must be understood in the light of the incarnation of Jesus

---

[1]Inst. 2 : 10 : 2.

[2]Comm. on Ps. 50 : 14, C.R. 31 : 502. . . . *caeterum idem cultus quoad substantiam, externa tantum specie diversus est.*

Though Calvin affirms so strongly, as will be seen in this chapter, the efficacy of the Old Covenant and its substantial identity with the New, he nevertheless looks on this property as being transferred to the Old Covenant by virtue of the New which it foreshadowed, in the same way as the promises are contained in the law. The Old Covenant is thus proleptically conditioned by the New. Cf. comm. on Jer. 31 : 33, C.R. 38 : 691. *Patres qui olim regeniti fuerunt, id fuisse adeptos Christi gratia, ita possumus dicere illud fuisse quasi translatitium. Non igitur residebat in lege haec virtus, ut animos penetraret, sed fuit translatitium bonum ab evangelio ad ipsam legem.* Cf. serm. on Gen. 14 : 20–24, C.R. 23 : 670. *Si on prenoit tous les umbrages qui ont esté en usage pour un temps, qu'ils ne profiteroyent rien et que tout seroit frivole sinon qu'on vienne au vray patron.*

Christ and interpreted as related to that one event. We must not forget that "at the time when the ancient prophets uttered their predictions concerning the death of Christ, He Himself, who was the eternal wisdom of God, was sitting upon the invisible throne of His glory".[1] Before Christ was born at Bethlehem, the light that was to come into the world in His person shed abroad its beams, as in a morning twilight, to enable men to live and walk in the light of the coming Redeemer. Prior to His coming, God gave the "primordial manifestation of His glory".[2] All revelation, whether under the Old or the New Covenant, is thus a participation in the one light shed over every age by the coming of Jesus Christ. In a remarkable passage in his commentary on John's Gospel Calvin likens the revelation given in the earthly life of Jesus to one day. "His bodily presence was a true and remarkable *day of the world*, the lustre of which was diffused over all ages.[3] From whence did the holy fathers in ancient time, or whence do we now, desire light and day, but because the manifestation of Christ has always darted its rays to a great distance, so as to form one continued day?"[4] Revelation took place there and then in that short earthly life lived by our Lord, and all previous and subsequent revelation derives its reality only by virtue of that one event. Those who enjoyed revelation in Old Testament times partook of the light of that day as those who lived in its dawning.

Revelation under the Old Covenant is thus never simply a preparation made before the event of conditions under which the event can now take place, but is a real participation in the event. The effect of the Old Covenant was not merely a stirring up of men's hearts by bare promises expectantly to await something they cannot already see and grasp, but an actual experience of the thing itself. The light of Christ shone into the world before He was born at Bethlehem, and men lived by it. But there cannot be light without life. There can be no participation in the knowledge of God without a sharing in the life of God. Therefore in the act of revelation, even under the Old Covenant,

[1]Comm. on Matt. 17 : 3, C.R. 45 : 486.
[2]Comm. on Ps. 86 : 9, C.R. 31 : 794.
[3]*Verus et singularis dies mundi cuius splendor in omnia saecula diffusus fuerit.*
[4]Comm. on John 9 : 5, C.R. 47 : 220. . . . *Christi exhibitio semper radios suos longe emisit qui perpetuum diem texerent.*

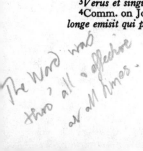

the Mediator always communicated His life and power to men. They not only saw Christ but they partook of Christ and of all the benefits of His death and resurrection. Christ "communicated Himself to the fathers under the signs of the law".[1] Before His body existed, the virtue of the salvation wrought out in that body was given to the men of the Old Testament. "All the fathers from the beginning of the world drew from Christ all the gifts which they possessed; for though the law was given by Moses, yet they did not obtain grace by it."[2] "The scholastic. dogma . . . by which the difference between the sacraments of the Old and New dispensations is made so great that the former did nothing but shadow forth the grace of God, while the latter did actually confer it, must be altogether exploded."[3]

Calvin can describe this participation in Christ given under the Old Covenant in terms of union with God. The fathers "both had and knew Christ the Mediator, by whom they were united to God".[4] He can speak of the Ark as a pledge or sign of the union which subsisted between God and the Israelites.[5]

2. True Christian experience mediated under the forms of the Old Covenant

Since under the Old Covenant the fathers partook of Christ, it follows that the Children of Israel throughout the course of their history were really a living Church. They fulfilled their historical destiny as a living part of the body of which Christ was the Head, and the ceremonies which constituted the ritual of their religious cult were not only means of revelation but also sacraments through which the participants received the benefits and blessings of Christian redemption.

It is quite startling to read Calvin's estimate of the experiences and privileges which the pious Israelites enjoyed through

[1]C.R. 9 : 176.
[2]Comm. on John 1 : 16, C.R. 47 : 17.
[3]Inst. 4 : 14 : 23. *Scholasticum autem illud dogma . . . quo tam longum discrimen inter veteris ac novae legis sacramenta notatur, perinde acsi illa non aliud quam Dei gratiam adumbrarint, haec vero praesentem conferant, penitus explodendum est.*
[4]Inst. 2 : 10 : 2.
[5]Comm. on Ps. 78 : 60, C.R. 31 : 740–1. Cf. Inst. 2 : 10 : 8.

their religious institutions, and the various accidents of their
history. "They were favoured with the same benefits as we this
day enjoy."[1] "God promised salvation to His ancient people
and also regenerated His chosen and illuminated them by His
Spirit."[2] When David writes, *I will magnify the Lord who hath
given me counsel*, "the counsel of which David makes mention is
the inward illumination of the Holy Spirit".[3] When making
expiatory sacrifices at the temple the worshippers there experienced a true reconciliation with God. Sins under the law were
"remitted through Christ".[4] Their ceremonies of cleansing and
purification before worship effected not only an outward "civil"
cleansing of the body but a real cleansing of the soul from sin,[5]
giving them the same sense of reconciliation with God as we
ourselves have through our sacraments under the New Covenant.
"The ancients were reconciled to God in a sacramental manner
by the victims, just as we are now cleansed through Baptism."[6]
"Let not that profane imagination be listened to, that the sacrifices only publicly and as far as regarded man, absolved."[7]

This reconciliation enjoyed by the people of Israel is marked
by the same emotions of faith and repentance as are experienced
to-day when men deal with Jesus Christ. "These symbols were
useful as exercises unto faith and repentance (*exercitia ad poenitentiam et fidem*), so that the sinner might learn to fear God's
wrath and to seek pardon in Christ.[8] They found a pleasure in
the Word of God similar to that which the Christian finds in
the hearing of the Gospel. David's delight in the law is due to
its being for him "quickened by the Spirit of Christ". He found
in the law "the free promises of salvation, or rather Christ
Himself".[9] They had on occasion full assurance and certainty

[1]Comm. on 1 Cor. 10 : 1 and ff., C.R. 49 : 451.
[2]Comm. on Jer. 31 : 34, C.R. 38 : 697. *Deus promisit salutem veteri populo :
deinde regenuit tunc suos, et illuxit per spiritum suum.* Cf. on Heb. 8 : 10.
[3]Comm. on Ps. 16 : 7, C.R. 31 : 154.
[4]Comm. on Heb. 9 : 15, C.R. 55 : 112, and on Heb. 8 : 10, C.R. 55 : 103–4.
[5]Comm. on Heb. 9 : 13, C.R. 55 : 111.
[6]Comm. on Lev. 1 : 1, C.R. 24 : 507. *Modo sacramentali reconciliati fuerunt
Deo veteres per victimas, sicuti hodie abluimur per baptismum.*
[7]Comm. on Lev. 4 : 22, C.R. 24 : 519. *Atque ita facessat profanum figmen-
tum, politice tantum hominum respectu sacrificia eos a quibus offerebantur a culpa
et reatu absolvisse.*
[8]Comm. on Lev. 1 : 1, C.R. 24 : 507.
[9]Cf. comm. on Ps. 19 : 8–10, C.R. 31 : 201, and on Ps. 119 : 103, C.R.
32 : 258.

through God's word. Calvin contrasts the fact that Abraham obeyed without question the command to sacrifice Isaac, with Peter's protestation on being commanded in the vision to kill and eat unclean animals, and he attributes the difference to the fact that Abraham by the power of the Spirit was furnished with the superior certainty.[1] They had a sense of sonship with God. They called God Father, because they had confidence in his only begotten Son as Mediator.[2]

The children of Israel had, moreover, a living hope of immortality. Behind all the promises given to him by God of earthly prosperity and happiness, the true man of faith in Israel would discern a hidden promise of everlasting life in heaven. To suggest otherwise is to side not only with the Roman Schoolmen but with "the Anabaptists . . . who think of the people of Israel as they would do of some herd of swine, absurdly imagining that the Lord gorged them with temporal blessings here, and gave them no hope of blessed immortality."[3] When God offers the conveniences of the earthly life "it is not because He wishes that our attention should be confined to present happiness . . . but in order that by the contemplation of it, we may rise to the heavenly life. . . . More especially was God accustomed to act in this manner towards the ancient people, that, by tasting present benefits, as by a shadow, they might be called to the heavenly inheritance."[4] Moreover, the Children of Israel had "that solid participation in God (*solida Dei participatio*) which cannot exist without the blessing of everlasting life".[5] "Such presence cannot be enjoyed without life being, at the same time, possessed along with it. And though nothing more had been expressed, they had a sufficiently clear promise of spiritual life in the words *I am your God* (Exodus 6 : 7) . . . not to their bodies only, but specially to their souls. Souls, however, if not united to God by righteousness remain estranged from Him in death. On the other hand, that union (*coniunctio*), wherever it exists,

[1]Cf. comm. on Acts 10 : 14, C.R. 48 : 232.
[2]Comm. on Luke 1 : 32, C.R. 45 : 28.
[3]Inst. 2 : 10 : 1.
[4]Comm. on Isa. 1 : 19, C.R. 36 : 47–8. *Neque quod velit nos praesenti felicitate detineri . . . sed ut contemplatione ipsius in coelestem assurgamus . . . Hoc autem magis usitatum fuit populo veteri, ut bonorum praesentium gustu, velut imagine, ad haereditatem coelestem vocarentur.*
[5]Inst. 2 : 10 : 7.

will bring perpetual salvation with it."[1] Thus in the Old Testament what is said in the promises about earthly prosperity must be understood as referring also to the "manifestation of celestial glory"[2] and was indeed so understood by the pious among the people of Israel. "Their views were directed to another and a higher life to which the present was only preparatory."[3]

Therefore it would be absurd to imagine that believers who died before Jesus came into the world were throughout all their lives slaves of sin and death.[4] In the view of Calvin, no one can possibly understand or truly value the Old Testament without taking full account of the presence of Christ with His ancient people. "The external economy without the reality would have been mere folly."[5] If Christ is put out of sight all that is left of the ceremonies of the law is "profane butchery".[6] Worship meant to the Children of Israel no less than what it means to us. "That God truly dwelt in the midst of the people, is what the faithful experienced who sought Him."[7] "The ark of the covenant was not a vain and illusory symbol of the presence of God."[8] When they rightly worshipped God in the temple, according to His word, they stood, as it were, in His presence, and would actually experience that He was near to them.[9]

3. Revelation under the New Covenant superior to that under the Old

While insisting so forcibly on the substantial unity of Old and New Covenants, Calvin, however, concedes that there are many differences between the two dispensations. "Faith has its degrees in beholding Christ,"[10] and undoubtedly, as a general rule, the

[1] Inst. 2 : 10 : 8.
[2] Inst. 2 : 10 : 16.
[3] Comm. on Ps. 49 : 16, C.R. 31 : 490. *Mentibus in coelum sublatis cucurrisse per hunc mundum, donec stadium suum peragerent.*
[4] Comm. on Luke 1 : 68, C.R. 45 : 46.
[5] Comm. on Exod. 29 : 38, C.R. 24 : 491. *Exterior caeremonia sine re fuisset mera fatuitas.*
[6] Comm. on Exod. 29 : 38, C.R. 24 : 490.
[7] Comm. on Ps. 24 : 8, C.R. 31 : 249.
[8] Ibid.
[9] Cf. comm. on Ps. 132 : 14, C.R. 32 : 350. *Nam requies et habitatio Dei virtutis eius praesentiam hominum respectu significant.*
[10] Comm. on John 8 : 56, C.R. 47 : 214. *Fidem in Christi intuitu suos habere gradus.* Cf. serm. on Luke 1 : 1–4, C.R. 46 : 1. *Nous differons en degré.*

degree of vision under the Old Covenant is less than under the New. The latter dispensation has a superiority over the former that gives it the right to be called "New". "The New Testament flows from that Covenant which God made with Abraham and afterwards sanctioned by the hand of Moses. That which is promulgated for us in the Gospel is called the New Covenant, not because it had no beginning previously, but because it was renewed, and better conditions added."[1] "Though Christ is the substance of both He is not equally manifested in both."[2]

(i) Revelation under the New Covenant is more *rich and full* than under the Old.[3] The Holy Spirit was "more abundantly given" under the gospel than under the law,[4] when God gave His redemptive gifts "not so freely and extensively" as now. Commenting on the quotation from Joel in Acts 2 : 17, *I will pour out my spirit upon all flesh*, Calvin notes a "twofold antithesis" between the times of the two Covenants, "for the *pouring out* signifies a great abundance, whereas there was under the law a more scarce distribution. *All flesh* signifies an infinite multitude, whereas God in times past did vouchsafe to bestow such full participation of His spirit only upon a few."[5] After speaking of the Red Sea passage as a symbol of mortification and resurrection in Christ, and of the cloud as a symbol of purification, covering and protecting the Israelites from the sun, as the blood of Christ covers and protects the Christian from the wrath of God, Calvin then adds, "The mystery was then obscure and known to few."[6] It is true that "scarcely a person can be found in the Christian Church, who is to be compared with Abraham for the excellency of his faith", but Abraham was an exception. The ordinary people of the Old Covenant possessed a knowledge partaking more or less of the obscurity of the age.[7] Under the New Covenant the promise has at last been fulfilled that "*All shall know me*" whereby to-day those who are the least among the disciples of Christ are endued with as much light of know-

---

[1]Comm. on Ezek. 16 : 60, C.R. 40 : 393.
[2]C.R. 9 : 177. *Quia etsi commu nisutriusque substantia est Christus, non tamen aequalis est euis exhibitio.*
[3]C.R. 9 : 176.
[4]Comm. on Joel 2 : 28, C.R. 42 : 566 f.
[5]Comm. on Acts 2 : 17, C.R. 48 : 32.
[6]Inst. 4 : 15 : 9. *Et si vero tunc obscurum et paucis cognitum fuit mysterium.*
[7]Inst. 2 : 11 : 6.

ledge as the outstanding prophets and teachers of the older dispensation.[1]

(ii) Revelation under the New Covenant is more *vivid and distinct* than under the Old. Christ was formerly beheld àt a distance by the prophets, but now has made Himself familiarly and completely visible.[2] The Gospel differs from the law "only in respect of clearness of manifestation (*dilucidae manifestationis*)".[3] When Paul says that Christ at His advent *brought life and immortality to light through the Gospel*, "he claims for the Gospel the honourable distinction of being a new and extraordinary kind of embassy. . . . For though believers at all times experienced the truth of Paul's declaration, that *all the promises of God in him are Yea and Amen* inasmuch as these promises were sealed upon their hearts; yet because He has in His flesh completed all the parts of our salvation, this vivid manifestation of realities was justly entitled to this new and special distinction."[4] "As painters do not in the first draught bring out the likeness in vivid colours and expressively but in the first instance draw rude and obscure lines, so the representation of Christ under the law was unpolished—a first sketch, but in our sacraments it is seen drawn out to the life."[5] "Under the law was shadowed forth only in rude and imperfect lines that which is under the Gospel set forth in living colours and graphically distinct."[6] The ceremonies of the law had not the "last touch of the artist" and things were shown in them "at a distance"[7] which are now set before our eyes. What was "formerly concealed" is now made known to us in the Gospel, the ancient fathers having "nothing more than little sparks of the true light, the full brightness of which daily shines around us".[8]

(iii) Revelation under the New Covenant is more *satisfying* than under the Old. The men of the Old Covenant "had only a slight foretaste; to us is given fuller fruition".[9] They "could

---

[1]Comm. on Jer. 31 : 34, C.R. 38 : 694–5.
[2]Comm. on John 8 : 56, C.R. 47 : 214.
[3]Inst. 2 : 9 : 4.
[4]Inst. 2 : 9 : 2. . . . *Viva ipsa rerum exhibitio iure novum et singulare praeconium obtinuit.*
[5]Comm. on Col. 2 : 18, C.R. 52 : 110.
[6]Comm. on Heb. 10 : 1, C.R. 55 : 121.
[7]Ibid.
[8]Comm. on John 1 : 18, C.R. 47 : 19; cf. on Ps. 67 : 2.
[9]Inst. 2 : 9 : 1. *Quum eam modice delibaverint, uberior nobis offertur eius fruitio.*

not be satisfied with the state in which they were then, but
aspired to higher things".[1] After being granted at Peniel as full
a revelation of God as could then be given him, Jacob nevertheless utters the prayer then unanswerable, *"Tell me, I pray thee,
thy name."* "It is not to be wondered at," comments Calvin,
"that the holy man, to whom God had manifested Himself
under so many veils and coverings that he had not yet obtained
any clear knowledge of Him, should break forth in this wish;
nay it is certain that all the saints under the law, were influenced
with this wish."[2] The fathers *"inquired* as though they possessed
not what is now offered to us".[3] As a proof that they "desired
something more", Calvin refers to the example of Simeon, who,
"after seeing Christ, prepared himself calmly and with a satisfied
mind for death", thus showing that "he was before unsatisfied
and anxious".[4] The experience of men under the Old Covenant
had not the same degree of satisfying assurance which we enjoy
under the Gospel. The fathers enjoyed the forgiveness of sins
but, though forgiven, their sins were still remembered. The
benefit of the New Covenant is that there is under it "no remembrance of sins".[5] The regenerating power of the Holy Spirit
under the New Covenant "penetrates into the heart and really
forms us for the service of God", whereas under the Old it was
more a doctrine than an experience.[6] The sense of sonship to
God under the old dispensation, though so real that they called
God "Father", is now so much greater that we can boldly cry
"Abba Father".[7]

(iv) Revelation under the New Covenant is more *familiar* than
under the Old. The dispensation of the law is full of terror,
"but the Gospel contains nothing but love, provided it be

[1]Comm. on Heb. 7 : 19, C.R. 55 : 92. *Praesenti suo statu non poterant esse
contenti quin longius adspirarent.*

[2]Comm. on Gen. 32 : 29, C.R. 23 : 445. *Nec mirum est si sanctus vir in hoc
votum prorumpat, cui se Deus patefacerat sub multis involucris, ut nondum familiaris
esset nec liquida cognitio.*

[3]Comm. on 1 Pet. 1 : 10, C.R. 55 : 216.

[4]Ibid. Cf. serm. on Luke 1 : 1–4, C.R. 46 : 1.

[5]Comm. on Jer. 31 : 34, C.R. 38 : 696.

[6]Cf. comm. on Jer. 31 : 31–2, C.R. 38 : 688–9. *Fuit igitur haec quoque aliqua
novitas, quod Deus regenuit fideles spiritu suo, ita ut non esset literalis tantum
doctrina, sed efficax, quae non tantum verberaret aures, sed in animos penetraret,
atque vere formaret in obsequium Dei.*

[7]Comm. on Luke 1 : 32, C.R. 45 : 28.

received by faith".[1] Our New Testament Sacraments "present Christ the more clearly to us, the more familiarly (*propius*) He has been manifested to men".[2] "In the precepts of the law, God is seen as the rewarder only of perfect righteousness ... and on the other hand as the stern avenger of wickedness. But in Christ His countenance beams forth full of grace and gentleness towards poor unworthy sinners."[3] The knowledge of God under the law Calvin can refer to as "dark and feeble"[4] when comparing it to that in the Gospel, where it is "the face of God"[5] that appears to us. "He made himself familiarly and completely visible when he came down from heaven."[6]

(v) Revelation under the New Covenant is more *immediately substantial* than under the Old. Those who enjoyed revelation under the law were conscious that their present experience was but a small pledge of a future glorious reality. In their experience of revelation they were conscious of grappling with a hidden mystery, the secret of which would belong to a future generation. What they saw of Christ they really *saw*, but it was placed "at a distance" from them. There was nothing "realised" about their eschatology. Even though they knew themselves truly to possess what the coming Redeemer was to bring them, they possessed it as the promise of their future inheritance. Referring to the Old Covenant, Calvin can say, "There is nothing substantial in it till we look beyond it."[7] Under these former conditions "the minds of believers were always impressed with the conviction that the full light of understanding was to be expected only on the advent of the Messiah".[8] "His kingdom was as yet hid under coverings." Though they "partook of Christ", they nevertheless possessed Him "as one hidden and as it were absent—absent, I say, not in the power of grace, but because he was not yet manifest in the flesh".[9] "Until Christ was manifest

---

[1]Comm. on Heb. 12 : 19, C.R. 55 : 183.
[2]Inst. 4 : 14 : 22–3.
[3]Inst. 2 : 7 : 8.
[4]Comm. on Isa. 25 : 9, C.R. 36 : 420.
[5]Comm. on 1 John 5 : 20, C.R. 55 : 375.
[6]Comm. on John 8 : 56, C.R. 47 : 214–15. *Familiariter ac penitus se conspicuum reddidit quum e coelo descendit ad homines.*
[7]Inst. 2 : 11 : 4. *In ea quoniam nihil solidum subest, nisi ulterius transeatur.*
[8]Inst. 2 : 15 : 1.
[9]Comm. on 1 Pet. 1 : 12, C.R. 55 : 218. *Ergo eum non nisi absconditum et quasi absentem possidebant. Absentem dico, non virtute aut gratia, sed quia nondum in carne manifestatus erat. Quare et regnum eius sub involucris adhuc latebat.*

in the flesh all signs shadowed Him as absent, however He might inwardly exert the presence of His power and consequently of His person on believers."[1] "Grace was in a manner suspended until the advent of Christ—not that the fathers were excluded from it, but they had not a present manifestation of it."[2]

Under the New Covenant, however, this eschatological tension, though not removed, has been lessened. What was formerly possessed and enjoyed as at a distance has been made a present experience. Christ has "in a manner opened heaven to us so that we might have a near view of those spiritual riches which before were under types exhibited at a distance".[3] Jesus announced this momentous change when before the paralytic man He claimed to have power *on earth* to forgive sins. The use of the phrase *on earth* is, for Calvin, very significant. "Christ's meaning is that forgiveness of sins ought not to be sought for at a distance: for He exhibits it to men in His own person, and as it were in His hands. . . . Now as Christ descended to earth for the purpose of exhibiting to men the grace of God as present, He is said to forgive sins visibly, because in Him and by Him the will of God was revealed, which, according to the perception of the flesh, had been formerly hidden above the clouds."[4] It is true that our salvation like that of those in former ages is yet "in hope",[5] but Christ stretches out His hand directly to us that He may withdraw us from the world and raise us up to heaven, whereas those who lived before His coming were directed to Him only "by the circuitous course of types and figures".[6]

[1]Inst. 4 : 14 : 25. *Donec eium manifestatus est in carne Christus, omnia signa velut absentem eum adumbrabant: utcunque virtutis suae, suique adeo ipsius praesentiam fidelibus intus exsereret.*

[2]Comm. on Col. 2 : 14, C.R. 52 : 108. *Gratia quodammodo suspensa erat usque ad Christi adventum. Non quod ab ea excluderentur Patres sed non habebant praesentem eius ostensionem in suis caeremoniis.* Cf. comm. on Isa. 25 : 9, where Calvin speaks of the promises as being suspended "till the coming of Christ".
Cf. comm. on Jer. 31 : 34, C.R. 38 : 694. *Tenenda est . . . quod Deus populum suum teneret suspensum exspectatione melioris status.*

[3]Comm. on 1 Pet. 1 : 12, C.R. 55 : 218.

[4]Comm. on Matt. 9 : 6, C.R. 45 : 246. *Nempe dicere voluit Christus, ne procul quaerenda sit peccatorum remissio, in sua persona quasi ad manus esse hominibus exhibitam. . . .*

[5]Cf. comm. on Heb. 10 : 1, C.R. 55 : 121, where Calvin says that the "full fruition" of the promised blessings of the O.T. is "deferred to the resurrection and the future world". The good things to come "are not only future blessings as to the Old Testament but also with respect to us who still hope for them". Cf. comm. on Dan. 12 : 2.

[6]Comm. on Heb. 4 : 8, C.R. 55 : 48; cf. comm. on Heb. 7 : 12, C.R. 55 : 89.

(vi) Revelation under the New Covenant is more *simple* than under the Old.

God accommodated Himself to the "weaker and unripe apprehensions of the fathers by the rudiments of ceremony, while He has extended a simple form of worship to us who have attained a mature age".[1] Under the Old Covenant there were many and very diverse ceremonies and events through which revelation was given. By choosing such a variety of methods God meant to indicate to His people in those times that there was as yet nothing fixed as to the manner in which He might reveal Himself, and thus their expectations were continually stirred to look for something in the future which might be durable and final. "Variety was an evidence of imperfection."[2] "By this variety they were reminded not to stop short at such figures . . . but to expect something better."[3] And, indeed, the multifarious veils and coverings which God used in revealing Himself did have this effect on the fathers.[4] Because of the superior spiritual power of the New Covenant such outward variety is no longer required, and its absence is a sign that at last the final revelation that fulfils all prophecy has been given. "After Christ was revealed sacraments were instituted fewer in number but of more august significance and more excellent power."[5] Since Jesus Christ has been manifested in the flesh, and doctrine been much more clearly delivered, ceremonies have diminished. As we have now the body we should leave off the shadows.[6] The richness and abundance of the content which

[1]Comm. on Ps. 50 : 14, C.R. 31 : 502.
[2]Comm. on Heb. 1 : 1, C.R. 55 : 9–10.
[3]Inst. 4 : 18 : 20.
[4]Cf. comm. on Gen. 32 : 29, C.R. 23 : 445–6.
[5]Inst. 4 : 14 : 26, quoted from Augustine. *Numero pauciora : significatione augustiora : virtute praestantiora.*
[6]O.S. 1 : 525. *Plus que la doctrine a esté esclaircie, les figures ont esté diminuées. Puis doncq que nous avons le corps, il nous fault delaisser les umbres.*

"It must be observed," says Calvin, "that musical instruments were among the legal ceremonies which Christ at His coming abolished; and therefore we, under the Gospel, must maintain a greater simplicity" (comm. on Exod. 15 : 20, C.R. 24 : 162). "The voice of man . . . assuredly excels all inanimate instruments of music" (comm. on Ps. 33 : 2, C.R. 31 : 325). The use of musical instruments in worship was part of the training of the law (comm. on Ps. 71 : 22, C.R. 31 : 662–3), fitted for those "yet tender, like children" (comm. on Ps. 81 : 2, C.R. 31 : 760). Instrumental music for Calvin is an "unknown tongue" in which we are now forbidden to praise God (1 Cor. 14 : 13).

gives rise to this final simplicity of form give us reason to designate this age as the last days.

It must again be stated, however, that in spite of all his concessions as to the superiority of the new dispensation to the old, Calvin very often, immediately after he has made such a concession, adds some statement to guard against giving the impression that there is after all any really substantial difference between the Covenants. He approaches the Old Testament with a realistic imagination. "Sacrifices, indeed, were undoubtedly not very pleasant and agreeable to behold, for the revolting act of taking away life, the reeking blood and the stench of the smoke, might have a repulsive effect."[1] Nevertheless, he goes on to point out that "in these things the honour of God shone brightly". Moreover, he is always ready to draw our attention to the fact that, compared with the full revelation that will be given in glory, the comparative difference between the two Covenants will appear as nothing.[2]

[1]Comm. on Isa. 34 : 6, C.R. 36 : 583.
[2]Comm. on John 14 : 2, C.R. 47 : 322–3.

Chapter IV

Unity of Revelation—Unity of Form

1. Calvin's distinction between the form and content
of revelation

WE have seen that Calvin admits a great difference in form between revelation under the Old Covenant and that under the New. In several places he sums up his view on this matter by saying that while the New Covenant is the same in content or "substance" (*substantia*) as the Old, the form (*forma*) or administration (*administratio*) is nevertheless greatly different and vastly superior. "Let us now see why He promises to the people a *New* Covenant. It, being new, no doubt refers to what they call the form; and the form or manner, regards not words only, but first Christ, then the grace of the Holy Spirit, and the whole external way of teaching. But the substance remains the same. By substance I understand the doctrine, for God in the Gospel brings forth nothing but what the Law contains."[1] "The newness was not as to substance but as to the form only. . . . He does not promise anything different as to the essence of the doctrine, but he makes the difference to be in the form only."[2] "The Covenant of all the fathers is so far from differing substantially from ours, that it is the very same; it only varies in the administration."[3]

---

[1]Comm. on Jer. 31 : 31, C.R. 38 : 688. *Nunc videndum est cur promittat foedus novum populo. Non dubium est quin hoc referatur ad formam, sicuti loquuntur. Forma autem haec non tantum posita est in verbis, sed primum in Christo, deinde in gratia spiritus sancti, et tota docendi ratione externa : substantia autem eadem manet. Substantia intelligo doctrinam, quia Deus in evangelio nihil profert, quod lex non contineat.*
Cf. comm. on Ezek. 16 : 61, C.R. 40 : 396. *Et tamen novum foedus ita a veteri manare, ut fere sit idem quoad substantiam, tametsi distinguenda sit forma.*
[2]Comm. on Jer. 31 : 33, C.R. 38 : 691.
[3]Inst. 2 : 10 : 2 (cf. comm. on Exod. 12 : 14, C.R. 24 : 290). In comm. on Heb. 8 : 6, C.R. 55 : 100, Calvin makes the distinction as between the *forma* and *materia* of the two Covenants.

2. Old Testament forms of revelation closely related to those of the New Testament

The complicated and manifold, obscure and carnal forms under which revelation took place have been replaced by ordinances of the New Covenant which are more simple and more spiritual. Nevertheless, even in the midst of this diversity Calvin also sees a close and highly significant connection between the forms taken by revelation in the Old Testament and those in the New—such a close connection that it may be called a real unity of form. The forms of revelation under the Old Covenant are greatly varied but never chosen haphazardly. All the differing forms of the old revelation shadow forth the outward form that revelation is to take in Jesus Christ and under the New Covenant. They are prophecies of what is to come. They are typical of Jesus Christ and of the sacraments of the Gospel. Behind them all there is a unity, the key to which is the flesh and blood of Jesus Christ. The *divers manners* in which at *sundry times* God spoke to the fathers all foreshadow Him. Moreover, it is through these Old Testament forms that we are given the categories through which we can understand and proclaim the true significance of Jesus Christ.

Though the validity of these forms as a means of revelation in actual concrete fact has been abolished, and we can no longer expect God to use such means in real life, nevertheless the account of them is still preserved to serve us as an authoritative interpretation and proclamation of Jesus Christ, and they are there for us to study in this light. This is for Calvin the key to the true interpretation of the Old Testament. "The prophets ministered more abundantly to us than to their own age."[1] "Their ministry was more useful to us because we are fallen on the ends of the world . . . what else then was this but that they spread the table that others might afterwards feed on the provisions laid on it?"[2] "We have in Christ whatever has been shadowed forth by the ancient sacrifices . . . yet it assists our faith not a little, to compare the reality with the type, so that we

[1]Comm. on 1 Pet. 1 : 10, C.R. 55 : 216.
[2]Comm. on 1 Pet. 1 : 12, C.R. 55 : 218.

may seek in the former what the latter contains."[1] This point
is well brought out by Calvin in his exposition of the story of the
transfiguration, where he asserts the abolition of the law and the
prophets in the light of Jesus, and yet at the same time their
present validity is a means of conducting us to Jesus that we
may understand Him. Christ is "the only teacher" who "by the
brightness of His gospel causes those sparks which shone in the
Old Testament to disappear", yet He is "as truly heard at the
present day in the law and in the prophets as in his Gospel".[2]
"When it is said that in the end they saw Christ *alone*, this means
that the law and prophets had a temporary glory, that Christ
alone might remain fully in view. If we would properly avail
ourselves of the aid of Moses, we must not stop with him, but
must endeavour to be conducted by his hand to Christ, of whom
both he and all the rest are ministers."[3]

3. The form of Christ as foreshadowed in the
Old Testament

It is on the basis of this unity of form between the covenants
that Calvin therefore expounds the Old and the New Testaments, and his views on this subject may be clarified and further
expounded by a study of his commentaries.

(i) *The form of Christ as foreshadowed in the historical form of Israel*

In the varied circumstances that came upon the people of
God in the course of their history Calvin seeks to lead us to discern the lineaments of the human form which Jesus was to
assume when He came in the flesh. The Children of Israel
were by the grace of God always a true Church, organically
connected to Christ as members to the head of a body. But it
is impossible to be so joined to Christ without such a union
becoming at least dimly apparent in some outward resemblance

[1]Comm. on 1 Pet. 1 : 19, C.R. 55 : 225.
[2]Comm. on Matt. 17 : 5, C.R. 45 : 488.
[3]Ibid, C.R. 45 : 489.

between head and members. Our own sacrament of Baptism bears witness to the fact that as Christ the Head died and rose so also His members must have the marks of death and resurrection engraven upon their outward form. Therefore we should expect to see in the historical existence and career of the Old Testament Church some faint outline of Jesus Christ. "We must note the proportion between the members and the head,"[1] says Calvin, dealing with one of the Old Testament prophecies, "for as the truth of this prophecy was found whole and perfect in Christ alone, as in the Head, so it takes place in all the members according to the measure and order of every man."[2] "Under the name of Israel, by which he means Christ, Isaiah includes the whole body of the people as members under the head."[3]

Calvin thus sees foreshadowed in the historical events of the Old Testament not only our own present condition as a Church but also, more faintly yet discernibly, the condition which Jesus Christ Himself was subject to in His earthly career. The sufferings of the faithful in Israel are adumbrations of the sufferings of Christ. "The ancient fathers submitted themselves wholly to bear the affliction of Jesus Christ . . . for it is not said, Moses bore the shame of Abraham, but of Jesus Christ. Thus the ancient fathers . . . offered themselves to God in sacrifices, to bear most patiently the afflictions of Christ."[4] The great historical deliverances in Israel's history are patterns or types of the eternal salvation which all the members of Christ in every age should experience under the leadership of their Head, Jesus Christ. Such experiences as the rescue by the Lord of His people from their low and desperate condition in Egypt and Babylon can really be called the death and resurrection, the rebirth and renewal, of the nation. But such experiences were brought upon Israel not simply as the natural outcome of their previous way of life but also for the sake of God's redemptive purpose, in order that there might be foreshadowed in Israel, under earthly figures, a real prelude to the sufferings, death,

[1]Comm. on Acts 13 : 36, C.R. 48 : 303. *Notanda est inter membra et caput proportio.*
[2]Ibid.
[3]Comm. on Isa. 49 : 3, C.R. 37 : 192.
[4]Serm. on 2 Tim. 1 : 9–10, C.R. 54 : 63.

resurrection and ascension of Jesus Christ. "Now that same carnal restitution did figure the true renewal of the Church of God, which is accomplished in Christ."[1] Referring to the Exodus, Calvin says, "That deliverance of the people did shadow the redemption of us all, for whose sake Christ was to be sent of his Father, that he might take upon him the shape of a servant together with our flesh.[2] This is why Calvin, for example, justifies Matthew's reference to Hosea 2 : 1, *Out of Egypt have I called my son*, when seeking a scripture parallel to the return from Egypt of the holy family. The passage in the original refers, it is true, not to the Messiah but to the nation, and Calvin admits a superficially apparent opposition between the original and the application at which "scoffers" might take occasion, "but," he goes on to say, "I think that Matthew had more deeply considered the purpose of God in having Christ led into Egypt . . . Christ cannot be separated from His Church, as the body will be mutilated and imperfect without the head. What, then, happened formerly in the Church, ought at length to be fulfilled in the Head. . . . It was then the full nativity of the Church when Christ came forth from Egypt to redeem His Church. God, when He formerly redeemed his people from Egypt, only showed by a certain prelude the redemption which He deferred till the coming of Christ."[3]

The deliverance of the Jews from Babylon is, in Calvin's view, a far more significant act of God even than that from Egypt.[4] "The deliverance from Babylon was but a prelude to the restoration of the Church, and was intended to last, not for a few years only, but till Christ should come and bring true salvation, not

[1]Comm. on Rom. 9 : 27, C.R. 49 : 191. *Iam restitutio illa carnalis veram ecclesiae Dei instaurationem figuravit, quae in Christo peragitur.*

[2]Comm. on Acts 7 : 30, C.R. 48 : 144. *Illa populi redemptio nostram omnium adumbravit. . . .*

Cf. serm. on Deut. 4 : 36–8, C.R. 26 : 220. *Il monstre que ceste redemption qui n'estoit que pour le corps, ie di de prima face, combien qu'elle fust figure du salut que desia Dieu avoit promis en la personne du Redempteur;* and serm. on Deut. 4 : 39–43, C.R. 26 : 224. *Vray est que nous ne sommes point sortis d'Egypte : mais Dieu nous a retirez de la servitude du diable et de mort.*

[3]Comm. on Hos. 11 : 1, C.R. 42 : 433. *. . . Tantum quodam praeludio ostendit redemptionem quam distulit ad Christi adventum;* cf. comm. on Matt. 2 : 15, C.R. 45 : 99. *Facit autem haec analogia, ne videri debeat absurdum, quod partem aliquam pueritiae suae Christus in Aegypto transegit.*

[4]Cf. comm. on Isa. 43 : 19, C.R. 37 : 94–5.

only to their bodies, but likewise to their souls."[1] "The return
of the people is closely connected with the renewal of the Church,
which was accomplished by Christ; for what God began by
bringing His people out of captivity He continued till Christ,
and then brought to perfection; and so it is one and the same
redemption."[2] Calvin calls the return of the Jews from Babylon
"the beginning of the full and solid liberty which was at length
made manifest in Christ",[3] and he regards the subsequent
rebuilding of the temple as the commencement of the reign of
Christ which continues until the end of this world.[4]

In the Messianic prophecies in the Old Testament (except for
a few passages which he insists can have no other reference than
to the person of Christ Himself)[5] Calvin finds a threefold reference. First, they refer actually and literally to some historic
situation in Israel, with reference either to some person or to
the whole nation. Calvin disallows interpretations that restrict

[1]Comm. on Isa. 9 : 2, C.R. 36 : 190. *Redemptio babylonica veluti praeludium
fuit instaurandae ecclesiae . . .* ; cf. on Isa. 9 : 3, C.R. 36 : 192. In his comment
on Isa. 9 : 6, C.R. 36 : 194, Calvin calls the same deliverance the *initium
renovationis ecclesiae.*

[2]Comm. on Isa. 43 : 8, C.R. 37 : 86.

[3]Comm. on Ezek. 17 : 22, C.R. 40 : 417. *Praeludium plenae et solidae
libertatis, quae tandem in Christo patefacta fuit.*

[4]Ibid. Calvin also refers to the calls of David to Kingship as the foundation
of the Kingdom of Christ; cf. on Ps. 118 : 25, C.R. 32 : 210; on Ps. 78 : 70,
C.R. 31 : 745. It should be noted that in the midst of the historical forces
which operated to open up the way for Israel to leave Babylon and Egypt Christ
Himself was also active, working in a spiritual and sacramental manner upon
the souls of His people, i.e. the actual historical deliverances which marked
Israel's history were for those who participated in them real sacramental
experiences. Cf. on Isa. 49 : 1, C.R. 37 : 190; on Isa. 9 : 6, C.R. 36 : 194–5.
"While the Lord relieved the necessities of the body He at the same time provided for the everlasting welfare of souls" (comm. on 1 Cor. 10 : 3, C.R. 49 :
453) is a principle which can apply to the whole of Old Testament history.
"Whenever, therefore, God assisted His ancient people, He at the same time
reconciled them to Himself through Christ; and accordingly, whenever famine,
pestilence and war are mentioned, in order to hold out a hope of deliverance,
He places the Messiah before their eyes" (comm. on Isa. 7 : 14, C.R. 36 : 156).
"That people was a figure of the Christian Church, in such a manner as to be a
true Church. . . . Their sacraments served to prefigure ours in such a way that
they were . . . true sacraments, having a present efficacy (comm. on 1 Cor.
10 : 11, C.R. 49 : 460) cf. comm. on Rom. 15 : 8. The coming in the flesh
of Christ perfects what has already been begun and continued (comm. on Isa.
43 : 8, C.R. 37 : 85–6) and brings to the light what is already there (comm. on
Ezek. 17 : 22, C.R. 40 : 417).

[5]Cf. comm. on Isa. 42 : 1, C.R. 37 : 58; on Matt. 12 : 17–21, C.R. 45 : 330
and ff.; on Ps. 45 : 6–8, C.R. 31 : 451 f.; on Ps. 2 : 8, C.R. 31 : 47; on Ps. 89 :
24 f., C.R. 31 : 819–20.

such passages to the person of Christ.[1] In the second place, such passages have also a Messianic reference, and Calvin accordingly also seeks to interpret them Christologically as being fulfilled truly when God sent His Son as redeemer. But such passages have, thirdly, a further reference to the state of the Church of Christ in this present world and should also be applied by the true expositor to what is daily and continually being fulfilled in the life of the Church, for[2] they are also meant by the Holy Spirit to have this reference. Take, for example, the verse, *In his quiver hath he hid me*.[3] Calvin first interprets this verse as referring to Christ and then adds, "The present question is not about the person of Christ; but about the whole body of the Church. We must indeed begin with the Head, but we must next come down to the members; and to all the ministers of the Word must be applied what is here affirmed concerning Christ." Such passages can also refer to the second advent of Christ.[4]

(ii) *The form of Christ as foreshadowed in individuals within Israel*

Within Israel there arose individual figures who, in union with the coming Mediator, shadowed out in their own individual experience not only what was to be the experience of all the true children of God but also what was to be the incarnate experience of the Word when He was made flesh. On Jacob's conflict with the Angel of the Lord at Peniel Calvin says, "Although this vision was particularly useful to Jacob himself, to teach him beforehand that many conflicts awaited him, that he might yet certainly conclude that he might be conqueror in them all; yet there is not the least doubt that the Lord exhibited in His person a specimen of the temptations—common to all His

---

[1]Cf. comm. on Ezek. 17 : 22, C.R. 40 : 417; on Isa. 52 : 8 and 10, C.R. 37 : 248–50; on Isa. 59 : 19, 60 : 15, 62 : 11.

[2]Cf. comm. on Ps. 41 : 10, C.R. 31 : 422.

[3]Comm. on Isa. 49 : 2, C.R. 37 : 192. Cf. also the verse, *Prepare ye the way of the Lord*. This is historically addressed to *Cyrus*, who under the hand of God opens a way for Israel to return from Babylon. "But that was a shadowy anticipation of redemption. When the spiritual truth is about to appear, *John* is sent to remove obstacles, and even now the same voice sounds in *our* ears . . . that we may take out of the way those sins which obstruct the Kingdom of Christ." Comm. on Matt. 3 : 3, C.R. 45 : 113; cf. comm. on Isa. 40 : 3, C.R. 37 : 7–8; on Isa. 35 : 7, C.R. 36 : 594–5.

[4]Comm. on Ezek. 17 : 22, C.R. 40 : 417.

people—which await them, and must be constantly submitted to, in this transitory life. Wherefore it is right to keep in view this design of the vision, which is to represent all the servants of God in this world as wrestlers. . . . Therefore what was once exhibited under a visible form to our father Jacob, is daily fulfilled in the individual members of the Church."[1] In Joseph's[2] trial in prison before his resurrection to glory and honour Calvin sees a figure of the death and resurrection of Christ and of all believers in Christ, and writes, "Thus the promise of God which had exalted him to honour, almost plunges him into the grave. We, also, who have received the gratuitous adoption of God amid many sorrows experience the same thing. For, from the time that Christ gathers us into His flock, God permits us to be cast down in various ways so that we seem nearer Hell than Heaven. Therefore let the example of Joseph be fixed in our minds that we be not disquieted. . . . For I have before showed, and the thing itself clearly testifies, that in Joseph was adumbrated what was afterwards more fully exhibited in Christ, in order that each member may form itself to the imitation of his example."[3]

It is, however, more particularly when he deals with the history of David[4] that Calvin makes most use of this interpretative principle. The life of David as reflected in the Psalms shadows forth in all its details the actual concrete historical circumstances

[1]Comm. on Gen. 32 : 24, C.R. 23 : 442. . . . *Ergo quod sub visibili forma semel demonstratum fuit patri nostro Jacob, quotidie in singulis ecclesiae membris impletur, ut cum Deo luctari in tentationibus necesse habeant.*

[2]In his sermon on Matt. 2 : 23, C.R. 46 : 453–4, Calvin discusses both Joseph and Samson as figures of Christ. *Ainsi donc puis que Ioseph a este comme Redempteur temporel de l'Eglise, il ne se faut point esbahir s'il a este figure de nostre Seigneur Iesus Christ . . . Quant à Samson, c'est un poinct assez notoire qu'il a representé nostre Seigneur Iesus Christ, d'autant qu'il a bataillé toute sa vie contre les ennemis de l'Eglise.* To justify the inclusion of Samson, Calvin reminds us that David too was a sinner in like respect, and adds, *Il n'est pas requis qu'il y ait perfection qui soit du tout pareille à la verite, quand on propose quelque figure.*

[3]Comm. on Gen. 37 : 18–19, C.R. 23 : 486. . . . *Iam enim supra admonui et res ipsa clare testatur adumbratum fuisse in Joseph quod plenius deinde in Christo ecclesiae capite exhibitum fuit, ut singula membra ad imitationem se forment.*

The fact that the mediating *angel* (see note on p. 10) appeared so often in the form of a man was a foreshadowing of the incarnation of God in a man (Inst. 1 : 11 : 3), a prelude to what was afterwards manifested in the flesh (comm. on Joshua 5 : 14, C.R. 25 : 464). Moreover, the role of leader and protector of the people which the Angel assumed so often is typical of Christ's leadership and protectorate of His Church (cf. comm. on Gen. 48 : 15, C.R. 23 : 584–5).

[4]Cf. comm. on Ps. 18 : 44 f., C.R. 31 : 190. *Christi personam sustinuit David.*

of the gospel story, and especially of the passion. In Psalm 22 David in describing his own sufferings, and in expressing his own genuine feelings, is at the same time describing Christ for us, since David's life is a prophecy of Christ's. "The heavenly Father intended that in the person of His Son these things should be visibly accomplished which were shadowed forth in David."[1] It is true, however, that David in writing the Psalm was dimly conscious that he was describing another, for he "speaks of himself in hyperbolic language and he does so in order to lead us beyond himself to Christ. The dreadful encounter of our Redeemer with death, by which there was forced from His body blood instead of sweat, His descent into Hell, by which he tasted the wrath of God which was due to sinners, and, in short, His emptying Himself, could not be adequately expressed by any of the ordinary forms of speech."[2]

The parallel which Calvin sees between David and Christ extends even to circumstantial details. The rejection of Jesus by the Jerusalem authorities and His sufferings at their hands were foreshadowed by the rejection of David by Saul, which in Calvin's view gave rise to the much quoted verse in the 118th Psalm about the stone which the builders rejected.[3] David's enemies are a type of Christ's enemies. Indeed, remembering that Jesus suffered at the hands of the Romans as well as at those of His own people, Calvin can suppose that David's enemies were composed of Gentiles as well as Jews, since this supposition "agrees better with the completeness of the type".[4] The Resurrection and Ascension of Christ whom God placed on the throne "contrary to the will of men" are thus "shadowed out (*adumbratum*) in David, whom, though rejected by the nobles, God took to give an instance and proof (*specimen ac documentum*) of what He would at length do in His Christ".[5] What was done in the person of David was thus "a prelude and figure of Christ".[6]

---

[1]Comm. on Ps. 22 : 18, C.R. 31 : 230.

[2]Comm. on Ps. 22 : 16, C.R. 31 : 228.

[3]Comm. on Ps. 118 : 25, C.R. 32 : 210–12.

[4]Comm. on Ps. 2 : 2, C.R. 31 : 42. *Adde quod figurae complemento melius quadrat, diversas hostium species coniungi.*

[5]Comm. on Matt. 21 : 42, C.R. 45 : 595.

[6]Ibid (*praeludium et figuram*), e.g. David in his warlike character in contrast to his gracious character "resembled Christ, who gently allures all men to

(iii) *The form of Christ as foreshadowed in the political institutions of Israel*

In Calvin's view, the political institutions of Israel are shaped in order to delineate the glory of the Kingdom of Christ and the relation of Christ to His Church. The Kingdom which God set up under David and his successors in office is a type or image of the spiritual Kingdom which the promised Messiah will set up. "God then gave a living representation of His Christ when He erected a Kingdom in the person of David."[1] "At the time when God erected David's·throne, He at the same time gave a visible sign of the more excellent Kingdom which was then secretly hoped for."[2] This typical significance applies not only to the person of David but to all his successors on the throne by virtue of their office.[3] Thus Calvin views Hezekiah as a "figure of Christ"[4] and calls his kingdom a "type of the Kingdom of Christ whose image Hezekiah bore". In the glory which the Davidic Kingdom acquired among the nations through David's victories, and in the tribute given by the surrounding nations for the rebuilding of Jerusalem after the exile, Calvin sees foreshadowings of the final glory and universality of the Kingdom of Christ.

repentance but breaks in pieces those who obstinately resist" (comm. on Ps. 18 : 38, C.R. 31 : 188).

David represents not only Christ but also the Church and the Christian. "Under the person of David, there is here described to us the Church, both in the person of Christ, who is the head and in His members" (comm. on Ps. 5 : 10, C.R. 31 : 70). Thus the personal tribulations of David can give us a foreshadowing not only of the Passion of Christ but also of the tribulation which marks the life of the ordinary Christian who has to be conformed to Christ. "David mourns over the injuries which he in particular was suffering, yet, in his own person, he represented Christ, and the whole body of the Church" (comm. on Ps. 109 : 1, C.R. 32 : 147). David is "the example after which the whole Church should be conformed—a point well entitled to our attention in order that each of us may prepare himself for the same condition" (comm. on Ps. 41 : 10, C.R. 31 : 422). Calvin works this out in detail in his view of the Christian life.

[1]Comm. on Hab. 3 : 13, C.R. 43 : 581. *Tunc ergo Deus familiarius expressit vivam picturam Christi sui dum erexit regnum in Davidis persona.* Cf. comm. on Ps. 20 (introduction).

[2]Comm. on Ezek. 17 : 24, C.R. 40 : 420. . . . *dedit signum visibile regni excellentioris, quod adhuc sub spe latebat.*

[3]Inst. 2 : 6 : 2.

[4]Comm. on Isa. 33 : 17, C.R. 36 : 572; (cf. on Mic. 4 : 6–7, C.R. 43 : 354–5). *Observandum est, regnum illud typum fuisse regni Christi cuius Ezechias imaginem gessit.* It is to be noted that Calvin in this passage, denying that this type of interpretation is an *allegoria*, uses the phrase: *mihi ergo placet ab Ezechia ad Christum anagoge . . . intelligamus.*

"From those tributes the temple of Jerusalem was rebuilt. But as that restoration was only the prelude to that accomplished by Christ, so likewise the homage which foreign nations rendered to the people of God was only the beginning of that homage which various nations rendered to the Church of God, after Christ had been revealed to the world."[1]

In the stability of the city of Jerusalem which, founded by God, continued unmoved amidst the varied commotions and revolutions which took place in the world and was restored after its destruction to show how steadfast the work of God was, Calvin sees adumbrated the eternity of the Kingdom of Christ and finds cause by which we can "comfort our minds regarding the stability of the Church" of which Jerusalem is a figure. "And now since Christ by His coming has renewed the world, whatever was spoke of that city in old time belongs to the spiritual Jerusalem, which is dispersed through all the countries of the world."[2] The fair physical situation of Zion, and the noble adornments of its architecture and battlements, are signs given beforehand of the spiritual gifts with which the Church "has been no less richly and magnificently adorned than Jerusalem, under the shadows of the law, was in old time surrounded and fortified with strong walls and towers".[3] "The beauty was indeed natural . . . but the agreeable appearance of the city had engraven upon it the marks of the favour of God."[4]

All this was indeed but a "kind of prelude, a shadowy representation of that greater grace, which was delayed and held in suspense, until the advent of the Messiah",[5] though even among the shadows Christ was there really confronting the people of Israel in the person of their King.[6] The prophets were conscious

[1]Comm. on Isa. 45 : 14, C.R. 37 : 140; cf. comm. on Ps. 47 : 1 and 2, C.R. 31 : 466–7; on Ps. 18 : 44 and 45, C.R. 31 : 190–1. Though the Church shares in this glory foreshadowed in the Davidic Kingdom, it is nevertheless at present largely concealed. The Church to-day more manifestly shares in the dissensions and strife described in the Psalms as marking even David's rule; cf. comm. on Ps. 18 : 44, C.R. 31 : 189–90; on Ps. 41 : 10, C.R. 31 : 422; on Ps. 5 : 10, C.R. 31 : 70.
[2]Comm. on Ps. 48 : 8–10, C.R. 31 : 477.
[3]Comm. on Ps. 48 : 12–14, C.R. 31 : 480.
[4]Comm. on Ps. 48 : 2, C.R. 31 : 473.
[5]Comm. on Gen. 49 : 10, C.R. 23 : 958. *Praeludium . . . ac umbratile specimen maioris illius gratiae quae in adventum Messiae dilata fuit ac suspensa.* Cf. comm. on Isa. 6 : 13, C.R. 36 : 140–2.
[6]Cf. comm. on Mic. 4 : 6 and 7, C.R. 43 : 353–5.

that the true meaning of the Davidic Kingdom could be found only when Jehovah Himself would come in the person of the Christ to give substance to the shadows. With the coming of Christ, who is Jehovah manifested in the flesh, this new and more spiritual Kingdom of which Jerusalem was a type has been set up. Christ is the "true David"[1] ruling over the Church as the latter ruled over his earthly kingdom. Calvin likens the Gospel or the preached word to the sceptre of the Kingdom[2] by which Christ rules in the Church, and to the sword[3] by which Christ slays for a sacrifice to God those who were formerly enemies, or delivers them over to everlasting destruction unless they repent.

(iv) *The form of Christ as foreshadowed in the ritual of the law*

The visible ceremonies of the law are shadows of spiritual things. "In the whole legal priesthood, in the sacrifices, in the form of the sanctuary, we ought to seek Christ,"[4] says Calvin. In his exposition of the scriptures, when he comes upon references to the temple, the Ark, or the tabernacle, Calvin painstakingly seeks to point out their reference to Christ. The Ark is always for him a sign of the presence of God, "not a vain or illusory symbol"[5] but a real sacramental object. Before the temple was built the Ark had no fixed dwelling place but only a shifting tabernacle, "being from time to time transported from one place to another like a wayfaring man".[6] Under these conditions, all pious Israelites desired something more settled for their centre of worship. In all their wanderings with the Ark and tabernacle the servants of God were stirred up "to pray that a certain settled place might be appointed".[7] Their prayer was partly answered, for at last the temple was built, "a sumptuous

[1]Cf. comm. on Hos. 1 : 11, C.R. 42 : 221.
[2]Comm. on Ezek. 17 : 24, C.R. 40 : 420.
[3]Comm. on Ps. 149 : 9, C.R. 32 : 440; cf. on Isa. 11 : 4, C.R. 36 : 238; and on Mic. 4 : 3, C.R. 43 : 346.
[4]Comm. on Luke 24 : 27, C.R. 45 : 807. Cf. serm. on Deut. 6 : 20–25, C.R. 26 : 488–9. *Moyse n'a point edifié le tabernacle, sinon que Dieu en ait donné le patron : et le tout pour monstrer qu'il y avoit une conformité entre ces choses externes, et la verité qui devoit estre manifestee en nostre Seigneur Iesus Christ.*
[5]Comm. on Ps. 24 : 8, C.R. 31 : 249; cf. on Ps. 14 : 7, C.R. 31 : 141; on Ps. 20 : 3, C.R. 31 : 208; on Ps. 132 : 8, C.R. 32 : 346.
[6]Comm. on Ps. 24 : 7, C.R. 31 : 248.
[7]Cf. also comm. on Ps. 122 : 2, C.R. 32 : 303–4.

building exceeding the tabernacle in magnificance", but especially superior in that it had a permanent situation. When the Ark was taken into the temple to its final resting place there, God gave the promise, *This is my rest for ever*,[1] and in the courts of the temple generations of God's people worshipped, knowing that here the Lord was with them and that here His presence, symbolised by the Ark, had found a place of rest.

Calvin teaches that all this is a foreshadowing of the incarnation.[2] The temple was not God's rest for ever. It was transitory in significance. It was destroyed, and at the time of its rebuilding by the Jews returned from captivity a prophecy was given of One who would come and rebuild the *true* temple of Jehovah to give Him a truly eternal place of abode. "*And he shall rebuild the temple of Jehovah.* This is a remarkable passage; it hence appears that the temple which the Jews had then begun to build, and which was afterwards built by Herod, was not the true temple which Haggai had prophesied when he said, *The glory of the second house shall be greater than that of the first* (Hag. 2 : 9). For though the temple of Herod was splendid, yet we see what the Spirit declares in this place—that to build the temple was Christ's own work. . . . Christ alone has been chosen by the Father to build this temple. Christ indeed Himself was a temple as to his body, for *the fullness of the Godhead dwelt in Him* (Col. 2 : 6),[3] but He built a temple to God the Father when He raised up everywhere pure worship, having demolished superstitions, and when He consecrated us a royal priesthood."[4] The entry of the Ark into the Temple spoken of in the 24th Psalm is thus a foreshadowing of the incarnation of God in Jesus Christ, in whom God finds His true place of abode amongst men.

[1] Comm. on Ps. 132 : 14, C.R. 32 : 350.

[2] "The material temple which was built at Jerusalem was no less than a figure. Indeed we know that it was only a shadow. But in our Lord Jesus Christ all fullness of the Godhead took up residence . . . bodily and in true substance" (serm. on Matt. 25 : 51 ff., C.R. 46 : 869).

[3] "Jesus Christ having made His appearance, the old shadows of the law are taken away; let us content ourselves, therefore, seeing we have a temple which is not material nor visible; yea all the fullness of the Godhead dwelleth in our Lord Jesus Christ. It is sufficient for us that He reacheth out His hand being ready to present us before God, and that through Him we have an entrance into the true spiritual sanctuary, that God receiveth us, that the veil of the temple is rent" (serm. on 1 Tim. 2 : 8, C.R. 53 : 187).

[4] Comm. on Zech. 6 : 12 f., C.R. 44 : 213–14.

The tabernacle in its form was "a sort of visible image of God",[1] and Calvin at times gives the details of its construction a Christological reference.[2] Of special interest are Calvin's remarks on the vail of the temple as a symbol of the *mystery* of the incarnation. "By the vail the obscurity of the shadows of the law was principally denoted, that the Israelites might know that the time of full revelation had not yet come, but that the spiritual worship of God was as yet enshrouded in a veil; and thus might extend their faith to their promised Messiah, at whose coming the truth would be discovered and laid bare.[3] Yet although there is now no vail to prevent us from openly and familiarly looking upon Christ, let us learn from this figure that the manifestation of God in the flesh is a hidden and incomprehensible mystery."[4]

The Levitical priesthood also foreshadows Christ in various ways. "The Levitical priest was ordained that he might be a type (*umbra*) of the true Mediator."[5] Aaron was an "image of God's only begotten Son and our only Mediator".[6] Calvin notes that the priesthood was surrounded by safeguards to preserve its dignity in the eyes of the people, lest through its being brought into contempt the priesthood of Christ should also be brought into contempt.[7] It was for this reason that Aaron was spared public punishment when he had deserved it,[8] and given the power to work a spectacular miracle before the people. For this reason, too, Aaron and his sons and their posterity were dressed in gorgeous and rich garments "which symbolise the more than angelic brightness of all virtues which is represented in Christ".[9]

[1]Comm. on Heb. 9 : 19, C.R. 55 : 115.

[2]Cf. comm. on Ps. 132 : 17, C.R. 32 : 352; comm. on Exod. 26 : 1, C.R. 24 : 414–17.

[3]Cf. Matt. 27 : 51.

[4]Comm. on Exod. 26 : 31, C.R. 24 : 417. . . .*Discamus tamen ex figura illa reconditum et incomprehensibile mysterium esse, quod Deus in carne manifestatus fuit.* Calvin can go further into detail in discussing the temple, e.g. the purifying water at the entrance is "a figure of the blood of our Lord Jesus Christ" (serm. on 1 Tim. 2 : 5–6, C.R. 53 : 173. Cf. serm. on 1 Tim. 2 : 8, C.R. 53 : 192). The candlestick always burning shows that the grace of the Spirit always shines in the Church, the seven candlesticks signify the variety of spiritual gifts, etc.; comm. on Zech. 4 : 1–6, C.R. 44 : 181 and ff.

[5]Comm. on Exod. 28 : 1, C.R. 24 : 427.

[6]Comm. on Num. 12 : 9, C.R. 25 : 184.

[7]Comm. on Lev. 21 : 7, C.R. 24 : 454.

[8]Comm. on Num. 12 : 9, C.R. 25 : 184.

[9]Comm. on Exod. 28 : 2, C.R. 24 : 428. *Voluit Deus hoc symbolo plusquam angelicum virtutum omnium splendorem, qui in Christo exhibendus erat.*

"Why were these costly and splendid vestments used with which God commanded Aaron to be adorned while performing holy rites, except that they were symbols of a holiness and excellency far exceeding all human virtues?"[1] What is thus "fulfilled in Christ by the hidden and celestial power of the Spirit, was shadowed forth under the law by ointment, various vestments, the sprinkling of blood, and other earthly ceremonies".[2] But Aaron and his successors were thus gorgeously dressed because "the reality did not exist".

It was obvious to anyone who could contrast what the priest was in himself and his outward garb that he was merely a type shadowing a reality yet to come whose excellence of character could not be represented by any man who was not thus adorned.[3] "The external ornaments denoted the want of those which are true and spiritual; for if the priest had been absolutely and entirely perfect, these typical accessories would have been superfluous."[4] Thus the office of priest points forward to the Person of the Mediator.[5]

In his exposition of the passages relating to the sacrifices performed by the priests in the sanctuary we have in Calvin the same patient care to bring out the faint traces they bear of the form of Christ. "The sacrifices were types of Christ."[6] By them God desired to bear witness that He would not be reconciled to them otherwise than through the sacrifice of a victim.[7] The freedom from blemish required by the law represents "the

[1]Comm. on Heb. 7 : 26, C.R. 55 : 94.
[2]Comm. on Heb. 7 : 15, C.R. 55 : 90.
[3]Cf. comm. on Lev. 16 : 3, C.R. 24 : 501–2.
[4]Comm. on Exod. 28 : 2, C.R. 24 : 428. *Ornatus exterior veri et spiritualis defectum notavit. Nam si omnibus perfectionis numeris absolutus fuisset sacerdos, supervacua erat umbratilis accessio.*
[5]Calvin finds a typical meaning even in the detailed construction of the Aaronic vestments, e.g., referring to the twelve precious stones: "inasmuch as Christ deigned to ingraft us into His body we are precious stones" (comm. on Exod. 28 : 4 f., C.R. 24 : 429–30). The names of the tribes engraven upon the priest's shoulders signify Jesus bearing our sins on the Cross (serm. on 1 Tim. 2 : 5–6, C.R. 53 : 169). Interpreting the bells and pomegranates on the edge of the robe, Calvin is unusually far-fetched: "Although there was no smell in the pomegranates, yet the type suggested this to the eyes; as if God required in that garment a sweet smell as well as a sound to cover up our stink through the foulness of our sins. God would give the bells a sound because the garment of Christ does not procure favour for us except by the sound of the gospel" (comm. on Exod. 28 : 31 f., C.R. 24 : 432–3).
[6]Comm. on Lev. 1 : 1 f., C.R. 24 : 506f.
[7]Comm. on Exod. 12 : 21, C.R. 24 : 136.

celestial perfection and purity of Christ".[1] The once-yearly offering on the day of atonement was "a symbol of the one offering, so that believers might understand that the sacrifice, whereby God was to be propitiated, was not often to be repeated".[2] The daily offerings enacted round this one offering showed that "although Christ was once offered . . . yet by the benefit of his death pardon is always ready for us",[3] this arrangement also being a symbol of the manner in which the intercession of Christ consecrated the daily prayers of the Church.[4] The accompaniments of the offerings are also significant. The prescribed oil-cake and wine are signs to the worshippers of the insufficiency of what was already offered in the sacrifice, "that the people should not rest in bare and empty figures, but should acknowledge that something better and more excellent underlay them", and also that they might add themselves "the sacrifices of faith and repentance".[5] The frankincense and oil were a type of the "sacrifice of praise" which we offer to God continually.[6] The salt added to the sacrifices teaches that "the true seasoning which gives grace to sacrifices is found nowhere except in God's word".[7] The regulations commanding outward cleanliness in the performance of the ceremonies are likewise in their intention spiritual. They are certainly in themselves expedient for sanitary reasons, but their main purpose was not to prevent disease spreading among the people but to serve as "useful aids to piety". They are outward signs of the inward holiness which God requires, and thus admonitions to us that "we should cleanse ourselves from all filthiness of the flesh and spirit".[8] The fire which consumed the offering represents the efficacy of the Holy Spirit, "for unless Christ had suffered in the Spirit He would not have been a propitiatory sacrifice".[9]

Those who participated in the sacrifices knew that, regarded by themselves, these ceremonies had no reality. David and the

[1]Comm. on Exod. 12 : 5, C.R. 24 : 288.
[2]Comm. on Lev. 16 : 2, C.R. 24 : 501; cf. on Heb. 9 : 11.
[3]Comm. on Exod. 29 : 38, C.R. 24 : 491.
[4]Ibid.
[5]Comm. on Exod. 29 : 38 f., C.R. 24 : 490–1.
[6]Comm. on Lev. 2 : 1, C.R. 24 : 509.
[7]Comm. on Lev. 2 : 13, C.R. 24 : 510.
[8]Cf. comm. on Deut. 24 : 8, C.R. 24 : 317–8; on Exod 19 : 10, C.R. 24 : 198–9.
[9]Comm. on Lev. 1 : 5, C.R. 24 : 508.

prophets knew that without them the service of God could be perfectly performed, and that they were only "rudiments enjoined with some further end in view".[1] The very crudity of the ceremonies taught this lesson. God "abundantly taught them that unless they directed their faith to Christ, whatsoever came from them would be rejected; for neither would the purity of a brute animal have satisfied Him if it had not represented something better".[2] "What could be more childish than to offer the blood of an animal?"[3] Thus through the sacrifices the death of Christ was set before His ancient people, and thus we too are taught through these now outmoded forms to discern the meaning of the one true sacrifice.[4]

(v) *Christ as foreshadowed in the signs and visions given during various occasions of revelation in the history of Israel*

Calvin in his exposition of the Old Testament sees the form of Christ not only in the institutions of the law, and in the general course taken by the history of the chosen people, but also in many occasional and, on a superficial view, apparently accidental features related in the Biblical account of how revelation came to men. Thus, for example, interpreting the meaning of the ladder in Jacob's dream, Calvin writes, "To us, who hold this principle, that the covenant of God was founded in Christ, and that Christ Himself was the eternal image of the Father, in which He manifested Himself to the holy patriarchs, there is nothing in this vision intricate or ambiguous. . . . It is Christ alone, therefore, who connects heaven and earth; He is the only Mediator who reaches from heaven down to earth; He is the medium through which the fullness of all celestial blessings flows to us, and through which we, in turn, ascend to God. He

[1]Comm. on Ps. 40 : 8, C.R. 31 : 413. Cf. on Ps. 50 : 8, C.R. 31 : 499.
[2]Comm. on Lev. 1 : 1, C.R. 24 : 507.
[3]Comm. on Exod. 12 : 21, C.R. 24 : 136.
[4]In the prescribed details of the legal ceremonies Calvin is always inclined to search out a typical meaning, e.g. the ceremony of banning the leper from the camp is typical of Church excommunication (comm. on Lev. 13 : 2 f., C.R. 24 : 320) but the regulation to shut him up for seven days before expulsion is a warning to Church courts to be cautious and not precipitate in judgment. The regulations commanding the washing of garments are all designed to impress on the people the horror of sin and the necessity for spiritual purity, sanitary considerations being entirely secondary (cf. comm. on Lev. 16 : 26, C.R. 24 : 505).

it is, who, being the Head over angels, causes them to minister to His earthly members. Therefore He properly claims for Himself this honour."[1] Calvin claims that this exposition is "not forced", that the figure "well suits the Mediator[2] for nothing was more suitable than that God should ratify His covenant of eternal salvation in His Son to His servant Jacob. Of equal interest are Calvin's remarks about Melchizedek: "We see in him the lineaments of Christ, as the form of the living man may be seen in his picture, while yet the man is very different from that which represents him."[3]

(vi) *The spiritual and eternal as foreshadowed in the material and temporal*

It has already been pointed out that the Old Covenant is more "carnal" than the New. God's dispensation of temporal favours is greater under the law than under the Gospel.[4] He testified His kindness to the Children of Israel by carnal and earthly blessings. The prime indication of His favour was, of course, the possession of the land of Canaan, which by supernatural grace He made abundantly fertile and liberally provident of the needs of its inhabitants.[5] In the New Testament, however, God's dispensation of His providence is different from what it was previously. The promises holding out earthly prosperity and success to those who fear God, given e.g. in the Psalms, are not strictly and literally applicable to our case, though they were thus applicable for those to whom they were originally given. Our rewards are spiritual and eternal.

Such is the difference between the Covenants. But even through this difference there is achieved a very close unity, for the one Covenant is meant to lead up to the other and the

[1]Comm. on Gen. 28 : 12, C.R. 23 : 391.
[2]Ibid. *Ergo si scalam dicimus esse Christi effigiem haec expositio nihil habet coactum. Nam scalae similitudo optime convenit mediatori.*
[3]Comm. on Heb. 7 : 3, C.R. 55 : 84.
[4]Inst. 4 : 16 : 11. Cf. serm. on Deut. 28 : 9–14, C.R. 28 : 381. *Car pour ce qu'un petit enfant ne sera point capable de cognoistre le bien de son pere : pour luy donner courage, on luy dira : ie te donneray un beau bonnet, ie t'acheteray une belle robbe neufve : cela est selon la portee de l'enfant . . . Ainsi Dieu en a-il usé envers les Peres anciens.*
[5]A gift of fertility which was, according to Calvin, later withdrawn. Comm. on Exod. 3 : 17, C.R. 24 : 46; comm. on Deut. 8 : 7, C.R. 24 : 245.

spiritual blessings, given in smaller measure during the earlier dispensation and more fully during the later dispensation, are shadowed forth in the material benefits bestowed as a token of God's favour to His people in these early ages. Canaan is a visible outward symbol of the eternal inheritance of the people of God in Christ. What is spiritual in Christ is thus described in the Old Testament in earthly figures. Here are some quotations on this subject: "It was requisite for a people inexperienced and feeble to be trained gradually, by means of temporal benefits, to entertain a better hope."[1] "The Lord did not formerly set the hope of the future inheritance plainly before the eyes of the fathers (as He now calls us and raises us directly towards heaven), but he led them by a circuitous course. Thus He appointed the land of Canaan as a mirror and pledge to them of the celestial inheritance . . . that being aided by such helps, according to the time in which they lived they might by degrees rise towards heaven. . . . All the promises of God were involved, and in a sense clothed in these symbols."[2] "The better to commend the divine goodness to the people they (i.e. the prophets) used temporal blessings as lineaments to shadow it forth, and yet gave such a portrait as might lift their minds above the earth, the elements of this world, and all that will perish, and compel them to think of the blessedness of a future and spiritual life."[3] "He promised them the land of Canaan not that it might be the limit of their hopes."[4]

Thus it is that we must not understand even the 45th Psalm as referring to "some lascivious and carnal amours" but transfer the opulence and the "abundance of pleasures" there described spiritually to the Kingdom of Christ, for it is not an unusual manner of speaking "that what is spiritual in Christ should be described under the form of earthly figures".[5] "In the same way we should understand all the terrestrial promises which were given to the Jewish nation, the spiritual promise, as the head to

[1]Comm. on Ps. 112 : 2, C.R. 32 : 172–3; cf. on Ps. 128 : 3, C.R. 32 : 328.
[2]Comm. on Gen. 27 : 28, C.R. 23 : 378. . . . *Sic terram Chanaan coelestis haereditatis speculum et pignus illis esse voluit . . . ut pro temporis ratione talibus adminiculis adiuti, paulatim in coelum assurgerent. . . . Sicut autem omnes Dei promissiones externis illis symbolis implicitae erant, et quasi vestitae.*
[3]Inst. 2 : 10 : 20.
[4]Inst. 2 : 11 : 2; cf. 2 : 11 : 1.
[5]Cf. comm. on Ps. 45 : 6–7, C.R. 31 : 453.

which the others bore reference, always holding the first place."[1]
It is on this principle of interpretation that Calvin justifies the
Apostles' habit in the New Testament of using Old Testament
promises that obviously in the original held out purely earthly
blessings, as if they referred to our eternal inheritance.[2]

4. Conclusion

In his commentary on Psalm 102 : 23 Calvin sums up his
whole teaching on this subject of the relation between the
Covenants. "The manifestation of Christ was the goal of the
race which God's ancient people were running." They were
conscious that they were running such a race, and though "their
strength was afflicted in the way", the days were nevertheless
shortened "because they directed their view to the fullness which
did not arrive till Christ was revealed".[3] When He came He
found Himself, and the destiny He was to fulfil, portrayed in
their writings. *And the Father who hath sent me, himself hath
testified concerning me,* He said. "He says in the past tense, that
the Father *testified* in order to show that he did not come forward
as an unknown person, because the Father had long ago distinguished him by peculiar marks, that bringing them along
with Him, He might be recognised."[4]

[1]Inst. 4 : 16 : 11.
[2]Cf. Paul's use of Hab. 2 : 4 in Rome 1 : 17.
[3]C.R. 32 : 71–2.
[4]John 5 : 37.

Calvin points out frequently that Jesus deliberately conformed the outward
details and pattern of His life to the prophecies of the Old Testament concerning
Himself. Moreover, God providentially ordered His life to this end. This
Calvin regards as a proof of the truth of the Old Testament. The kiss of Judas
was foretold in the Old Testament, and when it was fulfilled in the Gospel
story Calvin comments, "It was necessary that the Son of God should be thus
marked that the Scripture might be so much the better attested, that men
might know that this was He whom God had elected as our Redeemer" (serm.
on Matt. 26 : 40, C.R. 46 : 854). In the details of the Passion even exaggerated
phrases used in the Psalms by David metaphorically to describe his sufferings
have to be literally and in all reality fulfilled by Jesus: "*They part my garments
among them, and cast the lot upon my vesture.* We must understand his meaning
to be that what David complained of as having been done to himself metaphorically and figuratively (*metaphorice et sub figura*) was literally and in reality
(*literaliter et re ipsa*) exhibited in Christ" (comm. on Matt. 27 : 35, C.R.
45 : 766; cf. comm. on Ps. 69 : 21, C.R. 31 : 646; comm. on John 19 : 28,
C.R. 47 : 419; comm. on Exod. 12 : 46, on Num. 19 : 3, on Lev. 16 : 26).
"Nothing happened to the Son of God which had not been testified beforehand

and figured out, in order that we might be more strongly persuaded that this is He who from the beginning of time had been established by God, since He bears such infallible marks" (serm. on Matt. 26 : 40 ff., C.R. 46 : 854).

The blessing with uplifted hands which Jesus gave to the apostles at His ascension was the fulfilment of what was typified in the law in the blessing which the priests gave to the people (Num. 6 : 26) after making sacrifice to God (cf. serm. on Gen. 14 : 18–20, C.R. 23 : 663). *Car c'est le sommaire de l'Evangile qu'il a voulu conformer à ce qui avoit este testifié auparavant : et que nous cognoissions par ce moyen que la Loy, les Prophetes et l'Evangile ne sont qu'un* (serm. on Luke 1 : 31–5, C.R. 46 : 80).

Chapter V

The Uniqueness of Revelation

1. Christ as the only valid and satisfying source
of revelation

FOR Calvin, Jesus Christ is the only source and centre to which men must come to know God and to share the life of God. "Hence He is called the image of the Father because He sets forth and exhibits to us all that is necessary to be known of the Father. For the naked majesty of God would, by its immense brightness, ever dazzle our eyes; it is therefore necessary for us to look on Christ. This is to come to the light."[1] "God is made known to us in no other way than in Christ."[2] "We are blind to the light of God until in Christ it beams upon us."[3] In Jesus Christ God has united heaven and earth and has revealed the one and only way by which man can come to God, the one channel through which God gives men life. In Jesus Christ God has shone a light that by its very brightness shows up all other light to be darkness. "It is Christ alone, therefore, who connects heaven and earth: He is the medium through which the fullness of all celestial blessings flow down to us and through which we in turn ascend to God."[4] "Nor can anyone find God except he to whom the man Christ becomes the door and the way."[5] "Such is the determination of God—not to communicate Himself, or His gifts to men, otherwise than by His Son."[6] Christ is "the only key for opening the door to us, if we are desirous to have access to the true God".[7] "The sum is this—that God in Himself, that is, in His naked majesty, is *invisible*,

[1] Comm. on 1 John 2 : 22, C.R. 55 : 325.
[2] Comm. on Heb. 1 : 3, C.R. 55 : 12.
[3] Ibid.
[4] Comm. on Gen. 28 : 12, C.R. 23 : 391. *Solus ergo Christus est qui coelum terrae coniungit : hic solus est mediator qui pertingit a coelo usque ad terram : ille idem est per quem omnium bonorum coelestium plenitudo deorsum ad nos fluit, nosque vicissim ad Deum conscendimus.*
[5] Comm. on Heb. 10 : 20, C.R. 55 : 129.
[6] Comm. on Col. 1 : 19, C.R. 52 : 87.
[7] Comm. on Col. 1 : 3, C.R. 52 : 78.

that not to the eyes of the body merely, but also to the under-standings of men, and that He is revealed to us in Christ alone."[1]

2. The folly and ingratitude of turning from Christ to other supposed sources

The thought of Calvin is thus controlled by this fact—that in Jesus Christ are hid all treasures of wisdom and knowledge. What we have in Christ cannot be found in any other source. "In Christ He shews us His righteousness, goodness, wisdom, power, in short, His entire self. We must, therefore, beware of seeking Him elsewhere, for everything that would set itself off as a representation of God, apart from Christ, is an idol."[2] "John calls us to this practical part of faith, that as God has given Himself to us to be enjoyed only in Christ, He is elsewhere to be sought in vain; or (if anyone prefers what is clearer) that as in Christ dwells all the fullness of Deity, there is no God apart from Him."[3] "All that the Father had, He deposited with His only begotten Son, in order that He might manifest Himself in Him, and thus by the communication of blessings express the true image of His glory. . . . The invisible Father is to be sought nowhere but in this image."[4] No attempt must be made to supplement this revelation by turning away from Christ, even for a moment, to explore other sources of knowledge which might be supposed to have something to say and to give us that might enrich us further. "But it is asked—Is Christ only a part, or simply the commencement of the doctrine of salvation, as the foundation is merely part of the building; for if it were so, believers would only have their commencement in Christ, and would be perfected without Him. I answer . . . He . . . who has learned Christ is already complete in the whole system of heavenly doctrine. . . . By *gold, silver, precious stones* he means

---

[1]Comm. on Col. 1 : 15, C.R. 52 : 85. *Summa est Deum in se, hoc est, in nuda sua maiestate, esse invisibilem : nec tantum corporeis oculis, sed humanis etiam mentibus, revelari autem nobis in solo Christo.* Cf. serm. on Job 1 : 1, C.R. 33 : 31. "Do we know Him? That must be in such wise as He hath uttered Himself."
[2]Comm. on Col. 1 : 15, C.R. 52 : 85.
[3]Comm. on 1 John 2 : 22, C.R. 55 : 325.
[4]Inst. 3 : 2 : 1. *In hunc finem quicquid habebat Pater, apud unigenitum deposuit, ut in eo se patefaceret : ut ipsa bonorum communicatione exprimeret veram gloriae suae imaginem.* . . . Cf. comm. on John 1 : 16, C.R. 47 : 16–17.

doctrine worthy of Christ . . . superstructure corresponding to such a foundation. Let us not imagine, however, that this doctrine is apart from Christ, but on the contrary, let us understand that we must continue to preach Christ until the very completion of the building."[1]

The slightest turning away from Christ towards any other supposed source of revelation in an attempt to build up a supplementary branch of theology to enrich Christian doctrine Calvin views as a step that will lead us soon into the danger of losing faith, and salvation too, for faith rests wholly in Christ and requires to be continually created in our hearts by a most close adherence on our part to Christ alone. "Therefore, the moment we turn aside from Him in the minutest degree, salvation, which resides entirely in Him, gradually disappears: so that all who do not rest in Him voluntarily deprive themselves of all grace. The observation of Bernard well deserves to be remembered: the name of Jesus is not only light but food also, yea oil, without which all the food of the soul is dry: salt, without which as a condiment, whatever is set before us is insipid; in fine, honey in the mouth, melody in the ear, joy in the heart, and, at the same time, medicine; every discourse where His name is not heard is absurd."[2] "We do not truly trust God except when we forsake every other protection, and flee for refuge to His sure protection, and feel assured that it is our only safe asylum."[3] "When water is blended with fire both perish; so when one seeks in part to trust in God, and in part to trust in men, it is the same thing as though he wished to mix heaven and earth, and to throw all things into confusion. It is, then, to confound the order of nature, when men imagine that they had two objects of trust."[4] "*Ye believe in God, believe also in me.* For although, properly speaking, faith rises from Christ to the Father, He intimates, that even when it leans on God, it gradually vanishes away, unless He Himself interpose to give it solid strength. The

---

[1]Comm. on 1 Cor. 3 : 11–12, C.R. 49 : 354. Cf. ibid. *Qui ergo Christum didicit, in tota coelesti doctrina iam est absolutus.*
[2]Inst. 2 : 16 : 1. *Itaque simulac vel minimum ab eo deflectimus, sensum evanescit salus, quae solida in eos residet. . . .*
[3]Comm. on Heb. 6 : 18, C.R. 55 : 80.
[4]Comm. on Jer. 17 : 5, C.R. 38 : 265. *Ac si vellet miscere terram coelo, et omnia pervertere. Hoc est igitur confundere naturae ordinem, uni homines volunt sibi duas spes imaginari.*

majesty of God is too high to be scaled up by mortals, who creep like worms on the earth. Therefore the common saying that God is the object of faith requires to be received with some modification."[1]

So complete, unique and exclusive is the revelation which God gives of Himself in Christ that it is not only madness to forsake it for any other source of knowledge but also the most base ingratitude, and a robbery from Christ of His Glory. "We are perfect in wisdom if we truly know Christ, so that it is madness to wish to know anything besides Him. For since the Father has manifested Himself wholly in Him, that man wishes to be wise apart from God, who is not contented with Christ alone."[2] "Whoever obtains Christ is in want of nothing; and, therefore . . . whoever is not satisfied with Christ alone, strives after something beyond absolute perfection."[3] "Papists in common with us acknowledge one and the same Christ; yet in the meantime how great a difference there is between us and them, inasmuch as they, after confessing Christ to be the Son of God, transfer His excellence to others, and scatter it hither and thither, and thus leave Him next to empty, or at least rob Him of a great part of His glory."[4] "All theology, separated from Christ, is not only vain, but is also mad, deceitful, and spurious; for, though the philosophers sometimes utter excellent sayings, yet they have nothing but what is short-lived and even mixed up with wicked and erroneous statements."[5] "The whole world, with all its pretended wisdom and righteousness, is regarded as nothing but darkness in the sight of God, because, apart from the Kingdom of Christ, there is no light."[6] "Those . . . who do not rest satisfied with Christ alone do injury to God and are ungrateful. . . . They seek elsewhere what they already have in Christ."[7] For Calvin "all corruptions in religion arise from this, that men abide not in Christ alone".[8] "We shall never be beyond the reach

[1]Inst. 2 : 6 : 4.
[2]Comm. on Col. 2 : 3, C.R. 52 : 100.
[3]Comm. on John 14 : 6, C.R. 47 : 324. *Quisquis potitur Christo, nihil illi deesse : ideoque ultra ultimam perfectionem eniti, quisquis eo uno contentus non est.*
[4]Comm. on Col. 1 : 12, C.R. 52 : 83. Cf. serm. on Eph. 4 : 11–4, C.R. 51 : 569.
[5]Comm. on John 14 : 6, C.R. 47 : 324–5.
[6]Comm. on Col. 1 : 13, C.R. 52 : 84.
[7]Comm. on Col. 2 : 10, C.R. 52 : 104.
[8]Comm. on Heb. 13 : 9, C.R. 55 : 190.

of danger except we cleave to Christ." "As soon . . . as we turn aside from Him, we cannot do anything else but wander in error."[1] "As soon as men depart from Christ they go fatally astray."[2] It is the first duty, and the only wisdom, therefore, of the Christian thinker to abide in Christ, and to find in Him all treasures of wisdom and knowledge. For a theologian to do otherwise is to betray a complete ignorance of the significance of Christ. "That man is ignorant of Christ who is not led by Him to the Father and who does not in Him embrace God wholly."[3] "For how comes it that we are *carried about with so many strange doctrines*, but because the excellence of Christ is not perceived by us? For Christ alone makes all other things suddenly vanish."[4] Our Christian task therefore must be to apply for our benefit everything that is given to us in Christ, for God has placed "His entire self" there that we may make Him our God.[5] Accordingly, Calvin appeals to us always to remember "*the man Christ* who gently invites us, and takes us, as it were, by the hand", when we are dealing with the things of God.[6]

3. The place of natural religion as a source of the knowledge of God

Such is Calvin's teaching upon the completeness and uniqueness of the revelation given in Christ. It will be seen that, if Calvin does seem at times expressly to admit the validity for the Christian of natural theology, this discipline simply cannot have a prominent place in a Christian system of theology, and nature certainly cannot be made a source from which we can somehow supplement Christian dogma. There can be no doubt that when Calvin warns us of turning away from Christ he has in mind those who want to speak too much about "God in nature" and who want to ally theology too closely to philosophy.

Calvin, it is true, can go so far as to speak of the "very beautiful

[1]Comm. on 1 John 3 : 23, C.R. 55 : 345; cf. on Heb. 13 : 8, C.R. 55 : 189–90.
[2]Comm. on 1 Pet. 1 : 18, C.R. 55 : 225.
[3]Comm. on Col. 2 : 2, C.R. 52 : 99–100.
[4]Comm. on Col. 1 : 12, C.R. 52 : 82. . . . *Solus enim Christus facit ut subito alia omnia evanescant.*
[5]Cf. comm. on Col. 1 : 15, C.R. 52 : 85; on Heb. 7 : 25, C.R. 55 : 94.
[6]Comm. on 1 Tim. 2 : 5, C.R. 52 : 270.

fabric of the world" as the clothing in which God "comes forth into view" in order that we may cast our eyes upon Him.[1] Even more significant for Calvin than the mere fabric of nature is the "fair and beautiful order" observed by the heavenly bodies in their conflicting revolutions uninterruptedly maintained in the most perfect subordination and harmony for ages. In all this, "the glory of God shines forth more clearly".[2]

Calvin admits that the rays of Christ are diffused throughout the whole creation. He even suggests that pagan culture and religion owe much to Christ.[3] But such diffused knowledge, he insists, cannot lead us to God. "True indeed, the fountain of life, righteousness, virtue and wisdom is in God, but to us it is a hidden and inaccessible fountain. But an abundance of those things is exhibited to us in Christ, that we may be permitted to have recourse to Him."[4] Too often is nature merely the "terrible voice . . . which causes the hearts of men to beat in such a manner as to make them shrink from, rather than approach Him".[5] It is only when the faithful turn away from the temple of nature to the temple at Jerusalem that they hear His familiar and fatherly voice. Calvin would give the same verdict on the attempt to pursue God by looking within the heart of the natural man. "Although by nature the knowledge of God is engraven on the hearts of all men, yet it is so confused and dark, and entangled by so many errors, that, if the light of the word be not added to it, by knowing they know not God, but wander miser-

---

[1]Comm. on Ps. 104 : 1, C.R. 32 : 85. *Si de essentia euis agitur, habitat certe lucem inaccessam : sed dum irradiat totum mundum suo fulgore, haec vestis est in qua visibilis quodammodo nobis apparet qui in se ipso erat absconditus . . . Quare ut conspectu euis fruamur, prodeat in medium cum suo ornatu, hoc est, vertamus oculos ad pulcerrimam hanc mundi fabricam, in qua vult a nobis conspici.*

[2]Comm. on Ps. 68 : 33, C.R. 31 : 635. Cf. on Ps. 147 : 7, C.R. 32 : 428. "Were the same serenity always to continue, we would not have so wonderful a display of His power as when He suddenly veils them with clouds, etc."

[3]In the time of Cain, Abel and Noah there was a universal religious tradition (cf. comm. on Lev. 11 : 2, C.R. 24 : 345 f.; on Gen. 4 : 2 f., C.R. 23 : 83 f.; on Gen. 12 : 7, C.R. 23 : 180 f.). This was transmitted mainly through Shem (comm. on Gen. 33 : 20, C.R. 23 : 453), but adulterated forms of true ritual descended to the Gentiles and affected their rites (cf. on Exod. 29 : 38, C.R. 24 : 491; on Gen. 35 : 17 f., C.R. 23 : 473), the true religion being also imitated in a monkey-like manner (cf. comm. on Lev. 6 : 9, C.R. 24 : 531). On revelation to unbelievers see on Num. 22 : 5, C.R. 25 : 266 f.; on Gen. 41 : 1, C.R. 23 : 518 f.; on Dan. 2 : 2.

[4]Comm. on John 1 : 16, C.R. 47 : 16. *Apud Deum quidem est fons vitae, justitiae, virtutis, sapientiae : sed fons nobis occultus et inaccessus.*

[5]Comm. on Ps. 29 : 9, C.R. 31 : 290.

ably in darkness."[1] "In order truly to know God, and praise Him as His due, we need another voice than that which is heard in thunders, showers, and storms in the air, in the mountains and in the forests; for if He teaches us not in plain words, and also kindly allures us to Himself, by giving us a taste of His fatherly love, we will remain dumb."[2]

4. The place of the liberal arts and sciences as a source of the knowledge of God

"Even philosophers," says Calvin, "contributed nothing whatever that they might glorify God. All they say regarding religion is frigid and insipid. It is therefore in His word alone that there shines forth the truth which may lead us to true piety."[2] Calvin had a high respect for the liberal arts and sciences but the cultivation of these cannot lead us towards God. "Natural reason will never direct men to Christ; and as to their being endued with prudence for the regulation of their lives or born to cultivate the liberal arts and sciences, all this passes away without yielding any advantage."[3] Calvin admires in Daniel his superior natural abilities and learning, and his endowment with remarkable intellectual gifts, but points out that even then it was not through his own human industry or exertion that he acquired his spiritual knowledge. That knowledge came through prayer. "We know the profane to be endowed with singular talents, and other eminent faculties; and these are called natural, since God desires by His gracious gifts to shine forth in the human race by such examples as these." But when it comes to the knowledge of God such gifts are excluded from consideration as a means of achievement. "Daniel places revelation on a higher footing."[4] "Art and science cannot obtain the power of understanding the revelation of God, but a revelation from the Spirit must be

[1]Comm. on Isa. 55 : 5, C.R. 37 : 287. . . . *Noscendo non agnoscant, sed misere errent in tenebris.* Calvin here implies that precisely this natural knowledge of God, perverted into an idol, is the greatest hindrance to the acquisition of the true knowledge.

[2]Comm. on Ps. 29 : 9, C.R. 31 : 290.

[3]Comm. on John 1 : 5, C.R. 47 : 6-7. *Nunquam naturalis ratio homines ad Christum diriget. Iam quod prudentia ad regendam vitam instructi sunt, quod ad praeclaras artes ac disciplinas nati, id quoque totum sine fructu evanescit.*

[4]Cf. comm. on Dan. 2 : 30, C.R. 40 : 587.

waited for."[1] "We must carefully notice these two things—
that a knowledge of all the sciences is mere smoke when the
heavenly science of Christ is wanting; and man, with all his
acuteness, is as stupid for obtaining of himself a knowledge of
the mysteries of God, as an ass is unqualified for understanding
musical harmonies."[2] For though we have all the sciences in
the world stuffed inside our heads, what help will that be when
life fails us?"[3]

Calvin does not deny that in the writings of the philosophers
there are occasional shrewd and apposite remarks on the nature
of God, but these can help us forward no more than a flash of
lightning in the darkness, vanishing as soon as it has come, can
advance the benighted traveller. "To the great truths, What God
is in Himself, and what He is in relation to us, human reason
makes not the least approach."[4] "It is true that in Plato one will
find that there is intelligence in God. For when he speaks of
God, he says that God has always had His intelligence in Himself. Nearly all the other philosophers speak in this way. Now
those who are so curious as to want thus to show the agreement
between the philosophers and Holy Scripture think they are
doing a great service to the Christian Church when they can say
that the gospel writers have not been the only ones who have
spoken thus, and that the pagans themselves have known such
things well. This is all very much to the point! It is like covering
something clear with a veil. See! God gives us a perfectly clear
revelation in the doctrine of His Gospel, and we are going to throw
a veil across it, crying, 'Here, look at this! This will help you
to see the thing much more clearly'. It is quite true that God
wished that these same things should be known by pagan
Philosophers to render them so much the more inexcusable
before His Majesty. But that is not to say that His truth ought
to be proved by the things they have said. For it is obvious that,
the more they thought they were approaching God, the further
away they were putting themselves."[5]

[1]Comm. on Dan. 2 : 4 f., C.R. 40 : 562.
[2]Comm. on 1 Cor. 1 : 20, C.R. 49 : 325. *Fumus est omnium scientiarum
cognitio, ubi abest coelestis Christi scientia : et homo cum toto suo acumine perinde est
stupidus ad intelligenda per se Dei mysteria, atque asinus ineptus est ad symphoniam.*
[3]Serm. on Luke 2 : 1–14, C.R. 46 : 958.
[4]Inst. 2 : 2 : 18; cf. 3 : 2 : 14–16.
[5]Serm. on John 1 : 1–15, C.R. 47 : 475.

5. The perversity of man's mind as a barrier to any
true knowledge of God outside of Christ

The main barrier to our acquiring any living and true knowledge of God through the diffused and faint revelation which is
believed to be given in the natural realm is the perversity of
man's mind. Until this perversity is cured by the complete
renewal of the mind through contact with Christ, the natural
man is forced to turn even the faint glimmer of truth he possesses
into a vicious idol that is a mockery of the true God and whose
possession can only the more confirm man in his alienation from
the truth.[1] "What, then, these very sparks shine in the darkness
to render man without excuse. Behold, therefore, how far
man's reason prevails, that he may feel self-convinced that no
pretext for ignorance and error remains to him. . . . Therefore
man's intelligence is altogether useless towards guiding his life
aright. Perverseness (*perversitas*) more clearly appears in his
heart."[2] The poverty and untruth of all natural theology is thus
the condemnation of man and the proof of the perversity of his
mind, which should surely produce something better than a
lifeless idol from such a wonderful source of revelation as the
theatre of God's glory in the natural world! A further proof of
this perversity which closes man's mind against the possibility
of any natural revelation Calvin finds in the simple fact that in
Christ man is *wholly* regenerated and renewed in every part of
his being. This would not be necessary if, as the Papists believe,
some part of his reason were still sound and entire. "He gives
His elect one heart and a *new spirit*. It follows, therefore, that
the whole soul is vitiated, from reason even to the affections."[3]
Men are, therefore, "altogether, and in the whole of their mental
system, *alienated from God*",[4] and what has made us odious to
God has "taken possession of our whole mind".[5]

[1]Speaking of the inability of the natural man to profit from what "revelation"
he possesses, Calvin can say, "*Notons bien que les hommes ne pechent point ici
seulement par une simple ignorance, mais par une malice*" (serm. on Deut. 4 : 19–
24, C.R. 26 : 160).
[2]Comm. on Ezek. 11 : 19–20, C.R. 40 : 246.
[3]Comm. on Ezek. 11 : 19, C.R. 40 : 245. *Sequitur ergo, totam animam esse
vitiatam a ratione usque ad affectus.*
[4]Comm. on Col. 1 : 21, C.R. 52 : 90. *Penitus et toto mentis sensu abalienatos
a Deo.*
[5]Ibid.

Thus the natural man cannot profit from such traces of God
as mark the world of nature, since through the corruption of the
mind he cannot apply anything to its proper use—not even the
natural knowledge of God! He is bound only to corrupt and
abuse even what is good, and following this rule he turns the
very knowledge that might have saved him into an idol which
keeps him from the truth. "The demonstration of God, whereby
He maketh His glory apparent in His creatures, in respect of the
brightness thereof is clear enough, but in respect of our blindness
it is not sufficient."[1] The natural revelation of God, which we
must assert as present before the natural man, "avails only to
take away excuse", and differs greatly from "that knowledge
which brings salvation".[2] This perversity of mind, according
to Calvin, chiefly takes the form of an attitude of pride, standing
in which it is impossible for anyone to come to know God. God
can be apprehended only by the man who has completely
renounced all claims about his own ability to know Him, and it
is only the revelation of God in Christ that is sufficient to
destroy within the human heart this mental pride that makes him
a god to himself and so cuts him off from his Creator. "Where
is the man who renounces his own judgment, and is ready to
learn only from the mouth of God? . . . for the beginning of
piety is willingness to be taught, when we have renounced our
own judgment and follow where God calls."[3] "Until God reveal
Himself to us, we do not think that we are men, or rather we
think that we are gods; but when we have seen God, we then
begin to feel and know what we are. Hence springs true humility,
which consists in this, that a man makes no claims for himself,
and depends wholly on God."[4]

[1]Comm. on Rom. 1 : 20, C.R. 49 : 24. *Demonstrationem Dei qua gloriam
suam in creaturis perspicuam facit, esse, quantum ad lucem suam, satis evidentem :
quantum ad nostram caecitatem, non adeo sufficere.*
[2]Ibid.
[3]Comm. on Isa. 5 : 21, C.R. 36 : 118. . . . *Initium pietatis est docilitas, ubi
proprio sensu exinaniti sequimur quocunque vocat Deus.*
[4]Comm. on Isa. 6 : 5, C.R. 36 : 131.

Chapter VI

The Place and Function of Word and Sign in the Event of Revelation under the Old Covenant

1. The use of word and sign

THE God who speaks in the events of the Bible is shown to be One who in His communication with men uses not only spoken words but also concrete signs calculated to appeal to the other senses in the experiencing subject than that of hearing. Calvin uses the term "sign" generally to cover all the visible and tangible means which God uses along with the word to convey His grace to men. This includes e.g. the miracles by which God spoke to Gideon, Ahaz and Hezekiah.[1] "Our merciful Lord, with boundless condescension, so accommodated Himself to our capacity, that seeing how from our animal nature we are always creeping on the ground, and cleaving to the flesh, having no thought of what is spiritual, and not even forming an idea of it, He declines not by means of these earthly elements to lead us to Himself, and even in the flesh to exhibit a mirror of spiritual blessings."[2] The Brazen Serpent comes under the category of a sign, so also the tree of life in the garden of Eden, the rainbow shown to Noah, and the cloudy pillar.[3] Visions and dreams are signs.[4] There are thus natural signs and "preter-natural" or extraordinary signs. Signs need not be merely visible phenomena. There are audible signs such as the earthquake.[5] The Sabbath day, a purely temporal arrangement, is also a sign.[6] Under the New Covenant we find Jesus using miracles and signs alongside the word He spoke, and we have the sacraments as permanent signs appointed for our use.

[1]Comm. on Isa. 7 : 12, C.R. 36 : 152–3.
[2]Inst. 4 : 14 : 3. ... *Elementis etiam istis terrenis nos ad se deducere non gravetur, atque in ipsa carne proponere bonorum spiritualium speculum.*
[3]Cf. comm. on Gen. 9 : 13, C.R. 23 : 149; on Ps. 99 : 6 f., C.R. 32 : 52–3.
[4]Comm. on Gen. 15 : 12, C.R. 23 : 217–8.
[5]Comm. on Matt. 28 : 2, C.R. 45 : 794. The spoken word, for Calvin, is also a sign.
[6]Comm. on Ezek. 20 : 12, C.R. 40 : 483–5.

Calvin makes much of the fact that when God speaks there is thus normally a sign attached to the audible word, in order to enforce and supplement that word. The function of this chapter is to outline the place and function of word and sign in the event of revelation, and since the Word and Sacraments of the New Testament will be dealt with in detail later on, we will here confine our review mainly to the phenomena of the Old Testament, as a necessary preliminary to our later study.

2. In all revelation it is the word alone which can interpret and give meaning to the sign

Revelation, according to Calvin, never takes place without a word. There is never a genuine sign given without a voice which at some stage in the event comes from God to man. The word may be spoken in various ways. It may be put in the mouth of some figure in a dream. It may be spoken by an angel. It may come directly as if from heaven itself. It may be heard, as in the New Covenant, from the lips of one who preaches. However it comes, the voice must be there or it would not be revelation according to the true Biblical pattern. Revelation in the Bible is never a dumb event. "Whenever God offered any sign to the holy Patriarchs it was inseparably attached to doctrine without which our senses would gaze bewildered upon an unmeaning object."[1]   Commenting on Exodus 33 : 19, Calvin says, "Although a vision was exhibited to his eyes the main point was in the voice; because true acquaintance with God is made more by the ears than by the eyes.[2] A promise indeed is given that he shall behold God; but the latter blessing is more excellent, that God will proclaim His name so that Moses may know Him more by His voice than by His face, for speechless visions would be cold and altogether evanescent did they not borrow efficacy from words. . . . The soul of a vision is in the doctrine itself from which faith takes rise."[3] Therefore in all visions "the word of

[1]Inst. 4 : 14 : 4.

[2]Comm. in loc., C.R. 25 : 109. *Quamvis exhibita fuerit oculis visio, praecipuas tamen partes fuisse in voce, quia auribus magis quam oculis percipitur vera cognitio Dei.*

[3]. . . *Mutae enim visiones frigidae ac omnino evanidae essent nisi vigorem ex sermone mutuerentur. . . . Anima visiones est ipsa doctrina, ex qua nascitur fides.*

the Lord is as the soul which quickens them", the figure being
the "inferior appendage to the promise".[1] God always taught by
an annexed oracle what the visible symbol meant.[2]

The important place Calvin gives to the sacraments in the life
of the Church will be shown later. Nevertheless, in assessing
the value of the sacraments he argues from the Old Testament
to the New, and he puts the sacraments in the strictly subordinate position to the word which the visible element in the
Old Testament revelation has to the word spoken alongside of it.
Commenting on the action of the angel in cleansing Isaiah's lips
in his vision, he writes, "The angel does not here act the part of
a dumb man, but after having given the sign immediately adds
the doctrine in order to show what was intended by it, for it
would have been no sacrament if doctrine had not been added."[3]
Then he goes on to add: "Let us therefore learn that the chief
part of the sacraments consists in the Word and without it they
are absolute corruptions." "Figures are illusory without an
explanation. If the vision only had been offered to the eye of
the prophet, and no voice of God had followed, what would
have been the advantage? But when God confirmed the vision
by His Word, the Prophet is enabled to say with advantage, 'I
have seen the glory of God.' And this can be transferred to the
sacraments, because if signs only are presented to our eyes, they
will be, as it were, dead images. The Word of God then, throws
life into the sacraments, as it has been said concerning visions."[4]

3. The sign draws attention to the word that is spoken, serves to
confirm any promise or command therein given and also the
faith aroused by the word

"God illustrates and adorns His Word by external symbols,
that both greater clearness and authority may be added to it."[5]

[1]Comm. on Gen. 28 : 13, C.R. 23 : 392.
[2]Comm. on Gen. 15 : 12, C.R. 23 : 217; cf. serm. on Deut. 4 : 32–5, C.R.
26 : 205. *Les miracles n'eussent gueres servi, si la doctrine n'eust este coniointe avec.*
[3]Comm. on Isa. 6 : 8, C.R. 36 : 133.
[4]Comm. on Ezek. 2 : 3, C.R. 40 : 63. ... *Et hoc ad sacramenta etiam
transferri potest, quia si tantum signa ante oculos nostros versentur, erunt quasi
mortua spectra. Sermo igitur Dei quodammodo sacramenta vivificat sicuti et de
visionibus dictum fuit.*
[5]Comm. on Gen. 28 : 13, C.R. 23 : 392. *Externis symbolis Deus verbum
suum illustrat et ornat ut maior illi tum claritas tum autoritas accedit.*

Our minds are so constituted as to be arrested and held more readily and impressed more vividly when, on being addressed, we actually see someone or something in front of us that we can connect vitally with the sound we hear than if we merely hear a voice and see no form.   Samuel in the temple would have grasped the fact that God was speaking to him much more readily if he had been favoured with a vision as well as a voice.   It is thus the function of the sign to act as a seal attached to the word to draw attention to the importance and truth of what is being said. When God promised eternal rest to His people He sealed that promise by giving the Sabbath day as a "symbol or pledge or mark of the promise of God".[1] The continual recurrence of the Sabbath thus served to bring to mind the promises attached to the Sabbath day. "The dullness (*tarditas*) of men is so great that they do not perceive the presence of God unless they are put in mind by external signs."[2]

Miracles are regarded by Calvin as revelational signs attached to the word for its confirmation and illustration.   "Here we ought carefully to observe the use of signs, i.e. the reason why God performs miracles, namely to confirm us in the belief of His word. . . . Miracles added to the word are seals."[3] Miracles have thus the same function for the earlier form of revelation as the sacraments of the New Testament have for us.   "As Gideon was confirmed by an astonishing miracle, so are we confirmed by Baptism and the Lord's Supper, though our eyes behold no miracle."[4]   The miracles thus have the twofold function fulfilled by the sign in revelation: to "prepare the mind for faith, and when it is formed by the word, to confirm it still more".[5] Miracles "prepare the way for doctrine".[6] Thus, though faith in God does not come to men merely as a result of experiencing the miraculous or of seeing visions, for faith must rest

---

[1]Comm. on Ezek. 20 : 12, C.R. 40 : 485.   *Deus . . . voluit etiam symbolum aliquod et pignus vel tesseram exstare suae promissionis.*
[2]Comm. on Ps. 99 : 6 f., C.R. 32 : 53.
[3]Comm. on Isa. 7 : 10, C.R. 36 : 151. . . . *Coniuncta enim verbo miracula sigilla sunt.*
[4]Comm. on Isa. 7 : 12, C.R. 36 : 153.   *Quemadmodum enim admirabili portento confirmatus est Gedeon, ita et nos baptismo et sacra coena confirmamur tametsi nullum oculis nostris miraculum pateat.*
[5]Comm. on John 3 : 2, C.R. 47 : 53.   *Duplex sit miraculorum fructus, ut praeparent ad fidem, deinde ut eam ex verbo conceptam melius confirment.*
[6]Comm. on John 4 : 45, C.R. 47 : 99.

on the word alone,[1] nevertheless such signs can at least help
towards faith by serving the spoken word and drawing attention
to it. "Miracles when united to doctrine have no small weight."[2]
"Let us, therefore, learn reverently to consider the works of God,
that the wondering at them may make an entrance for doctrine."[3]

4. Signs, in varying degrees, testify to the real presence
of God on the scene of revelation

Where God gives a sign, there He comes Himself to be present
with men. The sign is thus a veil behind which He conceals His
presence on the scene of human affairs. When God revealed
Himself under the Old Covenant, "there were many signs under
the law to testify His presence".[4] Signs are means whereby God
"discovered (*exhibuit*) His presence".[5] They are focal points
for the meeting between God and man. Where the sign is, there
is indeed the "face of God".[6] "Under the appearance of the
cloud God testified that He met Moses."[7] Calvin can refer to a
prophetic vision as "a sign or symbol of the presence of God",[8]
likewise to the Ark[9] and to the Cloud at the Red Sea.[10] Those
who had such signs of God's presence given to them could be
absolutely confident that God was there with them to speak to
them and to save them and to bless them. "Whenever God
grants any token of His presence, He is undoubtedly present
with us."[11] He does not deceitfully expose the signs of His
presence to men's eyes.[12] The experience of the people of God

[1]Cf. pp. 124 ff.
[2]Comm. on John 10 : 41, C.R. 47 : 254; cf. on John 11 : 45, C.R. 47 : 271;
on Dan. 3 : 28.
[3]Comm. on Acts 3 : 9, C.R. 48 : 65–6.
[4]Comm. on Acts 7 : 40, C.R. 48 : 153. *Nam sub lege plurima erant symbola
ad testandam eius praesentiam.*
[5]Inst. 1 : 11 : 3, cf. serm. on Luke 1 : 26–30, C.R. 46 : 68. The Angel Gabriel
was not simply an angelic visitor, but a revelational sign to Mary of the hidden
presence of God there before her. Hence Mary's fear.
[6]Comm. on Ps. 42 : 2, C.R. 31 : 426–7.
[7]Comm. on Exod. 34 : 5, C.R. 25 : 113. *Sub specie nubis testatus est Deus se
Mosi occurrere.*
[8]Cf. comm. on Ezek. 9 : 3–4, C.R. 40 : 196–7.
[9]Comm. on Ps. 20 : 2, C.R. 31 : 208; on Ps. 14 : 7, C.R. 31 : 141.
[10]Comm. on 1 Cor. 10 : 2, C.R. 49 : 451–2.
[11]Comm. on Isa. 6 : 1, C.R. 36 : 126.
[12]Comm. on Exod. 13 : 21, C.R. 24 : 143.

made them so certain that He was true to His promise and granted His presence with the sign that they could actually in their manner of speaking transfer the name of the Lord Himself to the sign of His presence. Moses, thus describing the journey of the cloud before the Children of Israel, says, *The Lord went before them*,[1] and the Psalmist, describing the triumphal journey of the Ark, says, *God is gone up with triumph.*[2] "The name of Jehovah is here applied to the Ark; for although the essence or majesty of God was not shut up in it, nor His power and operation fixed to it, yet it was not a vain and idle symbol of His presence."

5. In many cases signs represent a spiritual gift which God actually wishes to bestow on His people in the presence of the sign, or which God pledges as their eternal inheritance

Not only do signs testify to the presence of God, but the form and nature of the sign bears testimony about the attitude in which God is present. In giving the sign, God "does not amuse us by idle and unmeaning shapes".[3] The form of the sign "perfectly agrees with the reality",[4] the sign being an attestation of the grace or power (*virtus*) of God towards the recipient.[5] Signs can thus testify to an invisible spiritual event in which God gives His grace to the souls of men. When, for example, Jesus by miracle cured men's bodies, He was not only drawing attention to His divine claims but giving an outward sign of what at the same time He was doing for men's souls. "What He bestowed upon their bodies was only a token of the far more abundant and excellent blessings which He imparts to our souls."[6] Thus the curing of physical blindness was a sign of the

[1]Exod. 13 : 21.
[2]Comm. on Ps. 47 : 6 f., C.R. 31 : 469.
[3]Comm. on Isa. 6 : 1, C.R. 36 : 126.
[4]Comm. on Isa. 42 : 3, C.R. 37 : 61.
[5]Comm. on Gen. 2 : 9, C.R. 23 : 38.
[6]Comm. on Isa. 35 : 5, C.R. 36 : 594. *Quod exhibuit corporibus, symbolum tantum fuit eorum quae abundantius multo ac praestantius animis nostris subministrat.* Cf. comm. on Matt. 14 : 34, C.R. 45 : 444; on Matt. 11 : 4, C.R. 45 : 300.

curing of spiritual blindness. When the Bible speaks of men as
seeing the heavens suddenly opened, we are to understand this
visible sign to mean that at that very moment God was removing
the spiritual distance between heaven and earth, and taking
away from within the mind the barriers which normally prevent
the man from knowing the mysteries of the heavenly realm. "It
follows therefore when God opens the heavens, that He also
gives new eyesight to His servants, to supply their deficiency to
pierce not only the intervening space, but even its tenth, or
hundredth part. So when Stephen saw the heavens open, his
eyes were doubtless illuminated with unusual powers of piercing
far more than men can behold. So at the baptism of Christ . . .
God made it appear to John the Baptist as if he were carried
above the clouds."[1] In discussing God's action in causing, as a
sign to assure Hezekiah that he was to be granted more years of
life, the turning back of the shadow on the sundial, Calvin notes
the resemblance between the sign and the gift. "The sign bears
a resemblance to the event itself (*analogiam cum re ipsa*) as all
other signs usually do."[2] Calvin likewise speaks of the Passover
feast as a sign of spiritual grace (*spiritualis gratiae symbolum*)[3]
with a form significant of the grace that is conveyed through its
celebration. He refers to the Manna and the Brazen Serpent as
having attached to them a spiritual mystery (*mysterium
spirituale*).[4] The Sabbath, regarded as a sign, is also for him an
outward symbol hiding and yet revealing a spiritual mystery,
"a visible figure of an invisible grace",[5] which grace was really
conveyed to those who observed with faith the promise of the
Sabbath. The land of Canaan is also referred to as a sign, though
in this case it is less a sign of a present spiritual blessing than a
pledge of an eternal inheritance.[6]

[1]Comm. on Ezek. 1 : 1 and 2. *Quum Deus coelos aperit, simul dare novos
oculos servis suis.* Cf. comm. on John 1 : 51, C.R. 47 : 36.
  [2]Comm. on Isa. 38 : 8, C.R. 36 : 652. Cf. comm. on John 1 : 32, C.R.
47 : 28. *Semper est signorum analogia cum veritate.*
  [3]Comm. on Exod. 12 : 1, C.R. 24 : 286.
  [4]Comm. on John 3 : 14, C.R. 47 : 63.
  [5]Comm. on Ezek. 20 : 12, C.R. 40 : 485. *Ostendit ergo duntaxat externum
esse symbolum, et quod sub se mysterium spirituale complectitur. Iam sequitur, ut
nuper attigi, sabbatum fuisse sacramentum quia visibilis fuit gratiae invisibilis
figura.*
  [6]Cf. Inst. 4 : 16 : 11; comm. on Gen. 27 : 28, C.R. 23 : 378; on Heb. 4 : 8.

6. Signs are aids by which man is made to realise the limits of his natural ability to apprehend the divine, and is thus in true humility raised up to the knowledge of God by grace alone

Man's mind, according to Calvin, is essentially earthly. The natural man through his mind and soul is unable to rise above the things of this earth to apprehend God. Moreover, because of his perversity, even what knowledge of God he might acquire would be used to "drag God down to earth"—and to make out of the truth of God a caricature of God in the form of an idol that man would be able to master, and manipulate according to his own self-will. "The sluggishness of our flesh hinders us from elevating our minds to the height of the divine majesty."[1] It suits us to form "gross and earthly conceptions of the heavenly majesty", thus disfiguring the glory of God, and turning His truth into a lie,[2] for then we have a God who does not disturb or challenge us overmuch, in dealing with whom we need not be converted, and in whose presence no mortal or healing wound is given to that human pride with which it is impossible to know the truth of God. "The human mind, stuffed as it is with presumptuous rashness, dares to imagine a God suited to its own capacity,"[3] says Calvin, giving the illustration of the Golden Calf, "the flesh is always restless till it has obtained some figment like itself, with which it may vainly solace itself as a representation of God. In consequence of this blind passion, men have, almost in all ages since the world began, set up signs on which they imagined that God was visibly depicted to their eyes."[4] Moreover, "as soon as a visible form is given to God, His power is also suffered to be annexed to it. So stupid are men that whenever they figure God they fix Him."[5]

God's purpose in revealing Himself to men through signs chosen by Himself is to prevent men from thus "fixing" God

[1]Comm. on Ps. 84 : 2, C.R. 31 : 780.
[2]Comm. on Ps. 42 : 1 f., C.R. 31 : 427. *Ubi vel crassum aliquid terrenumque concipimus de coelesti eius maiestate, fingimus meras larvas, quae Dei gloriam deformant, eiusque veritatem convertunt in mendacium.*
[3]Inst. 1 : 11 : 8. *Mens hominis ut superbia et temeritate est referta, Deum pro captu suo imaginari audet.*
[4]Ibid.
[5]Inst. 1 : 11 : 9. *. . . Ita stupidi sunt homines, ut Deum affigant ubicunque affingunt.*

under self-chosen and powerless forms. God, through the signs, seeks to give man something earthly to lay hold of with his mind, not in order that man may drag God downwards to become one standing on man's own level but in order that God may, by thus getting hold of the perverse and sluggish mind of his creature, raise him up from the earthly world to the heavenly mystery, and deliver him from small self-centred conceptions by giving him truly God-centred conceptions. "It pleases the Lord to employ earthly elements, as vehicles for raising the minds of men on high."[1] In giving signs, God's purpose is thus that His people should, by grasping the sign, at the same time be led by God's grace to grasp something transcendent beyond the sign, and thus really to lay hold of the spiritual gift which God offers in extending the sign of it to the consciousness of man.

Thus the signs, like the sacraments, are intended to act as ladders by which the mind of man can be raised to heaven. The visible symbolism of the tabernacle served the purpose of steps by which the Psalmist could "rise up to heaven", and, knowing the infirmity of his own mind, he longed for the sanctuary.[2] Men must beware, however, in using the visible symbols by which God seeks to direct our minds thus upwards, that they do not through their natural perversity seek to fix God to the sign and thus make an idol out of the very object through which He is graciously seeking to raise us to Himself. "Although the Lord intended that the Ark should be a testimony of His presence, yet He forbade these Jews to fix their whole and exclusive attention upon it, but commanded them to raise their eyes to heaven, and there to seek and adore God. He wished to be always worshipped in a spiritual manner (John 4 : 24) and the Ark was not to be adored instead of God."[3] "The Lord, though he holds intercourse with us by symbols and sacraments, yet wishes to be sought in heaven."[4] This is the reason why the temple is called the *footstool* of God, and the *place of His feet*. The visible sanctuary was

---

[1]Comm. on Gen. 9 : 13, C.R. 23 : 149. *Terrenis enim elementis uti placuit Domino, quae vehicula essent tollendis sursum hominum mentibus.* Cf. serm. on Job 1 : 2–5, C.R. 33 : 50. "The service of God is spiritual. We must mount far higher than these visible shapes: for they must lead us to a heavenly end and not hold us down here in the world without lifting up our minds to heaven."
[2]Comm. on Ps. 84 : 2, C.R. 31 : 780; cf. on Ps. 42 : 1, C.R. 31 : 426.
[3]Comm. on Isa. 46 : 2, C.R. 36 : 154.
[4]Ibid.

intended to serve the purpose of a "ladder" by which the minds of the godly were directed and conducted to the heavenly model (*ad coeleste exemplar*).[1] In the temple the discerning man of Israel could see the *face* of God indeed, and it is also described as the place where God's *face* shines upon His people; but to indicate that His *face* can be seen only if the worshipper allows his mind to be raised above the signs of God's presence and above the sanctuary, the latter is called but the *footstool* of God, as a reminder that the whole attention must not be fixed on the outward sign.[2]

In order to ensure that men cannot pervert the sign into a powerless idol, or imagine God as attached to the sign, God chooses as signs objects and figures that point beyond themselves and represent God as the mysterious and inconceivable God. "There were, no doubt, various appearances under which God made himself known to the holy fathers in ancient times; but in all cases he refrained from using signs which might induce them to make for themselves idols."[3] "It is true that the Lord occasionally manifested His presence by certain signs so that He was said to be seen face to face; but all the signs He ever employed were in apt accordance with the scheme of doctrine, and, at the same time, gave plain intimation of his incomprehensible essence, for the cloud, and smoke, and flame, though they were symbols of heavenly glory (Deut. 4 : 11), curbed men's minds as with a bridle, that they might not attempt to penetrate further. . . . The Holy Spirit appeared under the form of a dove, but as it instantly vanished, who does not see that in this symbol of a moment, the faithful were admonished to regard the Spirit as invisible, to be contented with His power and grace, and not call for any external figure."[4]

[1] Comm. on Ps. 84 : 2, C.R. 31 : 780.
[2] Cf. comm. on Isa. 60 : 13, C.R. 37 : 363–4; on Ps. 132 : 7, C.R. 32 : 345; on Ps. 99 : 5, C.R. 32 : 51–2.
[3] Comm. on Matt. 17 : 5, C.R. 45 : 487. . . . *Semper tamen a symbolis abstinuit, quae fabricandis idolis materiam praeberent.*
Cf. serm. on Deut. 4 : 11–14, C.R. 26 : 139. *Or cependant notons que Dieu a choisi ce signe, dont il est ici fait mention* (i.e. the cloud), *à ce que nous cognoissions qu'il ne nous faut point enquerir de sa Maieste plus que il ne nous est licite. Dieu ne s'est point monstré en forme visible, à ce qu'on pensast que son essence eust quelque figure, comme il en sera traitté demain au plaisir de Dieu : mais il a mis la nuee au devant, il a mis tenebres et obscurite. Et pourquoi? Afin que nous apprenions de nous humilier, et que nous sachions qu'il habite une clarte inaccessible.*
[4] Inst. 1 : 11 : 3.

It is only through his being encountered by God behind such mysterious and transcendent signs that the natural man can be cured of the pride and perversity and insolence of his mind, which otherwise make communion with God impossible. Ezekiel was shown as a sign of God's presence an appearance of brightness impossible to behold directly in order "to render him conscious of his weakness, so that he should not desire to know more than was lawful, but submit himself humbly to God."[1] "When the Lord gave tokens of His presence, He employed at the same time some coverings (*tegumenta*) to restrain the arrogance of the human mind."[2] God "suits Himself to our capacities, so that visions should be useful to us only when we avoid pride and are not carried away by foolish and bold curiosity".[3] Thus, confronted by the signs through which it pleases the true God to be known, man is humbled in order that he may know God, and the natural insolence that makes him desire to push his inquiries about the majesty of God beyond lawful limits is repressed.[4] Acquaintance with God must produce in us humility and submission, "nay it prostrates us entirely instead of elating us. But where pride is, *there* is ignorance of God".[5] Thus we should through the use of these signs submit ourselves to "come with pure hearts to seek Him in a spiritual manner", knowing that by their aid we can seek to behold even the glory of God which is hidden from the sight, knowing that through them we see the face of God.[6]

[1]Comm. on Ezek. 1 : 28, C.R. 40 : 60. *Ut conscius suae debilitatis non plus scire appeteret quam fas erat, sed Deo se modeste subiiceret.*
[2]Comm. on Matt. 17 : 5, C.R. 45 : 487.
[3]Comm. on Ezek. 1 : 27, C.R. 40 : 58. *Verum Deus se ita ad captum nostrum attemperat, ut visiones sint nobis utiles, modo ne superbiamus, vel ne efferamur stulta et audaci curiositate.*
[4]Cf. comm. on Isa. 6 : 4, C.R. 36 : 130.
[5]Comm. on 1 Cor. 8 : 2, C.R. 49 : 429; cf. comm. on Ps. 110 : 1, C.R. 32 : 161–2.
[6]Comm. on Ps. 42 : 2, C.R. 31 : 427.

Highly exalted view of preaching

Chapter VII

The Preached Word as the Word of God

1. Preaching as the Word of God

CALVIN takes note of the fact that, in communicating His Word to the children of Israel, God did not normally allow His voice to sound as thunder directly from heaven upon the ears of the assembled people. Usually when he had a word to speak He spoke it through the medium of a prophet, whose speech, however, in the act of speaking, God so closely identified with His own Word that it may be said that the mouth of the prophet was the mouth of God Himself. In this case man's speech can really become God's Word in the event of its being communicated to those who are intended to hear it. "The Word *goeth out of the mouth* of God in such a manner that it likewise *goeth out of the mouth* of men; for God does not speak openly from heaven but employs men as his instruments."[1] Commenting on the power of Haggai's word to stir up the people of his day to begin the work of building the temple, Calvin says, "The people received not what they heard from the mouth of mortal men, otherwise than if the majesty of God had openly appeared. For there was no ocular view of God given; but the message of the prophet obtained as much power as though God descended from heaven, and had given manifest tokens of His presence. We may then conclude from these words, that the glory of God so shines in His Word, that we ought to be so much affected by it, whenever He speaks by His servants, as though He were nigh to us, face to face."[2]

To-day the Word of God is normally heard by men in a similar

[1]Comm. on Isa. 55 : 11, C.R. 37 : 291. *Sic egreditur verbum ex ore Dei, ut simul ex ore hominum egrediatur. Nec enim loquitur palam e coelo Deus, sed hominibus tanquam organis utitur.*
[2]Comm. on Hag. 1 : 12, C.R. 44 : 95. *Tantundem efficaciae obtinuit prophetae legatio, ac si Deus e coelo descendens dedisset manifesta signa praesentiae suae. Ergo colligere ex his verbis oportet, sic fulgere Dei gloriam in eius verbo, ut perinde affici nos deceat quoties loquitur per servos suos, ac si facie ad faciem nobis esset propinquus.*

form, through the word of a man, a preacher of the Gospel, called
and appointed by God to this task. The task of the preacher of
the Word is to expound the scripture in the midst of the worshipping Church, preaching in the expectancy that God will do,
through his frail human word, what He did through the Word
of His prophets of old, that God by His grace will cause the
word that goes out of the mouth of man to become also a Word
that proceeds from God Himself, with all the power and efficacy
of the Word of the Creator and Redeemer. The word preached
by man can become "God speaking". "The Word of God is not
distinguished from the word of the prophet."[1] "God does not
wish to be heard but by the voice of His ministers."[2]

The task of preaching must therefore be undertaken, and the
word of the preacher should be heard, in the expectancy that
Christ the Mediator will come and give His presence where the
Gospel is preached, and cause men to hear His voice through
the voice of the minister. On John 10 : 4, *They know His voice*,
Calvin says, "Though he speaks here of ministers, yet instead of
wishing that they should be *heard* he wishes that God should be
heard speaking by them."[3] "This ought to add no small
reverence to the Gospel, since we ought not so much to consider
men as speaking to us, as Christ by His own mouth; for at the
time when He promised to publish God's name to men, He had
ceased to be in the world; it was not, however, to no purpose
that He claimed this office as His own; for He really performs it
by His disciples."[4] Christ is the sower who goes forth to sow,
in the gospel parable, but this does not mean that the parables
of sowing do not at the same time refer also to the sowing of the
Word by the ordinary preacher. "When Christ says not that
ministers of the Word sow, but that he alone sows, this is not
without meaning: for though this cannot be supposed to be
restricted to His person, yet as He makes use of our exertions
and employs us as His instruments for cultivating His field, so
that He alone acts by us and in us, He justly claims for Himself

[1]Comm. on Hag. 1 : 12, C.R. 44 : 94. *Neque enim hic sermo Dei a prophetae verbis discernitur.*
[2]Comm. on Isa. 50 : 10, C.R. 37 : 224.
[3]Comm. in loc., C.R. 47 : 237. *Deum per ipsos loquentum vult audire.*
[4]Comm. on Heb. 2 : 11, C.R. 55 : 29. *Quod non parum addere debet reverentiae Evangelio : si quidem non tam homines ipsos loqui reputandum est, quam Christum ipsorum ore. . . . Vere hoc per discipulos suos praestitit.*

what is in some respects common to His ministers. Let us therefore remember that the Gospel is preached not only by Christ's command, but by His authority and direction; in short, that we are only in His hand, and that He alone is the author of the work."[1] "Among the many noble endowments with which God has adorned the human race, one of the most remarkable is, that He deigns to consecrate the mouths and tongues of men to His service, making His own voice to be heard in them."[2]

2. Preaching as a sign of the presence of God

"Words are nothing else but signs."[3] Through the preaching of the Word by His ministers, Christ therefore gives His sacramental presence in the midst of His Church, imparts to men the grace which the Word promises, and establishes His Kingdom over the hearts of His hearers. The preaching of the Word by a minister is the gracious form behind which God in coming near to men veils that in Himself which man cannot bear to behold directly. "He consults our weakness in being pleased to address us after the manner of men by means of interpreters, that He may thus allure us to Himself, instead of driving us away by His thunder. How well this familiar mode of teaching (*familiaris docendi ratio*) is suited to us, all the godly are aware, from the dread with which the divine majesty justly inspires them."[4] "When the prophet says *by the breath of His lips*, this must not be limited to the person of Christ; for it refers to the Word which is preached by His ministers. Christ acts by them in such a manner (*sic enim Christus in illis agit*) that He wishes their *mouth*

---

[1]Comm. on Matt. 13 : 37, C.R. 45 : 369. *Porro quod Christus non verbi ministros seminare dicit, sed se unum, ratione non caret : quamvis enim ad eius personam hoc restringi minime conveniat, quia tamen nostra opera sic utitur, et ad culturam agri sui tanquam instrumenta nos adhibet, ut per nos solus et in nobis agat, merito sibi vindicat, quod eius ministris quodammodo commune est. Meminerimus ergo, non solum Christi mandato praedicari evangelium sed eius auspiciis et ductu, ut sumus tanquam eius manus, ipse autem unicus operis autor.*
[2]Inst. 4 : 1 : 5. . . . *Dignatur ora et linguas hominum sibi consecrare, ut in illis sua vox personet.*
[3]Inst. 4 : 14 : 26. *Nihil aliud sunt verba quam signa*, cf. comm. on Gen. 9 : 12, where Calvin speaks of Word and Sacrament together as a "vocal sign".
[4]Inst. 4 : 1 : 5. Cf. serm. on Eph. 4 : 11–14, C.R. 51 : 565. *Quand l'Evangile nous est presché, c'est autant comme si Dieu descendoit à nous, quand il s'accommode ainsi à nostre petitesse.*

to be reckoned as His *mouth*, and their *lips* as His *lips*."[1]

Christ, therefore, uses the preached word as a means of revelation and self-communication in much the same way as He uses the other signs of His presence and grace in His historic acts of revelation. Thus Calvin can refer to preaching as a token of the presence of God, and as a means whereby He comes near to us. "The Lord is said to 'come' when He gives any token of His presence. He approaches by the preaching of the Word, and He approaches also by various benefits which He bestows upon us."[2] In another place He takes note of the fact that Paul (in Rom. 10 : 8) equates God's being *near* to the preaching of the Gospel.[3] Preaching is the means whereby the gifts of Christ are conveyed to us. "The voice which is in itself mortal, is made an instrument to communicate eternal life."[4] "God has ordained His Word as the instrument by which Jesus Christ, with all His graces, is dispensed to us."[5]

3. Preaching as the instrument of Christ's rule

Preaching is, moreover, a means whereby Christ establishes His rule in the hearts of His people. On the verse, *He hath placed in my mouth a sharp sword*, Calvin says, "Christ hath therefore been appointed by the Father, not to rule, after the manner of princes, by the force of arms, and by surrounding Himself with other external defences, to make Himself an object of terror to His people; but His whole authority consists in doctrine, in the preaching of which He wishes to be sought and acknowledged."[6] David ruled over his earthly kingdom by a golden sceptre and sword of iron, but "how Christ designs to rule in His Church, we know; for the sceptre of His kingdom is the Gospel".[7]

[1] Comm. on Isa. 11 : 4, C.R. 36 : 240.

[2] Comm. on Isa. 50 : 2, C.R. 37 : 216–7.

[3] Comm. on Isa. 55 : 6, C.R. 37 : 288; cf. serm. on Deut. 4 : 6–10, C.R. 26 : 132. *Quand nous venons au sermon . . . nous ne pouvons point recevoir un seul mot qui nous soit publié et annoncé en son nom, que sa Maiesté ne soit presente, et que nous ne soyons devant lui.*

[4] Comm. on 1 Pet. 1 : 25, C.R. 55 : 231. *Vox quae per se mortua est, vitae aeternae sit organum.*

[5] O.S. 1 : 505. *Comme instrument, par lequel Jesus Christ, avec toutes ses graces nois soit dispensé.*

[6] Comm. on Isa. 49 : 2, C.R. 37 : 191. . . . *Totum eius imperium consistit in doctrina, in cuius praedicatione quaeri atque agnosci vult.*

[7] Comm. on Hos. 1 : 11, C.R. 42 : 221.

"Christ does not otherwise rule among us than by the doctrine of the Gospel."[1]

Calvin does not stop even here in his assessment of the function of preaching. He makes the final claim that preaching is such a mighty instrument in the hand of the Lord that through its means not only does Christ create and uphold and rule His Church, but also in a hidden way directs the whole course of history and creates the disturbance amongst the nations that is to bring about the consummation of His eternal purpose. Preaching is the *banner which shall stand for an ensign to the peoples.* "We know that this was fulfilled by the preaching of the gospel, and indeed was more illustrious than if Christ had soared above the clouds."[2] Preaching establishes the Kingdom of God far and wide wherever the disciples of Jesus go and proclaim His Word. Replying to the Apostles' question about the manner and time of the coming of the Kingdom, Jesus simply turned their thoughts towards their appointed task of preaching the Gospel. "For hereby he meant to drive out of His disciples the fond and false imagination which they had conceived of a terrestrial Kingdom, because He shows them briefly, that the Kingdom consists in the preaching of the Gospel. . . . They heard that Christ reigns whenever He subdues the world to Himself by the preaching of the Gospel."[3]

Preaching is not only the sceptre by which Christ rules within His Church but also the sword in the hand of the Church by which secretly and unknown even to itself the Church rules or brings judgment amongst the nations. "As to the Church collective, the sword now put in our hands is of another kind, that of the Word and Spirit, that we may slay for a sacrifice to God those who formerly were enemies, or again deliver them over to everlasting destruction unless they repent (Eph. 6 : 7). For what Isaiah predicted of Christ extends to all who are His members. *He shall smite the wicked with the Word of His mouth*

[1]Comm. on Mic. 4 : 3, C.R. 43 : 348; cf. on Ezek. 17 : 24, C.R. 40 : 420; on Isa. 11 : 4, C.R. 36 : 238. In serm. on Deut. 7 : 5–8, C.R. 26 : 514–6, Calvin shows that through the preached Word the Church is continually called sanctified, reformed, and held together in unity.

[2]Comm. on Isa. 11 : 10, C.R. 36 : 244.

[3]Comm. on Acts 1 : 8, C.R. 48 : 10. *Hac enim voce falsam de regno terreno imaginationem excutere voluit discipulis: quia breviter significat, in evangelii praedicatione consistere. . . . Audiunt tunc regnare Christum, ubi per evangelii doctrinam sibi mundum subiugat.*

and shall slay them with the breath of His lips (Isa. 11 : 4)."[1]
Thus Calvin applies many of the Old Testament prophecies of
the rule of the Messiah amongst the nations to the preacher of
the Word, for he regards Christ as acting in this world mainly
through the instrument of the preached Word. "This is why
Jesus Christ spoke so often of the Gospel, and called it the Kingdom of God. For unless we adhere to it, we are rebels against
God, and are banished from all His benefits. For we cannot
participate in these until we are reformed. . . . In fact, since
apart from this the Devil dominates everything, on account of
which he is also called the 'King of this World', so when Jesus
Christ causes His Gospel to be preached in a country, it is as if
He said, 'I want to rule over you and be your King.' "[2]

Calvin claims for preaching even the function of renewing the
whole fallen creation. He gives his views on this matter in his
application of Isaiah 51 : 16, *That I may plant the heavens*, "that
is, restore all things to its proper order". "Heaven and earth are
said to be restored by the doctrine of salvation; because *in Christ*,
as Paul says, *are collected all things that are either in heaven or
earth.* . . . Since, therefore, the whole face of the world is disfigured . . . there are good grounds for saying that godly teachers
renovate the world. . . . Thus, the *heavens* are said to be *planted
and the earth to be founded* when the Lord establishes the Church
by the Word."[3]

4. The preached Word effective to accomplish its commands and promises

Calvin has such an exalted view of the importance of preaching
in the Church and world that he regards the Word of God as

[1]Comm. on Ps. 149 : 9, C.R. 32 : 440. *Quantum ad totum ecclesiae corpus
spectat; alius nunc gladius nobis datur in manum, verbi scilicet, ac spiritus, quo
mactemus Deo in sacrificium qui prius fuerant hostes : vel etiam quo eos tradamus
in aeternum exitium nisi resipiscant.* . . . Cf. serm. on Job 4 : 7–11, C.R. 33 : 195.
*Il ne faut point que Dieu ait grand equippage quand il est question de reprimer ceux
qui sont ainsi revesches . . . qu'il souffle seulement, et voila tout abbatu . . . ses
ennemis sont confondus par sa simple Parole qui est comme un souffle.*

[2]Serm. on Acts 1 : 1–4, C.R. 48 : 598.

[3]Comm. on Isa. 51 : 16, C.R. 37 : 237. *Coelum et terra salutis doctrina
instaurari dicantur : quoniam in Christo colliguntur omnia, quae aut in coelis aut
in terra sunt, ut etiam ait Paulus . . . Ergo quum horribilis dissipatio totam mundi
speciem deformet, non abs re dicuntur pii doctores mundum renovare, ac si Deus
eorum manu coelum et terram de integro formaret.*

always mighty in power to effect what God promises or commands, even though that Word may be uttered through the frail human words of the preacher. God's Word cannot be divorced from His action. "He calls God true, not only because He is ready to stand faithfully by His promises, but also because whatsoever He says in words He fulfils the same in deed; for He so speaks that His command immediately becomes His act."[1] Isaac blessed Jacob "as the authorised interpreter of God, and the instrument employed by the Holy Spirit". He later found out that he had been deceived, but he could not go back on the word of blessing he had spoken, for it had been God's Word and had been efficacious in bringing into being what had been promised. *"Behold I have made him Lord,"* said Isaac. "He claims a certain fire and efficacy for his benediction," says Calvin in his comment, and then he adds, "In this way *they* are said to remit sins, who are only the messengers and interpreters of free forgiveness."[2]

Thus when God speaks through the mouth of the preacher offering forgiveness, those who hear the Word in faith are there and then really absolved from their sins, for the Word effects what it declares. "Christ puts forth His power in the ministry which He has instituted, in such a manner that it is made evident that it was not instituted in vain . . . for He is not separated from the minister, but on the contrary His power is declared efficacious in the minister."[3] "Christ through our instrumentality, illuminates the minds of men, renews their hearts, and in short regenerates them wholly."[4] *I will hear what God the Lord will speak, for He will speak peace to His people,* says the Psalmist, and Calvin comments, "The Psalmist might have spoken more plainly of divine providence, as for example 'I will look to what God will do,' but as the benefits bestowed upon the Church flow

[1]Comm. on Rom. 3 : 4, C.R. 49 : 48. *Deum veracem dicit non modo quia bona fide stare promissis paratus sit, sed quoniam opere implet quidquid loquitur : siquidem dicit, ut imperium mox quoque fiat opus.*

[2]Comm. on Gen. 27 : 37, C.R. 23 : 381. *Iterum notanda est loquutio qua suae benedictioni Isaac certam, vim et effectum asserit, ac si in eius voce inclusum fuisset imperium. . . . Sic remittere peccata dicuntur, qui tantum gratuitae veniae nuncii sunt ac interpretes.*

[3]Comm. on 1 Cor. 3 : 7, C.R. 49 : 351. *Sic in ministerio a se instituto potentiam suam exserit Christus, ut appareat, non frustra fuisse institutum . . . neque enim ipse separatur a ministro, sed potius vis eius in ministro efficax praedicatur.*

[4]Comm. on 2 Cor. 3 : 6, C.R. 50 : 40. *Christus per nos mentes illuminat, renovat corda, totos denique homines regenerat.*

from the divine promises He makes mention of God's *mouth* rather than of His *hand*."[1] "The voice of God is . . . living and conjoined with effect;"[2] "a powerful instrument for communicating strength;"[3] "nothing that has come out of God's holy mouth can fail in its effect."[4]

Calvin seldom refers to the preaching of the Gospel without speaking of it in such exalted language and without exhorting his readers to prize beyond all other gifts of God to the Church this incomparable treasure set in our midst by the grace of God, for it is the Word which is *able to save* the human soul. "It is a high eulogy on heavenly truth, that we obtain through it a sure salvation; and this is added, that we may learn to seek and love and magnify the Word as a treasure that is incomparable."[5] For, he reminds us, "The Gospel is not preached that it may only be heard by us, but that it may as a seed of immortal life, altogether reform our hearts,"[6] and "as often then as God's fatherly love towards us is preached, let us know that there is given to us ground for true joy, that with peaceable consciences we may be certain of our salvation."[7]

5. The preached Word effective only in the freedom and power of the Holy Spirit

It must be emphasised, however, in this discussion on the preached Word of God, that the word of the preacher can only become the Word of God through a sovereign and free act of the Holy Spirit, by whose power alone preaching can be effective. "Saving is not ascribed to the word, as if salvation is conveyed by the external sound of the voice, or as if the office of saving is taken away from God and transferred elsewhere."[8] "The work

[1]Comm. on Ps. 85 : 9, C.R. 31 : 788.
[2]Comm. on 1 Thess. 1 : 4, C.R. 52 : 142. *Vivam et cum effectu coniunctam.* Calvin in this context speaks of *spiritualem doctrinae energiam.*
[3]Comm. on Isa. 35 : 4, C.R. 36 : 592. *Nisi enim efficax esset organum huic vigori inspirando.*
[4]Comm. on Isa. 34 : 16, C.R. 36 : 588.
[5]Comm. on Jas. 1 : 21, C.R. 55 : 394.
[6]Comm. on 1 Pet. 1 : 23, C.R. 55 : 229.
[7]Comm. on John 15 : 11, C.R. 47 : 345.
[8]Comm. on Jas. 1 : 21, C.R. 55 : 394. *Non in hunc finem, servandi vis sermoni adscribitur, quasi aut salus in externo vocis sonitu inclusa foret, aut servandi munus Deo ablatum, alio transferretur.*

of the Spirit, then, is joined to the Word of God. But a distinction is made, that we may know that the external word is of no avail by itself, unless animated by the power of the Spirit. . . . All power of action, then, resides in the Spirit Himself (*residet igitur penes ipsum spiritum omnis agendi virtus*), and thus all power ought to be entirely referred to God alone."[1] "The whole power of ministers is included in the Word—but in such a way, nevertheless, that Christ must always remain Lord and Master."[2] Preaching may thus fail to be the Word of God. The act may remain on a merely human level throughout, in which case the preacher with all his eloquence and skill and fervour will accomplish nothing. When Paul calls himself a *minister of the Spirit* "he does not mean by this that the grace of the Holy Spirit and His influence were tied to his preaching so that he could whenever he pleased breathe forth the Spirit along with the utterance of the voice. . . . It is one thing for Christ to connect His influence with a man's doctrine (*adiungere suam virtutem*), and quite another for the man's doctrine to have such efficacy of itself. We are then, *ministers of the Spirit*, not as if we held Him enclosed (*inclusum*) within us, or as it were captive (*captivum*), not as if we could at our pleasure confer His grace upon all."[3] "God sometimes connects Himself with His servants and sometimes separates Himself from them: . . . He never resigns to them His own office."[4] "When God separates Himself from His ministers, nothing remains in them."[5]

6. The relationship between man's speech and God's Word

In the event of God's "connecting Himself" thus with the preacher, to make his act of speaking the effective Word of the Lord, a relationship is set up between the human act of the

[1]Comm. on Ezek. 2 : 2, C.R. 40 : 62.
[2]Comm. on 2 Cor. 10 : 8, C.R. 50 : 118. *Tota ministrorum potestas in verbo est inclusa, ut semper nihilominus maneat Christus solus Dominus et Magister.*
[3]Comm. on 2 Cor. 3 : 6, C.R. 50 : 40. *Non intelligit, gratiam spiritus sancti ac vim suae praedicationi esse alligatam : ut quoties libuerit, una cum voce spiritum e gutture proferat. . . .*
[4]Comm. on Mal. 4 : 6, C.R. 44 : 497. *Aliquando coniungit se Deus cum servis suis : aliquando autem ab illis se separat. Dum se coniungit, transfert ad eos quod apud ipsum tamen residere non desinit. Neque enim suas partes illis resignat.*
[5]Ibid; cf. also Inst. 4 : 1 : 6.

preacher and the divine action of grace which we may call a sacramental union. The nature of this relationship can be more fully discussed only when we deal with the subject of sacraments. At present, however, these points may be noted: when God graciously comes to give His presence and power along with the human word, there is the closest identity between the divine and human actions. "The Word of God is not distinguished from the words of the Prophet."[1] "He is not separated from the minister."[2] "God Himself who is the author is conjoined with the instrument, and the Spirit's influence with man's labour."[3] So close is this identity that the preacher can actually be called a *minister of the Spirit* and his work spoken of in the most exalted terms.[4] Indeed it may legitimately be said that it is the preacher who effects what is really effected by God. But even when all this happens there must remain at the same time the sharpest distinction between what is divine and what is human in this mysterious event. "We require to distinguish . . . we must set the Lord on one side and the minister on the other. We must view the minister as one that is a servant, not a master—an instrument, not the hand; and in short as man, not God."[5]

7. The preached Word effective to condemn where it is not received in faith

It must be emphasised that when the Word of God comes through preaching its effectiveness does not depend on the receptiveness of the hearer (though the nature of its effect may be so determined). As against those who dissolved the mystery of God's activity in preaching into a purely internal subjective effect in the hearts of the hearers Calvin says, "Delirious and even dangerous are those notions, that though the internal word is efficacious, yet that which proceeds from the mouth of man is lifeless and destitute of all power. I indeed admit that the power

[1] Comm. on Hag. 1 : 12, C.R. 44 : 94.
[2] Comm. on 1 Cor. 3 : 7, C.R. 49 : 351.
[3] Comm. on 1 Cor. 9 : 1, C.R. 49 : 438. *Deus ipse autor cum instrumento, et vis spiritus cum hominis opera coniungitur.*
[4] Comm. on 1 Cor. 3 : 7, C.R. 49 : 350.
[5] Ibid. . . . *Ministrum considerat ut est servus non dominus : ut est organum non manus : ut denique homo est, non Deus.* Cf. serm. on Luke 1 : 16–18, C.R. 46 : 39.

does not proceed from the tongue of man, nor exists in mere sound, but that the whole power is to be ascribed altogether to the Holy Spirit; there is, however, nothing to hinder the Spirit from putting forth His power in the word preached."[1] "The wickedness and depravity of men do not make the Word to lose its own nature."[2] The power is thus in the Word quite apart from the receptive hearing. "Though the Word of God does not always exert its power on man, yet it is in a manner included in itself (*in se inclusam*), as though He had said, 'If anyone thinks that the air is beaten by an empty sound when the Word of God is preached, he is greatly mistaken, for it is a living thing and full of hidden power (*occultae energiae*), which leaves nothing in man untouched.' "[3] Thus the true preaching of the Word of God, if it does not find a willing response through faith in the hearer, can, instead of bringing blessing and salvation, rouse within men the opposite effect and harden the heart instead of blessing it.

Calvin in his own day had the accusation thrown at him that Christian preaching made the world worse rather than better. He grimly admits a truth that lies in the reproach [4] and gives us the warning: "All who shall labour faithfully in the ministry of the Word will be laid under the necessity of meeting with the same result. We too have experienced it more than we could have wished. . . . We ought indeed to be deeply grieved when success does not attend our exertions. A part of the blame we ought even to lay on ourselves . . . yet . . . the truth must always be heard from our lips, even though there be no ears to receive it . . . for it is enough for us that we labour faithfully for the glory of God . . . and the sound of our voice is not ineffectual, when it renders the world without excuse. . . . That our faith may not fail, we ought to employ this support, that the office of teaching was enjoined upon Isaiah, on the condition that, in scattering the seed of life, it should yield nothing but death; and that this is not merely a narrative of what once happened, but a prediction of the future kingdom of Christ."[5]

[1]Comm. on Heb. 4 : 12, C.R. 55 : 51.
[2]Comm. on Matt. 13 : 19, C.R. 45 : 364.
[3]Comm. on Heb. 4 : 12, C.R. 55 : 50.
[4]Cf. comm. on Matt. 21 : 45, C.R. 45 : 598.
[5]Comm. on Isa. 6 : 10, C.R. 35 : 136.

This hardening of the heart against the Word Calvin attributes
to the satanic reaction to the inevitable advance of the Kingdom
of Christ through the preaching of the Word. "Although the
elect of God are reduced to submission by means of the Gospel,
nevertheless on the other hand we see that the enemies of truth become more proud and more rebellious, so that the world is plunged
into conflict, as experience to-day shows. For while there was
no preached Gospel, all the world was without care and at rest.
There was little to argue or dispute about. Why? The devil
reigned without any question. But since our Lord Jesus Christ
has appeared with the pure doctrine of the Gospel see how much
closer the skirmishes have become!"[1]

8. The twofold effect of the preached Word

Thus preaching has a twofold effect. It can either soften or
harden the heart. It can either save or condemn the hearer.
"The Gospel is never preached in vain, but has invariably an
effect, either for life or death."[2] "As the Word is efficacious for
the salvation of believers, so it is abundantly efficacious for the
condemning of the wicked."[3] Calvin regards Jesus' word to
Peter, '*whatsoever thou shalt bind on earth shall be bound in heaven,
and whatsoever thou shalt loose on earth shall be loosed in heaven,*'
as referring to the office of preaching. "The comparison of the
keys is very properly applied to the office of teaching. . . . We
know that there is no other way in which the gate of life is
opened to us than by the Word of God; and hence it follows
that the key is placed, as it were, in the hands of the ministers
of the Word. . . . As there are many, who are not only guilty of
wickedly rejecting the deliverance offered them . . . the power
and authority to *bind* is likewise granted to ministers of the
Gospel."[4] Calvin is, however, careful to add when he speaks in

[1]Serm. on Acts 2 : 1–4, C.R. 48 : 629. Cf. serm. on 1 Tim. 2 : 3–5, C.R.
53 : 155.
[2]Comm. on 2 Cor. 2 : 15, C.R. 50 : 34. *Nunquam frustra praedicatur quin
valeat aut in vitam aut in mortem.*
[3]Comm. on Isa. 55 : 11, C.7 : R.3 292.
[4]Comm. on Matt. 16 : 19, C.R. 45 : 475. Cf. serm. on Deut. 4 : 6–10, C.R.
26 : 132. *Quand il veut que sa parolle nous soit preschee, c'est autant comme s'il
nous appelloit à soy, et que nous fussions devant son throne, comparoissans là chacun
pour soy, afin de rendre compte comme devant nostre Iuge.*

this strain that this negative effect "does not belong to the nature
of the Gospel but is accidental".[1] "The doctrine of the Gospel
has in its own nature a tendency to edification—not to destruction. For as to its destroying, that comes from something apart
from itself—from the fault of mankind."[2] We must thus
"always distinguish between the proper office of the Gospel, and
the accidental one (so to speak) which must be imputed to the
depravity of mankind, to which it is owing, that life to them is
turned into death".[3]

Thus it is that it is a fearful thing for men to be confronted
with the grace of God offered through the preaching of the Word.
Grace can so easily be made by man's decision to show its other
side, which is judgment, and can indeed be turned into its very
opposite. Through the preaching of the Word the judgment of
the world is continually proceeding. In giving their inescapable
decision about the Word as it comes through the preacher, men
are giving their eternal decision about God. Since the Word is
the sceptre of Christ's Kingdom "it cannot be rejected without
treating Him with open contempt. . . . No crime is more offen-
sive to God than contempt of His Word."[4] "The reprobate . . .
though not softened, set up a brazen and an iron heart against
God's Word, yet . . . are . . . restrained by their own guilt. They
indeed laugh but it is a sardonic laugh; for they inwardly feel
that they are, as it were, slain; they make evasions in various
ways so as not to come before God's tribunal; but though unwill-
ing they are yet dragged there by this very Word which they
arrogantly deride; so that they may be fitly compared to furious
dogs, which bite and claw the chain by which they are bound
and yet can do nothing—they still remain fast bound."[5]

It may be added, in closing, that this twofold effect, which is so
characteristic of the true Word of God, can act even on its
negative side for the benefit of the Church and for the spiritual
health of the believer. It is through the Word's producing this
violent reaction of offence in the hearts of those who are hardened

---

[1]Comm. on Matt. 16 : 19, C.R. 45 : 475.
[2]Comm. on 2 Cor. 10 : 8, C.R. 50 : 118–9.
[3]Comm. on 2 Cor. 2 : 15, C.R. 50 : 34. *Semper ergo distinguendum est
proprium evangelii officium ab accidentali (ut ita loquar).* . . .
[4]Comm. on Matt. 10 : 14, C.R. 45 : 279.
[5]Comm. on Heb. 4 : 12, C.R. 55 : 50.

that the life of the Church is partly cleansed and those who are not Christ's sheep are by their own choice warded off from the fold. "The pastor ought to have two voices: one for gathering the sheep; and another for warding off and driving away wolves and thieves. The Scripture supplies him with the means of doing both."[1] Moreover, the believer himself must continually be assisted to mortify in himself those natural tendencies that run continually so counter to the Word of God. This mortification is effected by the Word of God, which, even in the heart of the children of God, can slay and subdue and cast out what is evil. This point will be dealt with more fully under the doctrine of Baptism. Meanwhile, let us note with Calvin that "there is a certain vivifying killing of the soul"[2] which continually slays the children of God in order that continually, under the Word of God, they may rise to new life.

[1]Comm. on Titus 1 : 9, C.R. 52 : 412. *Duplex esse vox pastoris debet ; altera ovibus colligendis, altera arcendis fugandisque lupis et furibus. Utramque facultatem scriptura suppeditat.*

[2]Comm. on Heb. 4 : 12, C.R. 55 : 50–1. *Est enim (ut diximus) vivifica quaedam occisio animae, quae fit per evangelium.*

Chapter VIII

The Written Word as the Word of God

1. Scripture as the only true source of the knowledge of Christ

I F anyone would proclaim the Word of God in the name of Jesus Christ, he must derive the word he has to speak from the witness to Jesus Christ given in the Scriptures of the Old and New Testaments. God, that we may hear His Word, has not left us to seek "daily oracles from heaven"[1] but has given us a written word to consult. The original purpose in having the law written down in the form of a book was to give the people an opportunity of knowing the Word of God apart from any oracular experience. "When it pleased God to raise up a more visible form of a Church, it was His will that His Word should be committed to writing in order that the priests might derive from it whatever they would communicate to the people."[2] In its early form the written Scripture was the record of the oracles with which God favoured the patriarchs, and which throughout their previous course of oral transmission had been carefully preserved by those that heard them, for they already bore the testimony of the Holy Spirit and men knew that they were marked off from all other oracles, as coming from God.[3] To this nucleus was added first the law and afterwards the oracles of the prophets, who were mainly interpreters of the law, adding nothing to it except prophecies of things to come.[4] Finally the writings of the New Covenant were written by the Apostles, whose office was merely to expound the ancient Scriptures and to show that the things delivered in it were accomplished in Christ.[5]

If we wish to know of Jesus Christ, and to bear witness to Him, it is to this source in the written word that we must turn, both

1Inst. 1 : 7 : 1. *Non quotidiana e coelis redduntur oracula.*
2Inst. 4 : 8 : 6.
3Cf. Inst. 1 : 4 : 2, 4 : 8 : 5.
4Inst. 4 : 8 : 8.
5Ibid.

for our necessary knowledge of the historical facts and for our understanding of the meaning of these facts. There can be no reliable source either for this knowledge or for this understanding other than the writings of the law, the prophets and the Apostles. They are thus for us the only authoritative witness to Christ, and we may trust them as reliable sources. "God has admirably provided for our sakes in choosing Moses His servant, who was the minister of their deliverance, to be also the witness and historian of it; and this too among those who had seen all with their own eyes and who, in their peculiar frowardness, would never suffer one, who was so severe a reprover of them, to make any false statements of fact. Since this is so then his *authority* is sure and unquestionable."[1] "Three only were then present (i.e. at the transfiguration of Jesus) but they were sufficient as witnesses; for they had through many miracles seen the glory of Christ, and had a remarkable evidence of His divinity in His resurrection. But we obtain certainty in another way; for though Christ has not risen before our eyes, yet we know by whom His resurrection has been handed down to us. And added to this is the inward testimony of conscience the sealing of the Spirit, which far exceeds all evidence of the senses."[2] "Whenever Satan attacks us, let us learn to meet him with this shield that it is not to no purpose that the son of God united us with the Apostles, so that the salvation of all was bound up, as it were, in the same bundle. . . . The Son of God . . . does not approve of any other faith than that which is drawn from the doctrine of the Apostles, and sure information of that doctrine will be found nowhere else than in their writings."[3] Therefore the writings of the Apostles are to be "received as the oracles of God";[4] and "others have no other office than to teach what is delivered and sealed in the sacred scriptures".[5] "Prophesying at this day

[1]Comm. on Exod. 14 : 28, C.R. 24 : 155.
[2]Comm. on 2 Pet. 1 : 16, C.R. 55 : 453. *Tres solum tunc aderant : illi nihilominus idonei fuerunt testes ; nempe quia tot miraculis intuiti erant Christi gloriam, et illustre divinitatis eius specimen in resurrectione habuerant. Nos vero aliter certi quatenus expedit : licet enim non resurrexerit ante oculos nostros Christus, scimus tamen a quibus de manu in manum prodita nobis fuerit eius resurrectio. Et accedit interius conscientiae testimonium ; illa inquam spiritus obsignatio quae omnes sensuum probationes longe superat.*
[3]Comm. on John 17 : 20, C.R. 47 : 386.
[4]Inst. 4 : 8 : 9.
[5]Ibid.

G

amongst Christians is almost nothing else than a right understanding of the Scripture, and singular gift of expounding the
same, since all old prophecies and oracles have been finished in
Christ and His Gospel."[1]

Therefore for us the Word of God is the Scripture. We cannot
have contact with the "Word which lies hid in the bosom of
God"[2] except through "that which has proceeded from His
mouth and has come to us",[3] and that Word is the word of the
Apostles and prophets by whom God has designed to speak to
us, and whose mouth is the mouth of the only true God. The
importance of the place which Calvin gives to the Scripture may
be summed up in two propositions from his commentary on St.
John's gospel: "Christ cannot be properly known in any other
way than from the Scriptures",[4] and "Christ is rejected when
we do not embrace the pure doctrine of the Gospel".[5]

We must recognise the providence of God in having completed
in the witness of the Apostles everything He has to say concerning His Son until the final consummation when He shall be
manifested in glory. "God will not in future, as in ages past,
speak from time to time by one and another. He will not add
prophecies to prophecies, or revelations to revelations, but He
has completed all branches of instruction in His Son (*omnes
docendi partes in filio complevisse*) . . . for which reason the whole
period of the New Testament . . . is designated as the last time,
in order that . . . we may learn neither to receive anything new,
nor to invent anything beyond it."[6] The Apostolic writings are
thus the "limits of revelation".[7] To try to establish contact with
God without the Scripture is like trying to "behold His face by
shutting our eyes" or like an almost blind person trying to see
without spectacles.[8] The Spirit of God is given to us to illuminate and quicken not any word but only the Word of Scripture.
"It is no less unreasonable to boast of the Spirit without the

[1]Comm. on Rom. 12 : 6, C.R. 49 : 239. *Prophetia hodie in christiana ecclesia
nihil fere aliud est quam recta scripturae intelligentia, et singularis eius explicandae
facultas.* Cf. Inst. 4 : 8 : 8.
[2]Comm. on 1 Pet. 1 : 25, C.R. 55 : 230.
[3]Ibid.
[4]Comm. on John 5 : 39, C.R. 47 : 125.
[5]Comm. on John 12 : 48, C.R. 47 : 303.
[6]Inst. 4 : 8 : 7.
[7]Comm. on 1 Pet. 1 : 25, C.R. 55 : 230. *Revelationis fines.*
[8]C.R. 8 : 427.

Word, than it would be an absurd thing to bring forward the Word itself without the Spirit."[1] "A strict adherence to the Word constitutes spiritual chastity."[2] This, of course, does not mean that God cannot reveal Himself without the Scripture, but it does mean that we cannot *expect* God to reveal Himself to us apart from the Scripture. We cannot expect revelation to come through heavenly oracles or private communications or visions or irregular signs, since the days for such modes of communication are long past. "When it pleased God to raise up a more visible form of a Church it was His will that His Word should be committed to writing."[3]

2. Scripture as the sole authority in the life of the Church

For Calvin the Bible is not only the sole source of Church proclamation but also the sole authority that must rule the life of the Church. It has been pointed out that through the preaching of the Word of God Christ rules within His Church. The preacher of the Word is bound to turn to no other source for his testimony than to the Scripture. This means that the Scripture

[1]O.S. 1 : 466.

[2]Comm. on Ps. 106 : 39, C.R. 32 : 132. *Haec spiritualis est castitas, verbo Dei prorsus adhaerere.*
The Scriptures are thus sufficient in themselves to furnish the people of God with all the inspiration and knowledge they require apart from any other source. Through them the Spirit leads us into *all truth*, and to imagine that this needs supplementing is "to do grievous injury to the Holy Spirit" (comm. on John 16 : 13, C.R. 47 : 362). "Everything that relates to the guidance of our life is contained in them abundantly" (comm. on Isa. 30 : 1, C.R. 36 : 507; cf. Inst. 1 : 6 : 1). Therefore we must approach the Scriptures with faith in their sufficiency, confident that they will give us all the light we need. This means, however, that we must let the all-sufficient Scripture mark for us the bounds of our research into the divine. "On the whole subject of religion one rule of modesty and soberness is to be observed; and it is this—in obscure matters not to speak or think, or even long to know, more than the Word of God has delivered" (Inst. 1 : 14 : 4). "Where the Lord shutteth His holy mouth, let us also stop the way to our minds going further" (comm. on Rom. 9 : 14, C.R. 49 : 180). The very silence of Scripture on many points should act as a "bridle to the waywardness of man's curiosity" (comm. on Rom. 9 : 20, C.R. 49 : 186), thus fulfilling the function of the sign in revelation (see pp. 78–81). Adoration rather than curiosity is the fitting attitude when searching out the secrets of revelation (comm. on Rom. 11 : 33, C.R. 49 : 230; on Rom. 9 : 20, C.R. 49 : 186; Inst. 1 : 14 : 4). Cf. serm. on Deut. 4 : 6–10, C.R. 26 : 131. *Le premier poinct de la Chrestienté c'est que l'Escriture saincte est toute nostre sagesse, et qu'il nous faut escouter Dieu qui parle là, sans y rien adiouster.*

[3]Inst. 4 : 8 : 6.

is set over the Church by God as the authority that must be allowed full freedom to rule the life of the Church. It must be given a place of unusurped honour within the Church. It was through the Word that the Church was brought into being; it is through the same Word always being given afresh that the Church is continually renewed in its life and preserved as a Church. We cannot admit the existence of a Church where the Word of God does not so rule, for "this is the perpetual mark by which our Lord has characterised His people: *Everyone that is of the truth heareth my voice* (John 18 : 37)".[1] No one must argue that it was the Church that produced the Word and that the Church, being therefore antecedent to the Word, is superior to it. "Paul testifies that the Church is *built on the foundation of the Apostles and Prophets* (Eph. 2 : 20). If the doctrine of the Apostles and prophets is the foundation of the Church, the former must have had its certainty before the latter began to exist. Nor is there any room for the cavil that, though the Church derives its first beginning from thence, it still remains doubtful what writings are to be attributed to the Apostles and Prophets, until her judgment is interposed. . . . The doctrine was certainly ascertained and sanctioned antecedently to the Church, since, but for this, the Church herself could never have existed."[2]

Even in recognising the canon of Scripture the Church merely recognised the obvious. "When the Church receives it and seals it with her suffrage she does not authenticate a thing otherwise dubious or controvertible."[3]   Calvin, in denying the Roman claim that the Church has the authority to judge Scripture, admits that it is the proper office of the Church to distinguish genuine from spurious Scripture, since the Sheep hear the voice of the Shepherd and will not listen to the voice of strangers. But "to submit the sound oracles of God to the Church, that they may obtain a kind of precarious authority among men, is blasphemous impiety. The Church is, as Paul declares, founded on the doctrine of Apostles and Prophets; but these men speak as if they imagined that the mother owed her birth to the daughter."[4]

---

[1] Inst. 4 : 2 : 4. *Haec enim perpetua est nota, qua signavit suos Dominus noster.* . . .
[2] Inst. 1 : 7 : 2.
[3] Inst. 1 : 7 : 2.
[4] C.R. 7 : 612–3.

By accepting the authority of Scripture the Church is allowing Christ to rule within its life and to be the sole inspiration of its life. 'Wherever, therefore, the doctrine of the Gospel is preached in purity, there we are certain that Christ reigns; and where it is rejected, His government is set aside."[1] "The government of the Church by the preaching of the Word is no human contrivance but a most sacred ordinance of Christ."[2] Calvin argues that such a mode of governing the Church is wise, for a Church governed purely by the Spirit without any definite word would be too unstable. "Seeing how dangerous it would be to boast of the Spirit without the Word, He declared that the Church is indeed governed by the Holy Spirit, but in order that the government might not be vague and unstable He annexed it to the Word."[3] For the Church to be governed by those in ministerial or priestly office would be equally dangerous. "The priest was only an interpreter of the law," says Calvin. "Whenever, then, God bids those pastors to be heard whom He sets over His Church, His will is . . . that He Himself should be heard through their mouth. In short, whatever authority is exercised in the Church ought to be subjected to this rule—that God's law is to retain its own pre-eminence and that men blend nothing of their own, but only define what is right according to the Word of the Lord."[4] God commits to ministers and teachers instruction only, "and on this condition, that the authority remains in Himself alone".[5]

3. The inner witness of the Holy Spirit as authenticating the authority of Scripture

The authority of Scripture is authenticated by the inner witness of the Holy Spirit. The reverence which the Church gives

[1]Comm. on Isa. 11 : 4, C.R. 36 : 240.
[2]Comm. on Eph. 4 : 11, C.R. 51 : 196.
[3]O.S. 1 : 465. *Quia enim providebat, quam periculosum foret absque verbo spiritum iactare, ecclesiam a sancto quidem spiritu gubernari asseruit : sed eam gubernationem, ne vaga et instabilis crederetur, verbo alligavit.*
[4]Comm. on Hag. 2 : 10–4, C.R. 44 : 111. *Denique ad hanc regulam exigere opportet quidquid autoritas est in ecclesia, nempe ut lex Dei retineat suum gradum, nec quidquam ex se ipsis homines comminiscantur, sed tantum definiant ex verbo Domini quid rectum sit.*
[5]Comm. on Mal. 2 : 9, C.R. 44 : 440.

to the Scripture is due primarily to the influence of the Holy Spirit in giving inward testimony to the believer that this word is the Word of God. Calvin is tireless in making the claim that to those who have faith you do not need to prove the authority of Scripture. It will be most readily accepted. To argue from the authority of Scripture is for him "the surest kind of proof with Christians".[1] To those who have faith, the Word of Scripture shines with a majesty of its own and a completely self-evidencing power. "The Word of the Lord constrains us by its majesty, as by a violent impulse, to yield obedience to it."[2] This majesty arrests and holds the human mind in a different and more powerful manner than ordinary human wisdom uses with its insinuating allurements and blandishments.[3] The testimony of the Spirit is superior to all reason.[4] "Those who are inwardly taught by the Holy Spirit acquiesce implicitly in Scripture."[5] But it is only on the minds of those who have faith that the Scripture so impresses itself. "It is foolish to attempt to prove to infidels that Scripture is the Word of God. This it cannot be known to be, except to faith."[6] "The volume of sacred Scripture very far surpasses all other writings . . . still, however, it is preposterous to attempt by discussion to rear up a full faith in Scripture."[7] "The Scripture, carrying its own evidence along with it, deigns not to submit to proofs and arguments, but owes the full conviction with which we ought to receive it to the testimony of the Spirit."[8]

4. A reverent approach to Scripture necessary

The authority of the Holy Scripture is such as to call for a reverent and humble approach to the Bible within the life of the

[1]Comm. on Rom. 3 : 10, C.R. 49 : 53. *Apud Christianos firmissima probationis species.*
[2]Comm. on 1 Cor. 2 : 4, C.R. 49 : 335. *Verbum enim Domini maiestate sua, tanquam violento impulsu, nos ad obediendum sibi cogit.*
[3]Ibid.
[4]Inst. 1 : 7 : 4. *Testimonium spiritus omni ratione praestantius esse respondeo.*
[5]Inst. 1 : 7 : 5.
[6]Inst. 1 : 8 : 13.
[7]Inst. 1 : 7 : 4.
[8]Inst. 1 : 7 : 5. *Scriptura . . . quidem esse αὐτόπιστον neque demonstrationi et rationibus subiici eam fas esse. . . .*

Church. Such humility before the Scripture is necessary if the Word of God is to be given freedom to do its work within the Church, and to authenticate itself to men. "We owe the Scripture the same reverence which we owe to God because it has proceeded from Him alone and has nothing belonging to man mixed with it."[1] Unless we approach the Scripture with such reverent expectancy of hearing through it the Word of God and with humble willingness to obey that Word we will not find through the Scripture the certainty and assurance that it was appointed by God to give us, and we will not find the book yielding to us its treasures of divine wisdom. "When we come to hear the sermon or take up the Bible, we must not have the foolish arrogance of thinking that we shall easily understand everything we hear or read. But we must come with reverence, we must wait entirely upon God, knowing that we need to be taught by His Holy Spirit, and that without Him we cannot understand anything that is shown us in His Word."[2] "Hereby it comes to pass that the reading of the Scripture profits few at this day, because we can scarcely find one among a hundred who submits himself willingly to learn. . . .[3] This is the true reverence of the Scripture when we acknowledge that there is wisdom laid up there which surpasses all our senses, and yet notwithstanding we do not loathe it, but, reading diligently, we depend upon the revelation of the Spirit and desire to have an interpreter given us."[4] This interpreter of Scripture is the Holy Spirit who is given to those who are humble before the word. The claim of the Roman Church was that the Church, in its superior position of authority over the word, has infallible power to interpret Scripture according to its own traditional or natural insights. Calvin, replying to such a claim, points out that "the prophecies can now be no more understood by the perspicacity of the human mind than they could at first have been composed by it. . . . We should pray to have their genuine meaning opened up to us by the Spirit of God. Nothing is to be given to ambition —nothing to arrogance."[5]

[1]Comm. on 2 Tim. 3 : 16, C.R. 52 : 383.
[2]Serm. on 1 Tim. 3 : 8–10, C.R. 53 : 300.
[3]*Qui se libenter ad discendum subiicat.*
[4]Comm. on Acts 8 : 31, C.R. 48 : 191–2.
[5]C.R. 7 : 613.

On Moses' action of sprinkling the book of the law with blood Calvin comments, "For this reason Christ in the Holy Supper commends His blood as the seal of the New Covenant; nay, whenever we take the sacred book into our hands, the blood of Christ ought to occur to our minds as if the whole of the sacred instruction were written therewith."[1] Note should be made of Calvin's use of the phrase "as if", here and in other places. We must approach Scripture "as if" it were the Word of God, and then we are in the position to find that it *is* the Word of God.[2] Part of this reverence consists in approaching the Scriptures with the right end in view. It is an insult to the majesty of the Scripture to seek to find within the book the answers to many of the idle and trivial questions that sometimes take hold of our human minds. We must not look upon the Bible as an answer to our questions, for we are not lords over God's Word. We must allow Him to prescribe the end we have to seek and the questions that must be answered. "It is unlawful to treat it (i.e. the Scripture) in an unprofitable manner; for the Lord, when He gave us the Scriptures, did not intend either to gratify our curiosity or to encourage ostentation."[3] "We are reminded not to read Holy Scripture so as to gratify our fancies, or to draw from it useless questions." Those who do so are "guilty of profaning a thing most holy".[4] Calvin can define the only end that is worthy of the dignity and majesty of this book. "We ought to read the Scriptures with the express design of finding Christ in them."[5] "The best method of seeking God is to begin at His Word."[6]

Part of the reverence due to Scripture, if we are to profit from it as the Word of God, is the belief that the *whole* Scripture is the gift of God, every part having significance for the Church, and the patient expectancy that those things which are yet obscure to us shall yet yield light and blessing if we adhere to

[1]Comm. on Exod. 24 : 5, C.R. 25 : 75.
[2]Cf. pp. 118-9.
[3]Comm. on 2 Tim. 3 : 16, C.R. 52 : 383. Cf. serm. on Acts 1 : 6-8, C.R. 48 : 605-13.
[4]Serm. on 2 Tim. 3 : 16, C.R. 54 : 287. Cf. serm. on Job 15 : 1-10, C.R. 33 : 709. *Voila quelle est nostre vraye sagesse, c'est que nous ne desirions point de plus savoir que ce que Dieu nous monstre en son escole.*
[5]Comm. on John 5 : 39, C.R. 47 : 125; cf. serm. on 1 Tim. 6 : 3-5, C.R. 53 : 560.
[6]Comm. on Gen. 48 : 15, C.R. 23 : 584. Cf. C.R. 9 : 825.

the Word of God. "Whatsoever, then, is set down in Scripture, let us labour to learn it; for it were contumely against the Holy Spirit if we should think that He hath taught anything which were not material for us to know."[1] "We must not pick and call the Scripture to please our own fancy, but must receive the whole without exception."[2] Calvin well understands the difficulties that will face those who seek to fulfil such an exhortation and to become reverent students of the whole Scripture. "Sometimes, perhaps, we shall have to wait long (i.e. for light!) but at length the Lord will rescue and deliver us if we are willing to obey Him."[3] Two passages in which he gives sympathetic and wise advice to the ordinary student of Scripture are well worth quoting: "He manifestly confesses his ignorance of the darker places. There be many things in Isaiah which need long exposition, as when he preaches of the goodness and power of God, partly that he may invite men unto faith, partly that he may exhort and teach them to lead a godly life. Therefore no man shall be so rude an idiot which shall not profit somewhat by reading that book and yet he shall, peradventure, scarce understand every tenth verse. Such was the eunuch's reading. For seeing that according to his capacity he gathered those things which served to edification, he had some certain profit by his studies. Nevertheless, though he were ignorant of many things, yet was he not so wearied that he did cast away the book. Thus we must also read the Scriptures. We must greedily, and with a prompt mind, receive those things which are plain, and wherein God opens His mind. As for those things which are hid from us, we must pass them over until we see greater light. And if we be not wearied with reading . . . Scripture shall be made more familiar by constant use."[4] "As the seed covered with earth lies hid for a time, so the Lord will illuminate us by His Spirit, and will cause that reading which, being barren and void of fruit, causes nothing but wearisomeness, to have plain light of understanding. The Lord never keeps the eyes so shut, but that, as soon as they are once entered, the way of salvation appears unto

[1]Comm. on Rom. 15 : 4, C.R. 49 : 271. . . . *Contumelia enim fieret Spiritui sancto, si putaremus illum docuisse aliquid, quod scire nostra nihil referat.*
[2]Serm. on 2 Tim. 3 : 16–17, C.R. 54 : 284.
[3]Comm. on Isa. 30 : 1, C.R. 36 : 507–8.
[4]Comm. on Acts 8 : 28, C.R. 48 : 191.

them in the Scripture; but that they profit ever now and then a little by the reading. Yet He suffers them to stick fast oftentimes, and permits their course to be hindered by some bar which is laid in the way both that He may try patience of faith in them, and also that He may teach them humility, by putting them in mind of their ignorance, that He may make them more attentive after that they have shaken off their drowsiness; that He may make them more fervent in prayer; that He may prick them forward to love the truth more dearly; that He may set forth the excellence of His heavenly wisdom, which is otherwise not so esteemed as it ought."[1]

5. The unique origin of Scripture as a basis for its authority

For Calvin the uniqueness and authority of the Scripture as a witness to Jesus Christ, and its right to be the sole source from which the Church derives its proclamation, arise, at least in part, from the fact that it has a unique origin. He attaches considerable importance to the inspiration under which the authors of the Scripture wrote. Calvin declares that the Holy Scripture will never be of any service to us unless we are persuaded that God is the author of it. The Scripture must not be read merely "as the history of mortal men".[2] "Since no daily responses are given from heaven, and the Scriptures are the only records in which God has been pleased to consign His truth to perpetual

---

[1]Comm. on Acts 8 : 34, C.R. 48 : 195.

Calvin continually asserts that those who take up the right attitude towards Scripture and who persevere in their search of its pages will find its teaching clear. He affirms the "*claritas*" of Scripture (cf. comm. on 2 Pet. 1 : 19, C.R. 55 : 457; on Isa. 45 : 19, C.R. 37 : 145) to those who "refuse not to follow the Holy Spirit as their guide" (comm. on 2 Pet. 3 : 16, C.R. 55 : 478; cf. comm. on Deut. 29 : 29, C.R. 24 : 255–6). "God does not propound to us obscure enigmas to keep our minds in suspense" (comm. on Deut. 30 : 11, C.R. 24 : 257). If we find it obscure and hard to understand this must be ascribed to the darkness of our understanding and not to the Scripture (comm. on Isa. 45 : 19, C.R. 37 : 145), or it may be that we are inflated with too much self-confidence (cf. serm. on Job 1 : 6–8, C.R. 33 : 63). "We look down, as it were from on high, on that doctrine which ought, on the contrary, to be reverently adored by us" (comm. on Zech. 4 : 12, C.R. 44 : 193). To this attitude the Scripture yields nothing. We must, however, learn to depend on the ministers of the word to illuminate the Scripture for us as well as the Spirit, in the same way as Zechariah had to depend on the angels to interpret his visions (comm. on Zech. 1 : 21, C.R. 44 : 151–2). Thus, "we need not despair when prophecies seem obscure to us" (comm. on Zech. 4 : 4, C.R. 44 : 183–5).

[2]Cf. serm. on 2 Tim. 3 : 16, C.R. 54 : 284 ff.

remembrance, the full authority which they ought to possess with the faithful is not recognised, unless they are believed to have come from heaven, as directly as if God had been heard giving utterance to them."[1] What Calvin means by the phrase "come from heaven" must now be the subject of our inquiry.

Calvin frequently uses phrases which suggest that he held the view that the Holy Scriptures were orally dictated from heaven. "The law and the Prophets are not a doctrine delivered according to the will and pleasure of men but dictated by the Holy Spirit (*a spiritu sancto dictatum*)."[2] "The ancient prophecies were dictated by Christ."[3] In his commentary on Isaiah 40 : 6, *The voice said cry*, etc., Calvin seizes on the analogy of a voice crying from heaven and another echoing the heavenly voice, as an explanation of the origin of the prophetic oracles. "There is also a beautiful comparison between the two *voices*, that we may receive with as much reverence what the prophets utter as if God Himself thundered from heaven; for they speak only by His mouth, and repeat as ambassadors what He has commissioned them to declare."[4] "He (Moses) wrote his five books not only under the guidance of the Spirit of God, but as God Himself had suggested them speaking out of His own mouth."[5]

There are many other passages in Calvin's writings, however, which seem to indicate that when Calvin speaks of a dictation of the words from heaven he really means not that the writers merely repeated a message that came to them, as it were, "out of the blue", but that they were inwardly moved to utter as the Word of God something that was at the same time the product of their own inspired thinking and feeling. "The prophets did not speak at their own suggestion but . . . being organs of the Holy Spirit they only uttered what they had been commissioned from heaven to declare."[6] "Prophets are the organs of the Holy

[1]Inst. 1 : 7 : 1. . . . *Non alio iure plenam apud fideles auctoritatem obtinent, quam unbi statuunt, e coeli fluxisse, acsi vivae ipsae Dei voces illic exauderentur.*
[2]Comm. on 2 Tim. 3 : 16, C.R. 52 : 383.
[3]Comm. on 1 Pet. 1 : 11, C.R. 55 : 217.
[4]Comm. on Isa. 40 : 6, C.R. 37 : 9. *Quia non loquuntur nisi ex eius ore, et quasi intermedii recitant quod suggessit.*
[5]Comm. on Exod. 31 : 18, C.R. 25 : 79. *Unde colligimus, quinque libros, non modo praeunte Dei spiritu scripsisse, verum sicuti Deus ipse ore ad os loquendo suggesserat.*
[6]Comm. on 2 Tim. 3 : 16, C.R. 52 : 383. *Scimus . . . non ex suo sensu loquutos esse prophetas, sed ut erant spiritus sancti organa, tantum protulisse quae coelitus mandata fuerant.*

Spirit."[1] The Holy Spirit "directed" David's tongue in the composition of his Psalms.[2] In giving forth their inspired utterance the prophets, though they "obediently followed the Spirit as their guide", were, however, "not bereaved of mind (as the Gentiles imagine their prophets to have been)".[3] Calvin no doubt means to emphasise that, though the resultant Word was really the Word that God intended should be uttered in all its details, nevertheless the prophet acted throughout as one who really experienced all that he said and who gave forth the message as one coming naturally from his own heart through a process of thought, on a psychological level, no different from that of ordinary human authorship. These points are brought out in his comments on Ezekiel 2 : 8. Ezekiel sees the roll of a book and this leads to the comment: "There is no doubt that this volume comprehended whatever the Spirit of God afterwards dictated to the prophet; and yet the effect was just as if God had made a mortal the channel of His Spirit: as if He had said, 'Now you shall utter nothing human nor terrestrial; because you shall utter what my Spirit has already written in this book.' " But then Ezekiel has to *eat* the roll of the book, and Calvin further comments, "The true servants of God . . . not only learn what they speak of, but, as food is eaten, so also they receive within them the Word of God, and hide it in their heart so that they may bring it forth as food properly dressed."[4] Calvin further adds, "God's servants ought to speak from the inmost affection of the heart."[5]

However much on a human level the mental process of the inspired writer may be, Calvin insists that in the resultant Word there is freedom from human error and from the marks of human infirmity. Ezekiel "put off, as it were, his human infirmities (*exuerit quodammodo hominem*) when God intrusted to him the

---

[1]Comm. on Ezek. 14 : 10, C.R. 40 : 312; cf. on Ezek. 5 : 16, C.R. 40 : 134.

[2]Comm. on Ps. 8 : 1, C.R. 31 : 88. *Davidis linguam direxit.* Cf. C.R. 47 : 469. *S. Jehan a donc bien este l'instrument et l'organe de Dieu, comme une plume escrira en la main de l'homme.*

[3]Comm. on 2 Pet. 1 : 20, C.R. 55 : 458. *Impulsos fuisse dicit, non quod mente alienati fuerint (qualem in suis prophetiis ἐνθουσιασμόν fingunt gentiles), sed quia nihil a se ipsis ausi fuerint, tantum obedienter sequuti sunt spiritum ducem, qui in ipsorum ore, tanquam in suo sacrario, regnabat.*

[4]Comm. on Ezek. 2 : 8 f., C.R. 40 : 72 and ff.

[5]Comm. on Ezek. 3 : 3, C.R. 40 : 76.

office of instructor".[1] Isaiah's writings contain nothing of his own imagination and "no human reasonings".[2] Daniel's writings are "free from any human delusion or invention".[3] Moses in writing Scripture acted "not as a man, but as an *angel* speaking under the impulse of the Holy Spirit (*angelus instinctu spiritus sancti loquens*), and free from all carnal affection".[4] The Apostle Paul brings forward "nothing but what he has *received from the Lord*, so as from hand to hand . . . to administer to the Church the pure word of God".[5] They all "dared not announce anything of their own, and obediently followed the Spirit as their guide, who ruled in their mouth as in his own sanctuary".[6] Moreover, the process of inspiration can endow the writer of Scripture with supernatural knowledge. Moses is "taught by the Holy Spirit concerning events still very remote",[7] and though he has never seen the Promised Land has through the same agency a knowledge of places there. Daniel's ability to describe "almost historically events previously hidden" is a proof that "he did not speak from his own discretion . . . but whatever he uttered was dictated by the Holy Spirit".[8] God thus opened the prophets' eyes "to perceive those things which otherwise they would not of themselves have been able to comprehend".[9] Amos could quote in his writings exactly the unuttered thoughts of the people he was ministering to because he "possessed the discernment of the Holy Spirit" by which he "penetrated into their hearts and brought out what was hid within".[10] The result is that in the Scripture we have a book of which we can say that its words "are those of God and not of men".[11] Even when Ezekiel in reaction to the contempt in which he was held by his hearers found it necessary to resort to exaggerated language,

[1]Comm. on Ezek. 1 : 2, C.R. 40 : 27.
[2]Comm. on Isa. 1 : 1, C.R. 36 : 27.
[3]Comm. on Dan. 10 : 21, C.R. 41 : 215.
[4]Comm. on Gen. 49 : 5, C.R. 23 : 595; cf. serm. on Deut. 9 : 8–12, C.R. 26 : 669—God withdrew Moses and hid him for 40 days (when He gave the law) in order to prove that the prophet was *exempté de toute condition humaine.*
[5]Comm. on 1 Cor. 15 : 3, C.R. 49 : 538.
[6]Comm. on 2 Pet. 1 : 20, C.R. 55 : 458.
[7]Comm. on Gen. 49 : 1 f., C.R. 23 : 590 f.
[8]C.R. 40 : 531.
[9]Comm. on Isa. 1 : 1, C.R. 36 : 27.
[10]Comm. on Amos 6 : 13, C.R. 43 : 117.
[11]Comm. on Heb. 3 : 7, C.R. 55 : 39. *Dei non hominum esse voces, quae ex prophetarum libris proferuntur.*

"heaping up forms of speech" which show he was a man under strain, he nevertheless adds to his threats and rebukes, *I Jehovah have spoken it.* "He sets God before them, by which he means that he (i.e. Ezekiel) was not the author of the threats, but spoke only from the mouth of God, as the organ of the Spirit (*organon spiritus*)."[1]

The question has been raised whether Calvin held the doctrine of the verbal inspiration of the Bible as it was later more definitely formulated by his successors in the reformed Church. This is a question to which an answer can be attempted only after a careful examination of many passages in which Calvin at one time seems to assert the doctrine in question most emphatically, and yet at another time seems quite indifferent on matters which are vital to those who hold the doctrine.

Many of the above-quoted phrases, for instance, seem to indicate that Calvin held the Scriptures to be verbally inspired and infallible in every detail. Moreover, in dealing with passages of Scripture that are liable to raise "difficulties" in the minds of those who have not simply annihilated their critical faculties, Calvin is always far more concerned to argue on the basis of their being true than to seek to give any justification of them.[2] The imprecations of the Psalmists have to be taken not as reflecting a natural incursion of human passion into the formation of the Scripture but as truly inspired expressions of God's judgment. "David did not allow himself recklessly to pour out his wrath even as the greater part of men, when they feel themselves wronged, intemperately give way to their own passion; but, being under the guidance of the Holy Spirit, he was kept from going beyond the bounds of duty."[3] "It may seem to savour of cruelty that he should wish the tender and innocent to be dashed and mangled upon the stones, but he does not speak under the impulse of personal feeling, and only employs words which God hath Himself authorised."[4] Indeed, the fact that there are such passages in Scripture can justify the use by Calvin himself of

---

[1]Comm. on Ezek. 5 : 16, C.R. 40 : 134.
[2]Cf. comm. on Exod. 16 : 14, C.R. 24 : 169–70.
[3]Comm. on Ps. 69 : 22 f., C.R. 31 : 647.
[4]Comm. on Ps. 137 : 9, C.R. 32 : 372. ... *Non impulsu proprio loquitur, sed verba petit ex ore Dei*; cf. comm. on Ps. 109 : 6, 12 and 17, C.R. 32 : 148–54; Ps. 59 : 5, C.R. 31 : 566.

the admittedly rather lurid language which he uses against the opponents of the faith. Commenting on the Baptist's use of the phrase *"offspring of vipers"*, Calvin says, "If John, the organ of the Holy Spirit, employed such severity of language . . . how ought we now to act towards the avowed enemies of Christ? . . . Those whose ears are so delicate, that they cannot endure to have any bitter thing said against the Pope, must argue, not with us, but with the Spirit of God."[1] Further indications of Calvin's view of the importance of the verbal form of Scripture in its detail may be drawn from such a passage as his comment on *God hath spoken once, twice have I heard this.* "Nothing more is meant than that the truth referred to had been amply confirmed, it being usual to reckon anything certain or fixed which has been repeatedly announced. Here, however, it must be remembered that every word which may have issued from God is to be received with implicit authority, and no countenance given to the abominable practice of refusing to receive a doctrine unless it can be supported by two or three texts of Scripture. This has been demanded by an unprincipled heretic. . . ."[2]

All this might seem to justify our ranking Calvin's view on this subject alongside that which is to-day called "fundamentalism". There are, however, other most important considerations which indicate that Calvin did not hold such a view and must qualify our opinion on this matter.

Calvin, while he affirms the general accuracy of Holy Scripture in historical matters,[3] is at times careless about details. After discussing possible reasons for the discrepancy between Luke's figure of seventy-five with Moses' figure of seventy as the number who accompanied Joseph to Egypt, he goes on to add, "We

---

[1]Comm. on Matt. 3 : 7, C.R. 45 : 117.

Aware of the dangers, however, he adds this caveat: "Yet let Godly teachers beware, lest while they are influenced by holy zeal against the tyrants of the Church, they mingle with it the affections of the flesh, and as no vehemence which is not regulated by the wisdom of the Spirit can obtain the Divine approbation, let them not only restrain their feelings, but surrender themselves to the Holy Spirit, and implore His guidance, that nothing may escape through inadvertency."

[2]Comm. on Ps. 62 : 12, C.R. 31 : 591.

[3]Cf. serm. on Job 1 : 1, C.R. 33 : 26. "There is no cause why we should doubt whether this man lived or no . . . for the record of Ezekiel and also of St. James shew right well that there was a Job indeed, and further, seeing that the story itself declareth it, we cannot in any wise deface the thing which the Holy Ghost meant to utter so precisely."

ought rather to weigh the miracle which the Spirit commendeth unto us in this place than to stand long about one letter whereby the number is altered."[1] On a difficulty about chronology in the gospels he can say, "Anyone who will consider how little care the evangelists bestowed on pointing out dates will not stumble at this diversity in the narrative."[2] "In Scripture, it is well known, things are not always stated according to the strict order of time in which they occurred."[3] On the difficulty about the exact number of people slain by Phinehas he can say, "We know that the exact account of numbers is not always observed."[4] Moreover, Calvin shows complete indifference about whether the Apostles in the New Testament writings quote the Old Testament accurately or not. He notes that the Apostles took "complete freedom" in quoting Scripture. "They never had any hesitation in changing the words provided the substance of the text remained unchanged."[5] The Apostles in this matter "were not squeamish, for they paid more attention to the matter than to the words".[6] The Apostle is also free to accommodate the meaning of Old Testament passages to a new sense not necessarily implied in the words of the original writer,[7] and to change the expression of text without undue care.[8] There are also passages in which Calvin seems to betray like indifference about the quality of the science taught by Scripture. The writers when referring to scientific matters can be supposed to speak "in mere accommodation to mistaken, though generally received, opinion".[9] Since the Biblical writers were addressing the "humble and unlearned" they did not need to have any care about the profundity or accuracy of their statements on such matters as astronomy.[10]

[1]Comm. on Acts 7 : 14, C.R. 48 : 137.
[2]Comm. on Matt. 21 : 10 ff., C.R. 45 : 597; cf. on Matt. 13 : 12 and 16, C.R. 45 : 359, 362.
[3]Comm. on Ps. 51 : 9 f., C.R. 31 : 517.
[4]Comm. on Num. 25 : 9, C.R. 25 : 299; cf. on Num. 28 : 26, C.R. 24 : 495.
[5]Comm. on Ps. 8 : 6, C.R. 31 : 92. *Quare modo de summa rei constaret verba mutare, nulla illis fuit religio.*
[6]Comm. on Isa. 64 : 3, C.R. 37 : 409; cf. on Rom. 3 : 4, C.R. 49 : 49.
[7]Cf. comm. on Rom. 10 : 6, C.R. 49 : 198–9; on Ps. 8 : 5.
[8]Comm. on Eph. 4 : 8 f., C.R. 51 : 193–4; cf. on Hos. 13 : 14, C.R. 42 : 493–4.
[9]Comm. on Ps. 58 : 4, C.R. 31 : 561. *Nisi forte magis placeat ex communi vulgi errore loquutum esse Davidem.*
[10]Cf. comm. on Ps. 136 : 7 f., C.R. 32 : 364–5; on Ps. 19 : 4, C.R. 31 : 198.

In making our judgment about Calvin's doctrine of Scripture we must, furthermore, give full weight to his frequent assertion that, even though there is much that is divine and heavenly about the book, its form at times is of the earth, very earthly. "God comes down to *earth* that He may raise us to *heaven*. It is too common a fault that men desire to be taught in an ingenious and clever style. . . . Hence many hold the Gospel in less estimation because they do not find in it high sounding words to fill their ears. . . . But it shows an extraordinary degree of wickedness that we yield less reverence to God speaking to us, because He condescends to our ignorance: and therefore when God prattles to us in Scripture in a rough and popular style, let us know that this is done on account of the love He bears us."[1] "It is not without an admirable arrangement of providence that the sublime mysteries of the Kingdom of heaven have for the greater part been delivered with a contemptible meanness of words (*sub contemptibili verborum humilitate*)."[2] Not only in style is the humanity of the book manifest but also at times even in its matter. Calvin clearly admits this in his comments on the 88th Psalm: "I think he rather gave utterance to those confused conceptions which arise in the mind of a man under affliction, than that he had an eye to the ignorant and uninstructed part of mankind. Nor is it wonderful that a man endued with the Spirit of God was, as it were, so stunned and stupified when sorrow overmastered him, as to allow unadvised words to escape from his lips."[3]

It must be remembered that, however much stress Calvin may have laid on the divine origin of the Word of Scripture, for him it is Jesus Christ who is the Word of God, and that the Scripture is the instrument that Christ uses for the manifestation of His presence. Moreover, it is an imperfect and inappropriate instrument at its very best. "Nothing can be said of things so great and so profound, but by similitudes taken from created things. . . . We must allow that there is a degree of impropriety (*improprium*) in the language when what is borrowed from

[1]Comm. on John 3 : 12, C.R. 47 : 61. . . . *Ergo quod crasse et plebeio stylo nobiscum balbutit Dominus in Scriptura, hoc sciamus causa nostra fieri.*

[2]Inst. 1 : 8 : 1; cf. comm. on Gen. 3 : 1, C.R. 23 : 53; on Exod. 7 : 8, C.R. 24 : 88; on Ps. 78 : 3, C.R. 31 : 722; on 1 Cor. 1 : 17.

[3]Comm. on Ps. 88 : 6, C.R. 31 : 807; cf. on Ps. 39 : 6 and 13, 88 : 14, 89 : 46; C.R. 31 : 400, 405, 810, 828.

H

created things is transferred to the hidden majesty of God."[1]
All the other instruments and signs which God uses in revelation
partake of a true worldliness and humanity. It would be consistent with Calvin's doctrine of revelation were he at this point
to insist that the word of Scripture also partakes of the same
human frailty as the other signs through which God reveals
Himself and is also "flesh".

It seems, moreover, quite impossible that Calvin, if assailed
on this point, would give sanction to any doctrine of inspiration
that presupposed a different relation between the divine and
human elements than the sacramental relation which is so
important a feature in Calvin's theology.[2] In this relation the
human action remains throughout real human action, and the
divine action remains divine grace throughout. The divine
character never becomes inherently and inseparably connected
with the human element, though it is true that the human action
and indeed the human element can be *spoken* of as if it did so
partake of the divine nature. Finally it must be remembered
that Calvin was not faced in his day with the urgent necessity of
examining and criticising his own position on this matter, and
possibly of bringing it more closely and more clearly into line
with his general doctrine of revelation and with his Christology.
The question to be decided is whether Calvin's theology required
that the doctrine of Scripture be made the starting place for the
rest of his theology, a doctrine to be defined before anything else
is defined, or whether, in the light of subsequent theological
discussion, a better start cannot be made for understanding
Calvin from his more dynamic doctrine of God's action in
revelation, from his discussion of the problems of Christology,
and by refusing to discuss the doctrine of the Word apart from
the doctrine of the Sacrament. It is possible that Calvin himself,
while retaining his close adherence to the Scripture as the working basis of all his thought, might, if he had lived to-day, have
placed his chapter on Scripture a little further back in his
Institutes.

[1]Comm. on Heb. 1 : 3, C.R. 55 : 11–12. *Nam de tantis rebus tamque reconditus
nihil potest dici, nisi similitudine a creaturis mutuo sumpta. . . . Fatendum est,
improprium quodammodo esse quod a creaturis ad arcanam Dei maiestatem
transfertur.*
[2]Cf. pp. 161–171.

Chapter IX

The Ministry as Interpretation of Scripture

~ Not for individual interpretation

1. The ministry of the Word as a gift to the Church

GOD, while giving to the Church the written Word to be the source of its life and wisdom, gives also to the Church a ministry through whose act of interpreting and expounding the Scripture, the Word of God finds its true place at the heart of the Church and exercises its true function of ruling the thought and life of the Church. "What is more useful than to produce the true and complete perfection of the Church? And yet the work so admirable and divine is here declared by the Apostle to be accomplished by the external ministry of the Word."[1] God has not given to the ordinary member of the Church by himself the power of rightly understanding the Scriptures. "This is a beautiful metaphor," says Calvin on 2 Timothy 2 : 15. "Since we ought to be satisfied with the Word of God alone, what purpose is served by hearing sermons every day, or even the office of pastors? Has not every person the opportunity of reading the Bible? But Paul assigns to teachers the duty of dividing or cutting, as if a father in giving food to his children were dividing the bread and cutting it in small pieces."[2] "Observe well it is not said that God has left the Scriptures for everyone to read but has appointed a government that there may be persons to teach."[3]

Calvin sees great significance in the fact that it was Philip and not an angel who was sent by God to guide the eunuch in the

---

[1]Comm. on Eph. 4 : 12, C.R. 51 : 199. *Quid enim praestantius quam constitui Christi ecclesiam, ut iusta sua et perfecta integritate constet? Atqui tam praeclarum opus et divinum externo verbi ministerio perfici apostolus hic praedicet.*

[2]Comm. on 2 Tim. 2 : 15, C.R. 52 : 367.

[3]C.R. 8 : 412. Cf. serm. on Deut. 4 : 6–10, C.R. 26 : 133. *Car Dieu a voulu que son Evangile se publiast. Et comment? ce n'est pas seulement en cachette et en l'oreille des personnes : mais il veut qu'il y ait une instruction commune, qu'on s'assemble, voire, et qu'on s'assemble, afin qu'il soit presché, qu'il y ait bonne unite de foy, et que nous tendions tous à ce but d'estre recueillis et assemblez à nostre chef Jesus Christ.*

meaning of what he was reading in his chariot. "Frantic men require inspirations and revelations from heaven and in the mean season they contemn the ministers of God, by whose hands they ought to be governed. Others who trust too much on their own wit, will vouchsafe to hear no man and they will read no commentaries. But God will not have us despise these helps. . . . The Scripture is not only given us but interpreters and teachers are also added to be helps to us. For this cause the Lord sent rather Philip than an angel to the eunuch. . . . This is assuredly no small commendation of external preaching, that the voice of God sounds in the mouth of men to our salvation when angels hold their peace."[1] Therefore it is not for each man to decide for himself the meaning of the Scripture without asking what the teachers of the Church have taught throughout the ages, and teach to-day. Christ has given to the Church the "gift of interpretation which should throw light upon the Word".[2] It is a gift of grace that we have in the Church this ministry. "God will not come down from heaven, neither will He send His angels to bring us revelations from above; but He will be made known to us by His Word. Therefore He will have ministers of the Church preach His truth."[3]

Daniel should be our example when faced by our difficulties in understanding the Christian faith. When the visions of his head frightened him Daniel *came unto one of them that stood by him and asked him the truth.* We have no angels standing by, it is true, "but, since Scripture is obscure to us, through the darkness in which we are involved, let us learn not to reject whatever surpasses our capacity . . . but let us fly . . . to Christ Himself, who in these days teaches us familiarly by means of the pastors and ministers of the Gospel".[4] "To Christ we owe it that we have ministers of the Gospel, that they abound in necessary qualifications, that they exercise the trust committed to them. All is His gift."[5] "We are fed by the Lord as by the head of the family, when the word is offered to us (Tit. 1 : 3), for teachers go forth not of themselves, but when they are sent

[1]Comm. on Acts 8 : 31, C.R. 48 : 192.
[2]Inst. 4 : 17 : 25. *Donum interpretationis . . . quod lucem verbo afferat.*
[3]Serm. on 1 Tim. 3 : 14–15, C.R. 53 : 308.
[4]Comm. on Dan. 7 : 15 and 16, C.R. 41 : 65.
[5]Comm. on Eph. 4 : 11, C.R. 51 : 196–7.

from above. As, then, the head of the family provides meat and sustenance for his children and servants, so also the Lord supplies us daily with spiritual food by true and faithful teachers, for they are, as it were, His hands."[1] Therefore among the judgments with which God can visit His Church the prophet mentions especially the withdrawal of this gift of the preaching of sound doctrine.[2]

2. The authority and effectiveness of the ministry dependent on divine calling

Since the ministry of the Word is an office of such high importance in the fulfilling of God's purpose with His Church, it follows that no man has any right to take upon himself the authority of this office without being definitely and particularly called to exercise it by God Himself. "We must now recollect— that what is asserted about John is required of all teachers of the Church that they be called of God; so that the authority of teaching may not be founded on any other than God alone."[3] "There are no regular teachers but those upon whom God has conferred the office; and it is not enough to have the Word of God if there be not likewise a special calling."[4] "The Apostles did not appoint themselves but were chosen by Christ; and, at the present day, true pastors do not rashly thrust themselves forward by their own judgment but are raised up by the Lord."[5]

It follows that if God calls men to the ministry He will with the calling give them sufficient gifts with which effectively to fulfil their ministry, and that in reality nothing more than a call is necessary to fit anyone to fulfil this high office. "It frequently happens that God selects vile and worthless persons to instruct and warn us, in order to subdue our pride."[6] "That the Lord

[1]Comm. on Amos 8 : 11 and 12, C..R. 43 : 152. ... *Ita etiam Dominus quotidie nobis spiritualem cibum suppeditat per probos et fidos doctores, quia sunt quasi eius manus.*
[2]Ibid.
[3]Comm. on John 1 : 6, C.R. 47 : 8.
[4]Comm. on Luke 3 : 2, C.R. 45 : 111. *Hinc collige, nullos esse veros doctores, nisi quibus iniunctum est a Deo munus : neque sufficit verbum Dei habere, nisi accedat etiam specialis vocatio.*
[5]Comm. on Eph. 4 : 11, C.R. 51 : 196. *Neque hodie qui veri sunt pastores, se temere ingerunt proprio arbitrio, sed a Domino excitantur.*
[6]Comm. on John 9 : 34, C.R. 47 : 231; cf. serm. on Luke 1 : 36–8, C.R. 46 : 94; and serm. on Deut. 20 : 2–9, C.R. 27 : 604.

... should employ inconsiderable men in publishing His Word may not be quite so agreeable to the human mind. But it tends to humble the pride of the flesh and try the obedience of faith, and therefore God approves of it."[1] Thus God, in this act of revelation through preaching, veils Himself to reveal Himself and through the sign seeks to create in us that humility by which alone we can come to know Him.[2] When we are addressed in the name of God by "a contemptible mortal who has just emerged from the dust, we give the best evidence of our piety and reverence towards God Himself if we readily submit".[3] Preaching—especially when we consider the man chosen to preach!—is indeed the Word made flesh.

Calvin realises that it must be hard for the ordinary Church member to submit, but he pleads for a right attitude towards the preacher.[4] The hearer should consider the alternatives! He should remember that this is a most gracious ordinance of God by which "He has provided for our infirmity, choosing to address us through the medium of human interpreters that He may sweetly allure us to Him rather than drive us away by His thunders".[5] Preaching is thus a truly "angelical office".[6] The preacher should be heard "not as a private individual, but as a public minister who has come from heaven".[7] He warns men that they reject God when they reject the person or word of one who has been called by God to this ministry. "Those are said to resist the Spirit who reject Him when He speaks in the prophets. . . . Therefore lest, like giants, we make war against God, let us learn to hearken to the ministers by whose mouth He teaches us."[8] There can be no arguing here. The ministry must simply be accepted as an ordinance of God. "There is no

---

[1]Comm. on Luke 2 : 17, C.R. 45 : 79.

[2]Cf. pp. 69–70.

[3]Inst. 4 : 3 : 1. *Verum ubi homuncio quis piam ex pulvere emersus in nomine Dei loquitur, hic nostram erga Deum ipsum pietatem et observantiam optimo testimonio declaramus, si dociles nos exhibemus eius ministro, quum nulla tamen in re nos excellat.*

[4]Cf. comm. on 1 Thess. 5 : 12–13, C.R. 52 : 171–2.

[5]Inst. 4 : 1 : 5. *Nostrae infirmitati consulit, dum per interpretes humano more nos mavult alloqui, ut ad se alliciat, quam tonando a se abigere.*

[6]Ibid. *Munus angelicum.*

[7]Comm. on Isa. 61 : 1, C.R. 37 : 372. *Non tanquam privatus homo, sed tanquam publicus minister e coelo profectus.*

[8]Comm. on Acts 7 : 51, C.R. 48 : 164. *Quare, ne gigantum instar cum Deo bellum geramus, ministros, quorum ore nos docet, discamus placide audire.*

need of inquiry here, why it is that we ought to obey the word preached, or the external voice of men, rather than revelations; it is enough to know that this is the will of God."[1] "If the edification of the Church proceeds from Christ alone, He has surely the right to prescribe in what manner it shall be edified."[2] Calvin, in one of his sermons, appeals to those who think the minister too long if he preaches for half an hour, and are yet willing to soak their ears night and day in "fables, lies, and things of no profit", to consider how necessary and glorious a thing it is to listen to the word that proclaims the length and breadth and height and depth of the love of Christ.[3]

3. The responsibility and dangers of the office of minister of the Word

The minister also has a most solemn responsibility laid upon him through this office. He must bind himself to the Scriptures and handle them with the utmost reverence,[4] without over-displaying his own skill for effect, or mixing his own ideas with the pure doctrine, or striving after novelty. "Christ *rose up to read*, not only that His voice might be better heard, but in token of reverence: for the majesty of Scripture deserves that its expounders should make it apparent, that they proceed to handle it with modesty and reverence."[5] "It is abominable boldness to use the Scripture at our pleasure, to play with them as with a tennis-ball as many before us have done."[6] "It often does happen that Christ is disfigured by the inventions of men, and is adulterated, as it were by their disguises."[7] Paul's doctrine was "not variable or ambiguous so as to present Him from time to time in a new shape after the manner of Proteus; as some persons make it their sport to make changes upon Him, just as if they were tossing a ball to and fro with their hand, simply for the purpose of displaying their dexterity."[8]

[1]Comm. on Hag. 1 : 12, C.R. 44 : 95.
[2]Comm. on Eph. 4 :12, C.R. 51 : 199.
[3]Serm. on Acts 1 : 6–8, C.R. 48 : 607–8.
[4]Cf. pp. 99 ff.
[5]Comm. on Luke 4 : 16, C.R. 45 : 140.
[6]C.R. 10 : 405. Cf. serm. on Job 15 : 1–10, C.R. 33 : 708–9.
[7]Comm. on 2 Cor. 1 : 19, C.R. 50 : 22. *Saepe accidit, ut hominum figmentis deformetur Christus, et quasi fucis adulteretur.*
[8]Ibid.

The minister must also strive to be a scholar. "None will ever be a good minister of the word of God, unless he is first of all a scholar."[1] "As for ministers of the Gospel, how many does one see who have only superficially glanced at Holy Scripture and are so pitifully poorly versed in it that with every new idea they change their views. Why? Because they have never taken the trouble to mould their minds completely to the language of the Holy Spirit as good scholars should."[2] But scholarship is not enough. He must have a knowledge of life and the gift of applying what the Scriptures teach to daily use. "Prophesying does not consist of a simple and bare interpretation of Scripture but includes also knowledge for applying it to present use."[3] "Though a man is faithful, and he lives a holy life, it does not follow that he has the ability in himself so to treat the word of God that it is well received. True doctrine, then, is not in everyone, and when there is the knowledge, it must, further, be applied (*idione*)."[4] It is not enough, in expounding the Word, "to discourse upon it as if it were mere history. . . . The office of a good and faithful shepherd is not barely to expound the Scripture, but he must use earnestness and sharpness, to give force and virtue to the Word of God."[5]

Such is the responsibility of the minister of the Word. Being in such an exalted position in the Church, he is also in danger. Calvin is insistent in uttering warnings against the temptation of giving way to ambition or of seeking to please the hearers by adulterating the Word of God or of hiding its unpleasant aspects in an impossible effort to be popular with all. "*Woe to you when all men shall applaud you.* This warning refers peculiarly to

[1]Serm. on Deut. 5 : 23–7, C.R. 26 : 406.

[2]Serm. on 2 Tim. 1 : 13–14, C.R. 54 : 68.

[3]Comm. on 1 Cor. 14 : 6, C.R. 49 : 519. *Prophetiam enim diximus, non simplici aut nuda interpretatione scripturae constare ; sed continere simul eius in praesentem usum accomodandae scientiam.* Cf. on 1 Thess. 5 : 20, C.R. 52 : 176.

[4]Serm. on 1 Tim. 3 : 1–4, C.R. 53 : 261. *Sainct Paul a ici mis une marque qui est propre et speciale aux prescheurs de l'Evangile, en disant qu'ils doyvent estre propres à enseigner.* (Ibid.)

[5]Serm. on 2 Tim. 3 : 16, C.R. 54 : 291. Cf. serm. on 1 Cor. 1 : 7, C.R. 49 : 614. *C'est une prudence que doyvent avoir ceux qui annoncent la Parole de Dieu, de regarder ce qui est convenable à un peuple . . . quand le peuple sera entaché de quelque mal et corruption, d'y parvenir et s'adresser là. . . . Car si seulement nous parlons en general, que Dieu condamnera les pechez des hommes . . . et que nous eussions cependant les yeux fermez à ce que nous verrons des scandales et corruptions entre nous, ce seroit comme desguiser la parole de Dieu, tellement qu'elle n'auroit plus nulle vertu.*

teachers, who have no plague more to be dreaded than ambition; because it is impossible for men not to corrupt the pure doctrine of God, when they *seek to please men*."[1] Like Joseph's task in declaring plainly the unpleasant interpretation of the dream to Pharaoh's baker, so the task of the minister of the Word is often unpleasant, but it cannot be shirked. "That freedom must be maintained by prophets, and teachers, that they may not hesitate by their teaching to inflict a wound upon those whom God has sentenced to death. All love to be flattered. Hence the majority of teachers, in desiring to yield to the corrupt wishes of the world, adulterate the word of God."[2] Nevertheless, in spite of the burden of responsibility he must bear, and the greatness of the danger in which he continually walks, the minister of the Word can rejoice with serene confidence and should continually magnify his office. It is the minister of the Gospel who is primarily referred to in Jesus' word, that the least in the Kingdom of heaven is greater than John the Baptist; for he stands in a more favoured position as a minister of the Word and exercises a more powerful ministry than that great prophet. "All the ministers of the Gospel are included. Many of them have undoubtedly received a small proportion of faith, and are therefore greatly inferior to John; but this does not prevent their preaching from being superior to his, because it holds out Christ as having rendered complete and eternal satisfaction by His one sacrifice, as the conqueror of death and the Lord of life, and because it withdraws the vail and elevates believers to the heavenly sanctuary."[3] Thus prophets and teachers "may take courage and . . . boldly set themselves against Kings and nations when armed with the power of celestial truth".[4] "They think not that they must give an account of their life, or they look only on a mortal man—'ah! who speaks? Is he indeed our God? Is he armed with celestial power? Do we not see a mortal man and one like ourselves?' We daily see that the ungodly do thus cast away every fear, and wilfully harden themselves. . . . It is not then

[1]Comm. on Luke 6 : 26, C.R. 45 : 166.
[2]Comm. on Gen. 40 : 16, C.R. 23 : 514. Cf. serm. on Job 15 : 1–10, C.R. 33 : 707. *Et quant à ceux qui ont la charge de porter et d'annoncer la parole de Dieu, s'ils voyent qu'on les reiette, qu'ils persistent constamment toutes fois, et que cela ne les desbauche point.*
[3]Comm. on Matt. 11 : 11, C.R. 45 : 303.
[4]Comm. on Jer. 1 : 10, C.R. 37 : 481.

without reason that the prophet bids the Jews seriously to consider who testifies of the rod; as though he said—I confess indeed that I am a mortal man, but remember who has sent me, for I go not forth as a private individual, nor have I presumptuously intruded into this office, but I am armed with God's command; nay, God Himself speaks through my mouth. If then ye despise me, the Lord is present, who will vindicate His own commands; for He will not suffer Himself to be despised in His servants: though they be contemptible according to the flesh, He will yet have the reverence which it deserves to be paid to His Word."[1]

[1]Comm. on Mic. 6 : 9, C.R. 43 : 396–7.

Chapter X

Man's Openness to Revelation

1. Revelation apprehended only by faith

IT is not enough that God, in the act of revealing Himself, should do no more than confront men with these outward forms that veil His presence, and leave it to man by the power of his own senses and mental ability to grasp what is revealed. It is "not by reason, nor by the perspicacity of the human understanding"[1] that we are enabled to discern the divine content behind the outward form when God reveals Himself. A man may stand full in the blazing light of revelation and yet not see that anything more is happening than a purely mundane event. God may speak, but man through spiritual deafness may not have the power to hear His voice. It is vain for God to reveal Himself, unless at the same time as He reveals Himself He also works within the mind and heart of man to create the power to grasp what is offered in the gracious act of revelation. This power is faith. "Faith beholds higher and more hidden things in God than what our senses can perceive."[2]

Faith is openness to revelation. It is the power to recognise the glory of God hidden in this act of His grace, and to receive the gift offered through it. It is the ability to hear the Word of God coming through the word of man. When the Apostle speaks of what he and his fellow-disciples have "seen" in Christ Calvin comments, "By seeing, he does not mean any sort of seeing, but what belongs to faith, by which they recognised the glory of God in Christ."[3] Thus revelation involves the giving

[1]Comm. on Col. 2 : 2, C.R. 52 : 99. *Verum hinc discamus, sola fide, non ratione, nec perspicacia humanae mentis, evangelium posse capi ; quia alioqui res est a nobis abscondita.*

[2]Comm. on Heb. 11 : 27, C.R. 55 : 163. *Fidem altiora et magis recondita in Deo intueri, quam quae sub sensus nostros cadant.*

[3]Comm. on 1 John 4 : 14, C.R. 55 : 356. *Aspectum non quemlibet intelligit sed fidei adiunctum, quo agnoverint in Christo Dei gloriam.*

Cf. serm. on Isa. 53 : 1–4, C.R. 35 : 617. *Les hommes ne pourront pas en leur sens naturel cognoistre qu'il a este envoyé pour leur salut, et qu'il ait toute puissance et de vie et de mort, et que toute plenitude de iustice, de sagesse, et de sainctete soyent en lui. Les hommes, di-ie, ne pourront concevoir cela en leur cerveau.*

of an inward illumination, of ears to hear and eyes to see, and a
mind to understand, and of a willingness to obey what is understood. It involves the reshaping, and opening out of the mind
and will of man in conformity to the Word of God. It involves
the giving of faith. When Stephen in his vision saw the heavens
opened, that was a sign to him that at that moment he was being
given this faculty to apprehend what is heavenly. "The miracle
was not wrought in heaven but in his eyes."[1] Faith is the working
of this miracle of openness to God in the mind of man.

2. Faith as response to the Word of God

When God reveals Himself, at the same time as He gives His
revelation He creates in man's heart this power of faith. Faith
arises as a response to revelation and is not normally otherwise
given. Moreover, faith arises in response not to the visible sign,
be it a vision or a miracle or a sacramental ceremony, but to the
spoken word that is always so central a part of revelation. "There
is no greater enemy of faith than to tie our minds to our eyes."[2]
"There is no faith without God's Word, for of His faithfulness
we cannot be convinced, until He has spoken . . . for we must
ever hold that there is a mutual relation between God's Word
and our faith."[3] We cannot persuade ourselves by any means
that God is gracious to us, or argue or excite ourselves into a
state of faith by our own cleverness or spiritual intensity. Faith
can come only through a humble and passive response to God's
Word. Faith is "rendering all our thoughts obedient to God's
Word".[4] One of Calvin's favourite texts is Romans 10 : 17.
Faith cometh by hearing and hearing by the Word of God. "Take
away the Word, then, and there will be no faith left."[5] Comment-

[1]Comm. on Acts 7 : 56, C.R. 48 : 168.
[2]Comm. on Rom. 4 : 18, C.R. 49 : 81. *Nihil fidei magis adversum est, quam
mentes nostras oculis affigere.* Cf. on Rom. 4 : 20, C.R. 49 : 84. Faith requires
"closed eyes". Cf. comm. on Luke 14 : 30, C.R. 45 : 413. *Fides a miraculis
non pendet, vel quislibet portentis, sed peculiare donum est spiritus, et nascitur ex
verbo.*
[3]Comm. on Heb. 11 : 11, C.R. 55 : 154. . . . *Semper enim tenenda est mutua
inter verbum Dei et fidem nostram relatio.*
[4]Comm. on 1 John 4 : 1, C.R. 55 : 348.
[5]Inst. 3 : 2 : 6. *Tolle igitur verbum et nulla iam restabit fides.* Cf. serm. on
Gen. 15 : 6–7, C.R. 23 : 737. *Voila donc la nature de la foy, que nous ayons les
yeux clos . . . il faut bien que nous ayons les oreilles ouvertes et attentives pour*

ing on the incident of healing the nobleman's son in which Jesus was seen to do nothing but merely give His Word that the son would be cured, Calvin says, "As soon as he heard a single word he seized it and fixed it in his heart. Though he did not entertain all the respect that he ought for the power of Christ, yet a short promise suddenly awoke new confidence in his mind so that he believed the life of his son to be contained in a single word of Christ. And such is the promptitude with which we ought to receive the Word of God."[1]

3. Faith as response to the promises of the Word

But Calvin fully recognises that there are words that God might speak more calculated to arouse within us this confident and assured faith than other words might be. The Word of Scripture contains threats as well as promises, words that might terrify us rather than invite us to Christ. Therefore Calvin qualifies his statement that faith arises from the Word of God by pointing out that it is the promises contained in the Word that are chiefly used by God in giving us the assurance of faith. "As faith is founded chiefly on the benevolence and kindness of God, it is not every word, though coming from His mouth, that is sufficient; but a promise is necessary as an evidence of His favour. Hence Sara is said to have counted God faithful who had promised. True faith, then, is that which hears God speaking and rests on His promise."[2] "The human heart is not excited to faith by *every* word."[3] "Therefore we need a promise of grace to assure us that He is our propitious Father."[4] Man

recevoir ce que Dieu nous dira. See also serm. on Luke 1 : 45–8, C.R. 46 : 111. *Quand il nous est parlé de croire en l'Escriture saincte, cela presuppose que Dieu se presente à nous . . . et nous testifie qu'il nous veut avoir agreables comme ses enfans . . . La foy contemple les promesses de Dieu.*

[1]Comm. on John 4 : 50, C.R. 47 : 102. *. . . Brevis promissio novam repente in eius animo fiduciam peperit, ut in uno Christi verbo filii sui vitam inclusam esse statueret. Atque hac promptitudine verbum Dei a nobis recipi decebat.*

In all that has been said in this section Calvin is laying down a general rule, but it is not an invariable rule. "When the apostle makes hearing the beginning of faith, he is only describing the usual economy and dispensation which the Lord is wont to employ in calling his people. . . . Many He certainly has called and endued with the true knowledge of Himself by internal means, by the illumination of the Spirit, without the intervention of preaching." Inst. 4 : 16 : 9.

[2]Comm. on Heb. 11 : 11, C.R. 55 : 154.

[3]Inst. 3 : 2 : 7.

[4]Ibid. Cf. Inst. 3 : 2 : 29.

when he lays hold of the promises of God is embracing God Himself as his Father. "All the promises of God . . . flow from the free mercy of God and are evidence of that . . . gratuitous adoption on which their salvation is founded. Therefore we do not say that Abraham was justified because he laid hold on a single word respecting the offspring . . . but because he embraced God as his Father.[1] And truly faith does not justify us for any other reason than that it reconciles us to God."[2] Thus this faith that comes in response to the promises of God is no mere intellectual assent to a doctrine or a fact but is nothing less than our response to the mercy of God in Jesus Christ by which we are saved.

Since faith is such a response to the Word of promise, faith is never an irrational act, a blind leap in the dark. Faith is as rational an act as the Word of God is rational event. Faith is a laying hold of that which reaches us by knowledge. "When *faith* is called *knowledge* it is distinguished not only from opinion, but from that shapeless faith which the Papists have contrived; for they have forged an implicit faith destitute of all light of the understanding. But when Paul describes it to be a quality which essentially belongs to faith—to know the truth, he plainly shows that there is no faith without knowledge."[3]

But faith is more than a mere response of the mind. Being a response to grace of God in the promises, it is the response of the whole heart and will, as well as of the mind. "Faith is the principal service which God asks of men. Truly, however, we must note that faith is not simply mental assent to the doctrines

---

[1]There is a "kind of faith which is only partial"—as when men lay hold of some particular promise of God when they are in danger or sickness, believing that they will be delivered in this instance. Calvin distinguishes this *"façon de croire particuliere"* which is not sufficient for salvation from the *"foy qui comprend toutes les promesses"*, which recognises God as the author of all good and which grasps His all-embracing Fatherhood. Serm. on Gen. 15 : 4-6, C.R. 23 : 690. In his sermon on Luke 1 : 18-25, C.R. 46 : 51-5, Calvin points out that even though the faithful hold the "general principle" that God will fulfil all His promises, it is at the same time possible, as in the case of Zacharias, to be unbelieving in particular matters. He contrasts Judas, who in certain particulars believed but was nevertheless without true faith.

[2]Comm. on Gen. 15 : 6, C.R. 23 : 212.

[3]Comm. on Titus 1 : 1, C.R. 52 : 404. *Quum fides "agnitio" nominatur, non ab opinione discernitur tantum, sed ab informi illo papistarum figmento. Fidem enim implicitam commenti sunt omni intelligentiae luce vacuam. At Paulus dum istud fidei quasi proprium assignat, veritatem cognoscere, nullam certe absque notitia esse fidem, palam ostendit.* Cf. comm. on Gal. 1 : 8, C.R. 50 : 173. *Nulla est fides ubi nulla est cognitio.* And serm. on Gal. 3 : 3-5, C.R. 50 : 482, *Nulle foy sans instruction de l'Evangile.* Also serm. on Mark 1 : 23-7, C.R. 46 : 736-9.

we are taught, but it is equally an affair of the heart and the
affections. . . . Faith is from the heart, then, and has its root
there. It is not pure and simple knowledge."[1] "Faith does not
consist solely in a person's giving his assent to true doctrine,
but . . . embraces something greater and loftier, that the hearer,
renouncing himself, devotes his life wholly to God."[2]

4. Faith as a gift of the Holy Spirit

It must be emphasised that the faith thus formed is not a
natural response to the Word of God but is an entirely miraculous act of the Holy Spirit[3] within the heart of the hearer of
God's Word. Man is as incapable as any inanimate object of
responding by himself through faith to the grace of God when
it is held out in the Word. "We may hear perfectly everything
that is spoken to us, but the words might as well be spoken to a
tree-trunk till God has taken away this insensibility which is in
our corrupt nature. Unless this happens we shall not understand
anything of what He says to us, for His Word exceeds our
capacity."[4] "Those who do not sufficiently know the darkness
of the human mind imagine that faith is formed naturally by
hearing and preaching alone."[5] An assurance of the nature of
faith is "above the capacity of the human mind (*humanae mentis
captu superior*), it is the part of the Holy Spirit to confirm within
us (*intus confirmare*) what God promises in His Word".[6] "The
outward preaching will be vain and useless if it be not accompanied by the teaching of the Spirit. God has two ways of teaching; for first He sounds in our ears by the mouth of men; and
secondly He addresses us inwardly by His Spirit and He does
this either at the same moment or at different times as He thinks
fit."[7] "Our Lord must make His Word available by the working

---

[1]Serm. on 2 Thess. 1 : 6–10, C.R. 52 : 227–8.
[2]Comm. on Matt. 21 : 32, C.R. 45 : 590.
[3]Cf. serm. on Isa. 53 : 1–4, C.R. 35 : 609. *Chacun de nous n'est point donné
la foy de son propre mouvement mais . . . Dieu nous a illuminez.*
[4]Serm. on Acts 1 : 6–8, C.R. 48 : 605.
[5]Comm. on John 15 : 27, C.R. 47 : 354. Cf. serm. on 1 Tim. 2 : 3–5, C.R.
53 : 158. *Et y viendrons-nous de nostre mouvement naturel? Helas non : car
nous luy sommes du tout contraires.*
[6]Comm. on 2 Cor. 1 : 21, C.R. 50 : 24.
[7]Comm. on John 14 : 25, C.R. 334–5.

of His Holy Spirit. He must bore into our ears or we shall never hear Him."[1] "The heavenly doctrine proves to be useful and efficacious to us only so far as the Spirit both forms our minds to understand it and our hearts to submit to its yoke."[2]

Even the revelation given in the days when Jesus on earth confronted His contemporaries in flesh and blood could not be recognised by those who had not the Spirit at work in their hearts.[3] Even when confronted by Jesus risen from the dead and radiant with divine glory the disciples did not recognise Him because *their eyes were restrained.* "The evangelist expressly states this," says Calvin, "lest anyone should think that the aspect of Christ's body was changed. . . . For though Christ remained like Himself, He was not recognised because the eyes of the beholders were held. . . . Hence we learn how great is the weakness of all our senses, since neither eyes nor ears discharge their office, unless so far as power is incessantly communicated to them from heaven."[4] The ability to recognise the glory of God in Christ "flows from the illumination of the Spirit".[5] Even Jesus as a teacher had to depend for the efficacy of anything He said on the inward working of the Holy Spirit in the hearts of His hearers. "Christ discharged the office of teacher but in order to make known the Father He employed the secret revelation of the Spirit and not the sound of His voice alone."[6]

5. The Spirit and the Word

We saw in a previous chapter that only by the power of the Holy Spirit can the word of the preacher become the Word of God. We can now make the further statement that even the Word of God can have no efficacy unless at the same time the Holy Spirit works in the hearts of the hearers, creating faith and

---

[1]Serm. on Job 26 : 1 f., C.R. 34 : 427.

[2]Comm. on Luke 24 : 45, C.R. 45 : 816. *Ut coelestis doctrina non aliter utilis sit nobis vel efficax nisi quatenus spiritus et mentes nostras ad eam intelligendam, et corda nostra ad subeundum eius iugum format.* Cf. comm. on Eph. 1 : 13, C.R. 51 : 153.

[3]See pp. 19f.

[4]Comm. on Luke 24 : 16, C.R. 45 : 803.

[5]Comm. on 1 John 4 : 14, C.R. 55 : 356.

[6]Comm. on John 17 : 26, C.R. 47 : 390. *Ad patrem manifestandum arcana spiritus revelatione, non autem solo vocis sonitu usus est.* Cf. Inst. 2 : 2 : 20.

making men's minds open to receive the Word. The Spirit with a "wondrous and special energy", "must form the ear to hear and the mind to understand".[1] There is a veil within that prevents us from seeing God even when He is there before us in His Word. The removal of this inward veil is the gracious work of the Holy Ghost. Every man is blind, until He also enlighten the eyes of his understanding. "Admitting that God gives light to us by His Word, the prophet here means that we are blind amid the clearest light, until He remove the veil from our eyes."[2] Thus the external voice can strike the ear to no purpose "unless Christ speaks to our hearts within by His Spirit, that we may receive by faith the life which is offered to us".[3] God in order to bring us salvation "must not only appoint men, and send them to teach us faithfully, but He must operate upon our hearts. He must touch us to the quick."[4] He must "correct our slowness of apprehension and render us docile by the secret influence of His Spirit".[5] "Herein consists the completeness of the faithful, in that God engraves on their hearts what He shows by His Word to be right."[6]

The piercing and opening of the ears[7] by the Holy Spirit does not, however, take place apart from the external word. The Spirit in creating faith works alongside of the Word and not apart from it. There is no more dubious and dangerous practice, according to Calvin, than to try to make contact with the Spirit of God by turning to any other source than the Word of God. "It is the Spirit of Satan that is separated from the Word, to which the Spirit of God is continually joined."[8] The Spirit has been promised for this reason, "to impress the truth of the Gospel on our minds. . . . It is no less unreasonable to boast of the Spirit without the Word, than it would be an absurd thing

[1]Inst. 2 : 2 : 20. *Nempe ubi aures ad audiendum et mentes ad intelligendum, spiritus mira et singulare virtute format.*
[2]Comm. on Ps. 119 : 17, C.R. 32 : 221. *. . . Intelligit Propheta donec velum ex oculis nostris abstulerit, nos caecutire in clara luce.*
[3]Comm. on John 5 : 25, C.R. 47 : 117. Cf. serm. on Deut. 31 : 14–17, C.R. 28 : 623–5.
[4]Serm. on 1 Tim. 2 : 3–5, C.R. 53 : 155.
[5]Comm. on Ps. 119 : 124, C.R. 32 : 270.
[6]Comm. on Ps. 119 : 133, C.R. 32 : 275. *Haec solida est fidelium perfectio, dum cordibus eorum insculpit Deus quod voce ostendit rectum esse.*
[7]Cf. comm. on John 5 : 25, C.R. 47 : 117.
[8]Comm. on Isa. 59 : 21, C.R. 37 : 352.

to bring forward the Word without the Spirit."[1] Here Calvin takes his stand against the "many fanatics who disdain outward preaching and who imagine that they can enjoy the inspiration of the Spirit of God in secret revelations and inspirations"[2] and against Mahomet and the Pope, "who agree in holding this as a principle of their religion, that Scripture does not contain a perfection of doctrine, but that something other has been revealed by the Spirit".[3] He insists that "Christ has joined these two things together"[4]—the Spirit and Word—and that "the Spirit that introduces any doctrine or invention apart from the Gospel is a deceiving spirit and not the Spirit of Christ".[5]

6. The Word and faith

We have noted the fact that there can be no faith apart from the Word of God. It is equally true to add—after this has been first said—that the Word of God cannot exert its power to save and bless where there is no faith. There is a reciprocal relation between the Word of God and faith. "We must observe the connection between the Word and faith. It is such that faith is not to be separated from the Word and that the Word separated from faith can confer no good; not indeed that the efficacy of the power of the Word depends on us, for were the whole world false, He who cannot lie would still never cease to be true, but the Word never puts forth its power except when faith gives it an entrance."[6] Calvin on this subject uses the illustration of a Fugue with two voices, each depending on the other for effect yet one being dominant and the other echoing it, the Word being the dominant voice and faith following as its corresponding echo.[7] He also likens the relationship between faith and the

---

[1] O.S. 1 : 466.
[2] Comm. on John 15 : 27, C.R. 47 : 354.
[3] Comm. on John 14 : 25, C.R. 47 : 335.
[4] Comm. on John 15 : 27, C.R. 47 : 354.
[5] Comm. on John 14 : 25, C.R. 47 : 335.
[6] Comm. on Heb. 4 : 2, C.R. 55 : 45.

[7] Serm. on Gen. 15 : 4–6, C.R. 23 : 689. *On pourra bein chanter à une voix : mais nous n'aurons point une melodie parfaite, sinon qu'il y ait plusieurs voix et bonne correspondance. Ainsi est-il de la foy : car si la parole de Dieu ne precede, et que la foy ne s'accorde avec icelle, il n'y aura nulle melodie. Ce sont deux choses inseparables, que la parole de Dieu et la foy.*

Word to that between the sun and the rays of the sun—so impossible is it to divorce the one from the other.[1]

Faith, once formed by the Word of God, is so closely attached to the Word that it will never seek to stand apart from it. It is of the nature of faith to be continually conscious of its own weakness and thus continually to seek fresh life and reality from the one source to which it owed its birth—the Word of God. Faith continually cries out, *Lord I believe, help thou mine unbelief*,[2] and seeks Him who alone can help, in the one source where He is likely to be found—His Word. Calvin is severely critical of those who, having come to faith in Christ through the Word, now act as if they had faith as a sure and perfect possession which they can hold independently of a continual recourse to the Word, or who imagine that this same faith can be sustained and nourished from any other source. "God does not bestow His Spirit on His people in order to set aside the use of His Word, but rather to render it fruitful."[3] "So long as faith shall wander in this manner, or rather, as soon as it shall have gone out of the sanctuary of God, it must become involved in miserable uncertainty. It must, therefore, be brought back to the inward and secret testimony of the Spirit, which, believers know, has been given them from heaven."[4]

Faith is so assailed amidst the many trials of life that it knows that it cannot live apart from the Word of God, but it also knows that it can continually triumph if it stands fast in the Word. "When the world rages on all sides, our only protection is that the truth of God, sealed by the Holy Spirit on our hearts, despises and defies all that is in the world; for if it were subject to the opinions of men, our faith would be overwhelmed a hundred times a day. . . . This single witness powerfully drives away, scatters, and overturns, all that the world rears up to obscure and crush the truth of God."[5] Faith submits humbly to the Word of God and knows no other master. "Faith owes no subjection except to the Word of God . . . and is not at all in sub-

[1] Inst. 3 : 2 : 6. *Principio admonendi sumus, perpetuam esse fidei relationem cum verbo, nec magis ab eo posse divelli, quam radios a sole unde oriuntur.*
[2] Cf. Inst. 4 : 14 : 8.
[3] Comm. on Luke 24 : 45, C.R. 45 : 816. *Neque enim spiritum Deus suis confert, qui verbi sui usum aboleat, sed potius qui fructuosum reddat.*
[4] Comm. on John 15 : 26, C.R. 47 : 354.
[5] Comm. on John 15 : 26, C.R. 47 : 353.

jection to human control".[1]   But before the Word of God the subjection of true faith is complete.

It is true that Faith is born through the *promises* of the Word, but it lives by the *whole* Word of God. "It rightly belongs to faith to hear God whenever He speaks, and unhesitatingly to embrace whatever may proceed from His sacred mouth. Thus far it has regard to commands and threatenings as well as to gratuitous promises. . . . Faith, then, though its most direct regard is to God's promises, yet looks on his threatenings so far as it is necessary for it to be taught to fear and obey God."[2] Our attitude towards the Word of God is, then, a test of whether we have true faith, indeed it is a test of whether or not we love God. "Wherefore, this is the chief point of His worship, obediently to embrace His promises; and true religion begins at faith."[3]

[1]Comm. on 2 Cor. 1 : 24, C.R. 50 : 26.
[2]Comm. on Heb. 11 : 7, C.R. 55 : 151. *Fides tamen utcunque recta in Dei promissiones se conferat, ad minas nihilominus intenta est, quatenus nos ad Dei timorem ac obsequium erudiri necesse est.*
[3]Comm. on Rom. 4 : 20, C.R. 49 : 84.

Chapter XI

The Sacraments of the New Covenant as Signs and Seals

1. Baptism and the Lord's Supper as sacraments of the New Covenant

WHEN God, under the New Covenant, holds forth Christ to us, offering us in Him "the treasures of heavenly grace", He gives us not only the Word, but also, along with the Word, sacraments or signs, which seal the promise given in the Word and make it more vivid and sure. A sacrament of the New Covenant is a ceremony instituted by Jesus Christ to fulfil the same function as the various signs which were such a marked feature of revelation in the Old Testament. They replace the much more complicated ceremonies which God formerly commanded men to use so that He might make them sure of His promises. Calvin defines a sacrament as "an external sign, by which the Lord seals on our consciences His promises of good-will towards us in order to sustain the weakness of our faith, and we in our turn testify our piety towards Him, both before Himself and before angels as well as men".[1] Calvin also gives with approval the definition of Augustine calling the sacrament a "visible sign of a sacred thing, or a visible form of an invisible grace",[2] with a warning that the brevity of this definition tends to make it obscure.

Calvin tested the various ceremonies practised in the Roman Church of his day as to whether they satisfied this definition. His rule was: "There must be a promise and command of the Lord"[3]—"a Word of God which promises the presence of the Holy Spirit."[4] He found in the words of Jesus such authority

[1]Inst. 4 : 14 : 1. *Externum symbolum quo benevolentiae erga nos suae promissiones conscientiis nostris Dominus obsignat. . . .*
[2]Inst. 4 : 14 : 1. *Rei sacrae visibile signum, aut invisibilis gratiae visibilis forma.*
[3]Inst. 4 : 19 : 1.
[4]Inst. 4 : 19 : 5.

for only two of the commonly practised rites of that Church—
Baptism and the Lord's Supper. These only have been instituted at the command of Jesus and have the promise of His grace
attached to them, so that they can be celebrated by the Church
with the confident expectancy that He will bless their use. Apart
from these two ordinances, he found the other ceremonies of the
Roman Church to be mainly man-made ordinances and thus
"empty shows",[1] for without the command and promises of
Christ it is foolish for us to seek to embellish the Word of God
by inventing unauthorised rites in the vain hope that Christ will
give His presence otherwise than along with the signs whose use
He has appointed. "No one can set forth a sign which is to be a
testimonial of His will and of some promise. He alone can give
the sign and bear witness to Himself. . . . There can never be a
sacrament without a promise of salvation."[2]   On the action of
Ezekiel in depicting the siege of Jerusalem on a tile, and in performing other strange acts as signs to his contemporaries of what
God was doing in their midst, Calvin comments: "This had been
a childish spectacle, unless God had commanded the prophet to
act so. And hence we infer that the sacraments cannot be distinguished from empty shows, unless by the Word of God. The
authority of God, therefore, is the mark of distinction by which
sacraments excel, and have their weight and dignity, and whatever men mingle with them is frivolous."[3]

[1]Calvin, however, admits the laying on of hands to be a sacrament "in true
and legitimate ordination" (Inst. 4 : 19 : 31). "This ceremony is effectual to
give the Spirit" (cf. comm. on Acts 9 : 17, C.R. 48 : 208). It is "highly useful
both to recommend to the people the dignity of the ministry, and to admonish
the person ordained that he is no longer his own master" (Inst. 4 : 3 : 11).
But it is not to be numbered among the ordinary sacraments (Inst. 4 : 14 : 20).
No doubt because of its entirely restricted reference Calvin prefers to call
confirmation "an appointed rite for prayer" (comm. on Heb. 6 : 2, C.R. 55 : 69;
cf. Inst. 4 : 19 : 12). Calvin also admits that anointing the sick was a sacrament
in the Apostolic age—"a visible token of spiritual grace", oil representing the
grace of the Spirit (comm. on Mark 6 : 12) and having no medical virtue in
itself (comm. on Jas. 5 : 15, C.R. 55 : 431–2). But since the gift of healing was
a "temporary seal of the doctrine of the gospel", and has been withdrawn, the
"sign ought not to be deemed perpetual" and we should not seek to "ape" the
Apostles in this matter.
[2]Inst. 4 : 18 : 19.
[3]Comm. on Ezek. 4 : 1, C.R. 40 : 104. Cf. pp. 247 ff.

2. The sacraments not valid or effectual apart from the Word

It follows that a sacrament can never be celebrated without at least a clear repetition of the command of Christ to which it owes its origin, and of the promise of Christ in the hope of which the Church fulfils His ordinance. "There is never a sacrament without an antecedent promise, the sacrament being added as a kind of appendix, with a view to confirming and sealing the promise."[1] Calvin calls the sacraments "appendages to the Gospel".[2] Apart from the Word, which must always be proclaimed alongside them, the sacraments are "nothing in themselves, just as seals of a diploma or a public deed are nothing in themselves, and would be affixed to no purpose if nothing was written on the parchment".[3] Calvin approves of the saying of Augustine that "the elements only become sacraments when the Word is added",[4] and himself adds the comment, "Certainly if a man only brings his eyes and shuts his ears they will differ in no respect from the profane rites of the heathen."[5] Christ delayed His own Baptism till the day when His preaching began, so that it might not be imagined by anyone that the sign of Baptism could have any validity without the Word. "This was also the reason why He delayed His Baptism till *the thirtieth year of His age.* Baptism was an appendage to the Gospel (*accessio evangelii*); and therefore it began at the same time as the preaching of the Gospel."[6]

Separated from the spoken word the human action in the sacrament has no spiritual efficacy,[7] the sacrament remaining a "lifeless and bare phantom"[8] with all its power gone and containing nothing sound and nothing pure.[9] Indeed, Calvin calls

---

[1]Inst. 4 : 14 : 3. . . . *Appendicem quandam adiungi, eo fine ut promissionem ipsam confirmet ac obsignet.*

[2]C.R. 7 : 736.

[3]Inst. 4 : 14 : 4.

[4]Hom. in John 80. Cf. Calvin comm. on Matt. 28 : 19, C.R. 45 : 823. *Quare teneamus doctrinae virtute fieri ut signa novam naturam induant.*

[5]C.R. 9 : 21. *Certe siquis oculos tantum illuc aufferat clausis auribus nihil a profanis gentium mysteriis different.*

[6]Comm. on Matt. 3 : 16, C.R. 45 : 126.

[7]Cf. serm. on Luke 1 : 36–8, C.R. 46 : 96–8.

[8]Comm. on Gen. 17 : 9, C.R. 23 : 240. *Mortuum et inane spectrum.*

[9]Comm. on Eph. 5 : 26, C.R. 51 : 224. *Verbo sublato perit tota vis sacramentorum.*

the sacraments without the Word "idle and unmeaning shadows",[1] "pure corruptions",[2] and "delusive signs".[3] But when the Word is given along with the signs not only is the Word effective in itself but it also causes the signs to "assume a new nature", so that what was apart from the Word simply the outward working of the flesh (*externa carnis lotio*) "now begins to be the spiritual pledge of regeneration (*spirituale regenerationis pignus*)".[4] The Word thus really makes the action of the sacrament efficacious in itself, though this efficacy is never given to it without the Word. Calvin skilfully brings out this point in his commentary on John 20 : 22, illustrating it from the relation between the action of the risen Jesus and His word when He breathed on His disciples and said, *Receive ye the Holy Ghost.* "With the visible and outward sign the Word is also joined; for this is the source from which the sacraments derive their efficacy; not that the efficacy of the Holy Spirit is contained in the word which sounds in our ears, but because the effect of all these things which the believers receive from the sacraments depends on the testimony of the Word. Christ *breathes* on the Apostles: they receive not only the *breathing* but also the *Spirit.* And why, but because Christ promises to them?"[5] Thus it is the *action* of Christ in the sacraments that is made efficacious because of the Word.

When he insists on the sacraments being accompanied by the Word Calvin means us to understand by his use of the term "word" not a "sort of enchantment" or "magical incantation" muttered in a scarcely audible voice and in an unknown tongue over the elements, "as if it were addressed to dead matter and not to men",[6] but one which "proclaimed aloud by the minister leads the people by the hand to that which the sign tends and directs us".[7] "By the word is here meant the promise which

[1]Comm. on Matt. 28 : 19, C.R. 45 : 823.

[2]Comm. on Isa. 6 : 7, C.R. 36 : 134.

[3]Cf. comm. on Exod. 24 : 5, C.R. 25 : 75. *Nisi enim praecedat doctrina, quae sit mutuae inter Deum et homines coniunctionis vinculum, lusoria et evanida erunt signa, quantumvis honorificis elogiis ornentur.*

[4]Comm. on Matt. 28 : 19, C.R. 45 : 823.

[5]Comm. *in loc.*, C.R. 47 : 439–40.

[6]Comm. on Eph. 5 : 26, C.R. 51 : 224; cf. Inst. 4 : 14 : 4.

[7]Inst. 4 : 14 : 4. *Clara voce a ministro praedicata, plebem eo manducat quo signum tendit ac nos dirigit.*

explains the power and use of the signs."¹ "The Word which gives life to the sacraments is . . . a clear and distinct voice which is addressed to men and avails to beget faith in them."² These conditions can best be fulfilled through the preaching of a sermon, and thus it is that Calvin urges that the sacrament if it is to be properly administered should be preceded by preaching —"a word which preached, makes us understand what the visible sign means".³ In the use of the sacraments it is of the utmost importance not only that the Word be given but that those who participate attend first to the Word and then relate the sacramental action to the Word that has been spoken, otherwise the sacraments will lose their value. "As soon as the sign itself meets our eyes, the Word ought to sound in our ears."⁴ Though God seals our salvation daily by the sacraments "yet the certainty of it must be obtained from the Word. Unless we yield such authority to the Word as to believe that, as soon as God has spoken by His ministers, our sins are undoubtedly forgiven, and we are restored to life, all confidence of salvation is overthrown."⁵ The sacramental activity of the Church must not be preferred to the Word, for neither can be ultimately separated from the other.

3. The sacraments as seals of the Word

One important function of the sacraments is to confirm and seal the Word. Though the sacraments are ineffective without the Word, nevertheless the bare word cannot have its full effect without the sacraments. The New Testament sacraments take the important place which miracles and visions and dreams and all the visible phenomena by means of which God revealed Himself had in the Old Testament times. Though the Word preached appeals to us through the ear and thus begets faith in our hearts,

¹Comm. on Eph. 5 : 26, C.R. 51 : 224.
²Comm. on Exod. 24 : 5, C.R. 25 : 75. *Addendum est, verbum quod sacramenta vivificat, non esse obscurum susurrum, qualiter in papatu magica incantatio . . . sed esse claram et distinctam vocem, quae ad homines dirigitur, et ad fidem gignendam valet.*
³Inst. 4 : 14 : 4.
⁴Comm. on Gen. 17 : 9, C.R. 23 : 240. *Sciamus tamen, simulatque in oculis signum ipsum incurrit, debere in auribus personare verbum.*
⁵Comm. on Matt. 8 : 10, C.R. 45 : 237.

nevertheless through the sacraments God reinforces the appeal and power of the spoken Word. Abraham's faith when he heard the promise of God was strong but it "was increased by the sight of the stars. For the Lord, in order more deeply to affect His own people, and more efficaciously to penetrate their minds, after He has reached their ears by the Word, also arrests their eyes by external symbols, that eyes and ears may consent together. Therefore the sight of the stars was not superfluous."[1] That man's carnal nature makes him in his religious life hunger for something apparently more concrete than invisible and spiritual realities is shown by the fact that in all pagan religions visible images and vivid ceremonies are prominent. Calvin takes this as an "indication that men could not be without such external signs of religion",[2] and God has provided sympathetically even for the needs of man's carnal nature, instituting the sacraments. "Because man who is carnal will have God with him according to the capacity of the flesh, this is the cause why men are so bold in all ages to make idols. And God indeed so far applies Himself to our rudeness (se ruditati nostrae accomodat) that He shows Himself visible, after a manner, under figures, for there were many signs under the law to testify His presence. And He comes down to us, even at this day, by Baptism and the Lord's Supper."[3] "Because His grace is invisible and hidden, a visible symbol of it is beheld in Baptism."[4]

Thus the sacraments confirm the word by making it more visible and concrete to the senses. "The Supper is added to doctrine instead of a confirmation."[5] The sacraments "attest and ratify the benevolence of the Lord towards us".[6] Calvin often draws a parallel between the function which miracles have in the Old Testament, and in the history of the early Church, and the part which the sacraments are meant to play in these

[1]Comm. on Gen. 15 : 4, C.R. 23 : 210. Cf. serm. on Deut. 4 : 27–31, C.R. 26 : 197, where Calvin bids the man who doubts his share in the promises of God say, "N'ay-ie pas este baptisé au nom de nostre Seigneur Jesus Christ? N'ay-ie pas la saincte Cene, qui m'est encores un second gage par lequel Dieu me monstre qu'il me recoit au nombre de ses enfans?

[2]Inst. 4 : 14 : 19.
[3]Comm. on Acts 7 : 40, C.R. 48 : 153.
[4]Comm. on Titus 3 : 5, C.R. 52 : 431.
[5]Comm. on Acts 2 : 42, C.R. 48 : 58. Coena autem ad doctrinam vice confirmationis accedit.
[6]Inst. 4 : 14 : 17.

days when they form the only visible element in God's ordinary revealing activity. Miracles in their day acted as seals to confirm the word of God. "Almost all the miracles done in all ages were performed . . . that they might be the seals of God's word (*verbi Dei sigilla*)."[1] The miracles of Jesus Himself were "seals of His doctrine which confirm His teaching".[2] But the day has passed when we can expect as seals of the Gospel such miracles as were granted to those who lived in former ages.[3] God's action towards us in Christ is to-day no less miraculous than it always was, indeed it is more miraculous, but to-day the miracle is inward and hidden, and the sign is natural, whereas formerly the miracle lay more in the sign than in the spiritual gift given. "There are two kind of signs. Some are extraordinary and may be called supernatural (*portenta*); such as that which the prophet will immediately add, that which, as we shall afterwards see, was offered to Hezekiah (Isa. 38 : 7). Some are ordinary and in daily use among believers, such as Baptism and the Lord's Supper, which contain no miracle, or at least which may be perceived by the eye or by some of the senses. What the Lord miraculously performs by His Spirit is unseen, but in those which are extraordinary the miracle itself is seen. Such is the end and use of all *signs*, for as Gideon was confirmed by an astonishing miracle, so we are confirmed by Baptism and the Lord's Supper, though our eyes behold no miracle."[4]

4. The sacraments as representations of the Word

The sacraments are more than mere seals added to the Word to confirm it. They are also true visible representations of the

[1]Comm. on Heb. 2 : 4, C.R. 55 : 23. The miracles of Jesus must not be regarded as ends in themselves. Cf. serm. on Mark 1 : 23–7, C.R. 46 : 734–5, and 745.

[2]Comm. on Acts 1 : 1, C.R. 48 : 1–2; cf. comm. on Matt. 24 : 23, C.R. 45 : 663.

[3]Cf. e.g. Calvin's comm. on Mark 16 : 17. "Though Christ does not expressly state whether He intends this gift to be temporary, or to remain perpetually in His Church, yet it is more probable that miracles were promised only for a time, in order to give lustre to the Gospel, while it was new and in a state of obscurity. It is possible, no doubt, that the world may have been deprived of this honour through the guilt of its own ingratitude; but, I think that the true design for which miracles were appointed was that nothing which was necessary for the proving of the doctrine of the Gospel should be wanting at its commencement."

[4]Comm. on Isa. 7 : 13, C.R. 36 : 153.

invisible spiritual things to which the Word directs us. Calvin on this point again quotes with approval a saying of Augustine to the effect that the sacrament is the "visible word". The sacraments are so designed that the man who is pointed to them by the Word is able to see in the form of the action and in the use of the elements the very promises of the Word set forth patently and visibly. "The testimony of the Gospel is engraven upon the sacraments."[1] "By the corporeal things which are produced in the sacrament, we are by a kind of analogy conducted to spiritual things."[2] The sacraments "represent the promises to life, as if painted in a picture".[3] They are a "sculpture or image of that grace of God which the word more fully illustrates".[4] Calvin approves of the use by Greek writers of the word "antitupon" with reference to the sacraments, every sacrament being a visible yet shadowy representation of what is invisible,[5] and he again turns to Augustine for a quotation, "Had not the sacraments some resemblance to the things of which they are sacraments they would not be sacraments at all."[6]

Thus in God's action there is a correspondence between the sign and the reality. When the Spirit was given to the Apostles they *saw* cloven tongues of fire "because the preaching of the gospel was to spread through all tongues and was to possess the power of fire". When the Spirit came upon Christ, He appeared in the form of a dove because "God intended to make a public representation of that mildness of Christ of which Isaiah speaks in such lofty terms".[7] So in the sacraments "God adapts the signs to the things to give similitude".[8] Calvin argues that the burning bush was "the fittest thing that could be shown to

---

[1]Comm. on 2 Cor. 5 : 19, C.R. 50 : 72. *Sacramentis insculptum est evangelii testimonium.*

[2]Inst. 4 : 17 : 3. *A rebus corporeis, quae in sacramento proferuntur, quadam analogia nos ad spirituales deduci.*

[3]Inst. 4 : 14 : 5. Cf. serm. on Gal. 3 : 1–3, C.R. 50 : 464.

[4]Comm. on Gen. 17 : 9, C.R. 23 : 239–40. *Imo nihil aliud est sacramentum, quam verbum visibile, vel sculptura et effigies gratiae Dei quae verbum melius illustret.*

[5]Comm. on Heb. 9 : 24, C.R. 55 : 117.

[6]C.R. 9 : 155. Quoted from Aug. ad Bonifac Ep. 23. *Si sacramenta, inquit, quandem similitudinem earum rerum quarum sacramenta sunt non haberent, omnino sacramenta non essent.*

[7]Comm. on John 1 : 32, C.R. 47 : 28; cf. comm. on Acts 2 : 3, C.R. 48 : 27.

[8]Comm. on Acts 7 : 30, C.R. 48 : 145. *Tritum est illud, Deum similitudine quadam rebus signa aptare.*

Moses to confirm his faith in the business that he had on hand".[1]
In the same way, the sacraments of the New Testament are in
their outward form devised to represent most fittingly the gifts
which God wills to bestow on man through their operation, and
the manner in which He bestows these gifts. Thus the sacraments in confirming the promises of the Word also clarify them,
and, as Calvin points out, it is precisely because they clarify them
that they are most effective in confirming them. "The clearer
any evidence is, the fitter is it to support our faith. But sacraments bring with them the clearest promises."[2] It is little
wonder, then, that Calvin likens them not only to a sculpture but
also to the pillars of a building.[3]

5. The sacraments as signs of man's acceptance of God's grace

In the very act of accepting the signs of God's grace given in
the sacrament and of observing the rites connected with these
signs man gives a sign that he on his part will live daily by the
grace figured forth in the sacraments, and will be a follower of
Jesus Christ. "There is a mutual agreement in the sacraments,
by which God binds us to Himself, and we mutually pledge our
faith. . . . They are mutual and reciprocal signs, as I may
express it."[4] Calvin does not lay a great deal of stress on this
aspect of the sacraments. Against those who held that according
to the meaning of the Latin word *sacramentum* the main significance of the sacraments lay in the fact that they were a pledge of
human loyalty to God before men Calvin writes, "We approve
not, that that which is a secondary thing in the sacraments is
by them made first and indeed the only thing. The first thing is

---

[1]Ibid. Cf. C.R. 9 : 184. *Exprimi debet inter rem et signum analogia.*

Discussing circumcision as a sacrament of the Old Covenant in his commentary on Gen. 17 : 11, C.R. 23 : 241, Calvin asks "whether any analogy is here
apparent between the visible sign and the thing signified?" and he finds it in
that the rite shows that whatever is born of man is polluted, and that whatever
men have peculiar to themselves by generation God has condemned. He brings
out the same kind of analogy between sign and reality in his discussion of
Jacob's thigh injury when wrestling with the angel (see comm. on Gen. 32 : 25,
C.R. 23 : 444).

[2]Inst. 4 : 14 : 5. *Nempe ut quaeque est manifestior, ita est ad fulciendam
fidem magis idonea. Sacramenta vero et promissiones afferunt clarissimas.*

[3]Inst. 4 : 14 : 6.

[4]Comm. on Ezek. 20 : 12, C.R. 40 : 485.

that they may contribute to our faith in God; the secondary, that they may attest our confession before men."[1] "The ends of the sacraments are to be marks and badges of Christian profession and fellowship or fraternity, to be incitements to gratitude, and exercises to faith and a godly life; in short to be contracts binding us to this. But among other ends, the principal one is, that God may by means of them attest, represent, and seal His grace in us."[2]

[1]Inst. 4 : 14 : 13.
[2]C.R. 7 : 737. *Notae ac tesserae christianae professionis et societatis, sive fraternitatis : ut sint ad gratiarum actionem incitamenta, et exercitia fidei, ac piae vitae : denique syngraphae ad id obligantes. Sed hic unus inter alios praecipuus, ut per ea nobis suam gratiam testetur Deus, repraesentet atque obsignet.*

Chapter XII

The Sacraments of the New Covenant as Signs of Union with the Body of Christ

1. Union with the body of Christ as the spiritual mystery figured in the sacraments

THE aspect of the Gospel which the sacraments chiefly bring before our eyes in clarifying for us the promises given in the Word is that of our mystical union with the body of Christ. For Calvin, this union with Christ is one of the most important doctrines for anyone to grasp who would understand the Christian faith and the Christian life and the Christian ordinances. "To that union of the Head and members, the residence of Christ in our hearts, in fine, the mystical union, we assign the highest rank, Christ when He becomes ours making us partners with Him in the gifts with which He was endued. *Immanuel* Hence we do not view Him at a distance and without us, so that His righteousness is imputed to us, but as we have put Him on and been ingrafted into His body, He deigns to make us one with Himself, and, therefore, we glory in having a fellowship of righteousness with Him."[1] "Let us mark well what this word, *Christianity*, meaneth: its meaning is to be members of the Son of God."[2] "When the apostle defines the Gospel, and the use of it, he says that we are called to be partakers of our Lord Jesus Christ, and to be made one with Him, and to dwell in Him, and He in us; and that we be joined together in an inseparable bond."[3]

The nature of this union with Christ is, however, such a spiritual mystery in itself that it is incomprehensible to the natural

[1]Inst. 3 : 11 : 10. *Coniunctio igitur illa capitis et membrorum habitatio Christi in cordibus nostris, mystica denique unio a nobis in summo gradu statuitur : ut Christus noster factus, donorum quibus praeditus est, nos faciat consortes. Non ergo eum extra nos procul speculamur, ut nobis imputetur eius iustitia : sed quia ipsum induimus, et insiti sumus in eius corpus, unum denique nos secum efficere dignatus est : ideo iustitiae societatem nobis cum eo gloriamus.*
[2]Serm. on 2 Tim. 2 : 19, C.R. 54 : 174.
[3]Serm. on Titus 1 : 7–9, C.R. 54 : 442–3.

mind. It is extremely difficult even for believers to grasp its meaning and reality. Therefore God appoints the two sacraments chiefly in order to depict visibly this particular mystery, so that by their use we may come to know and understand better the nature of our union with Christ. "As this mystery of the secret union of Christ with believers is incomprehensible by nature He exhibits its figure and image in visible signs adapted to our capacity, nay, by giving, as it were, earnests and badges, He makes it as certain to us as if it were seen by the eye; the familiarity of the similitude giving it access to minds however dull and showing that souls are fed by Christ just as the corporeal life is sustained by bread and wine."[1] "As the communion which we have with the body of Christ is a thing incomprehensible not only to the eye but to our natural sense, it is there visibly demonstrated to us."[2] It is in order to testify to this "spiritual mystery which can be neither seen by the eye nor comprehended by the human understanding"[3] that "both the preaching of the Gospel was appointed and the use of the sacraments".[4] Calvin, in speaking in the *Institutes* of the importance of this doctrine for the Christian life, points out that "this same doctrine is clearly seen in the sacraments".[5] "When we come to this holy table, we must know that our Lord Jesus Christ presents Himself to confirm us in the unity which we have already received by the faith of the Gospel, that we may be grafted into His body in such a manner that He will dwell in us and we in Him."[6] The sacrament, for Calvin, is "a looking-glass in which we may see that God not only dwelleth among us, but that He also dwelleth in everyone of us".[7]

---

[1]Inst. 4 : 17 : 1. *Quoniam vero mysterium hoc arcanae Christi cum piis unionis natura incomprehensibile est : figuram eius et imagem in signis visibilibus exhibet ad modulum nostrum aptissimis.* Cf. serm. on Luke 1 : 36–8, C.R. 46 : 98, and serm. on 1 Cor. 10 : 8–9, C.R. 49 : 624.

[2]O.S., 1 : 508.

[3]O.S., 1 : 509.

[4]C.R. 7 : 737; cf. Inst. 4 : 17 : 20.

[5]Inst. 3 : 11 : 9.

[6]Serm. on Titus 1 : 7–9, C.R. 54 : 443.

[7]Serm. on 1 Tim. 3 : 14–15, C.R. 53 : 314. Cf. serm. on Luke 2 : 1–14, C.R. 46 : 966. *Et voyla pourquoy aussi la saincte table nous est apprestee c'est asçavoir afin que nous cognoissions que nostre Seigneur Iesus estant descendu yci bas, et s'estant aneanti du tout, n'est pas pourtant separé d'avec nous, quand il est monté en sa gloire des cieux.*

2. The necessity of this union

Calvin teaches faithfully that Jesus Christ through His life and especially His death and resurrection performed in His human nature, and indeed in His human body, all that was necessary for the salvation of mankind. "What we constantly maintain is, that our righteousness and life are in the death and resurrection of Christ."[1] "Our salvation may be divided between the death and resurrection of Christ: by the former sin was abolished and death annihilated; by the latter righteousness was restored and life revived, the power and efficacy of the former being bestowed upon us by means of the latter."[2] "Though righteousness flows from God alone, still we shall not attain the full manifestation of it anywhere else than in the flesh of Christ, for in it was accomplished the redemption of man, in it a sacrifice was offered to atone for sins, and an obedience yielded to God to reconcile Him to us; it was also filled with the sanctification of the spirit and at length, having vanquished death, it was received into heavenly glory. It follows therefore that all the parts of life have been placed in it."[3] "Although Christ could never purify our souls in His own blood, nor appease the Father by His sacrifice, nor acquit us from the charge of guilt, nor, in short, perform the office of priest unless He had been very God, because no human ability was equal to such a burden, it is, however, certain that He performed all these things in His human nature."[4]

Since Christ has thus worked out our salvation in and through His human body and human nature, it follows that the benefits of His work are not available for us, unless we ourselves are brought into some kind of communion with the human nature, and indeed with the body, in which all the work of our salvation was performed. Participation in the blessings which Christ died and rose to win for us is inseparable from communion with His

[1]Inst. 3 : 11 : 12.
[2]Inst. 2 : 16 : 13. *Quare sic salutis nostrae materiam inter Christi mortem et resurrectionem partimur, quod per illam peccatum abolitum, et mors exstincta : per hanc iustitia reparata, et erecta vita : sic tamen ut huius beneficio vim efficaciamque suam illa nobis proferat.*
[3]Comm. on John 6 : 51, C.R. 47 : 152-3. . . . *Sequitur ergo, omnes vitae partes illic fuisse locatas.*
[4]Inst. 3 : 11 : 9.

person, and Calvin insists that this union can be attained only through participation in the "flesh" of Christ. "The flesh of Christ gives life, not only because we once obtained salvation by it, but because now, while we are made one with Christ by a sacred union, the same flesh breathes life into us, or to express it more briefly, because ingrafted into the body of Christ by the secret agency of the Spirit we have life in common with Him. For from the hidden fountain of the Godhead life was miraculously infused into the body of Christ, that it might flow from thence to us."[1] "I see not how anyone can expect to have redemption and righteousness in the Cross of Christ, and life in His death, without trusting first of all to true communion with Christ Himself. Those blessings could not reach us, did not Christ previously make Himself ours."[2] "The Lord Jesus, to communicate the gift of salvation which He has purchased for us, must first be made ours, and His flesh be our meat and nourishment, seeing that it is from it that we derive life."[3]

Time and again Calvin speaks in this strain, insisting that nothing which Christ did for us and nothing which He possesses is of any avail to us until we become one with Him,[4] through a union effected somehow through that "human nature", or "flesh", or "body", in which He wrought salvation.[5] "The materials of righteousness and salvation reside in His flesh; not that the mere man Himself justifies and quickens, but that God was pleased, by means of a Mediator, to manifest His own hidden and incomprehensible nature. Hence I often repeat, that Christ has been in a manner set before us as a fountain, whence we may draw what would otherwise lie without use in that deep

---

[1]C.R. 9 : 30–1. *Carnem ergo Christi . . . fatemur esse vivificam non tantum quia semel in ea nobis salus parta est, sed quia nunc dum sacra unitate cum Christo coalescimus, eadem illa caro vitam in nos spirat, vel ut brevius dicam, quia arcana spiritus virtute in Christi corpus insiti communem habemus cum ipso vitam. Nam ex abscondito deitatis fonte in Christi carnem mirabiliter infusa est vita, ut inde ad nos flueret.*

[2]Inst. 4 : 17 : 11.

[3]C.R. 9 : 10.

[4]Inst. 3 : 1 : 1.

[5]Cf. C.R. 15 : 723, *Ep. ad Vermigli* (where Calvin sums up his teaching on this and kindred subjects). *Neque enim aliter nos Deo mortis suae sacrificio reconciliat, nisi quia noster est ac nos unum cum ipso. Sic illum Pauli locum interpretor, ubi fideles in eius κοινωνιαν vocatos esse dicit (1 Cor. 1 : 9) Neque vero nomen consortii vel societatis mentem eius satis exprimere videtur, sed mihi sacram illam unitatem designat, qua filius Dei nos in corpus suum inserit, ut nobiscum sua omnium communicet.*

and hidden abyss which streams forth to us in the person of the Mediator."[1] Even though this "power" (*virtus*) communicated through the human nature of Christ to those united to Him comes from another source than that flesh itself (i.e. from the divine nature), nevertheless "His flesh as a channel, conveys to us that *life* which dwells intrinsically, as we say, in His divinity".[2]

This union between us and the human nature of Christ effects the completion' of the reconciling act of God in uniting to Himself in Jesus a human nature. In this union there takes place what Calvin calls a "wondrous exchange"[3] made by the boundless goodness of God, whereby Christ takes upon Himself what is ours, and transfers to us what is His own. "Seeing He was once pleased to become our brother, we must not doubt but that, in taking upon Him our poor and wretched state, He hath made an exchange with us that we may become rich through His grace."[4] "Having become with us the son of man, He has made us with Himself sons of God. By His own descent to the earth, He has prepared our ascent to heaven. Having received our mortality, He has bestowed on us His immortality. Having undertaken our weakness, He has made us strong in His strength. Having submitted to our poverty, He has transferred to us His riches. Having taken upon Himself the burden of our unrighteousness with which we were oppressed, He has clothed us with His righteousness."[5] "The work to be performed by the Mediator was of no common description, being to restore us to divine favour, so as to make us, instead of sons of men, sons of God;

[1]Inst. 3 : 11 : 9. *Simul tamen iustitiae et salutis materiam in eius carne docent : non quod a se ipso iustificet aut vivificet merus homo, sed quia Deo placuit quod in se absconditum et incomprehensibile erat in mediatore palam facere. Unde soleo dicere, Christum esse nobis quasi expositum fontem, unde hauriamus quod alioqui sine fructu lateret in occulta illa et profunda scaturigine, quae in Mediatoris persona ad nos emergit.*

[2]Cf. comm. on John 6 : 51, C.R. 47 : 152. *Quamvis haec virtus aliunde quam ex carne proveniat, nihil tamen obstare quin apte in eam competat hic titulus. Nam sicuti aeternus Dei sermo fons vitae est, ita caro eius veluti canalis vitam, quae intrinseca ut loquuntur in divinitate residet, ad nos diffundit.*

[3]Inst. 4 : 17 : 2. *Mirifica commutatio.* Cf. serm. on Isa. 53 : 4–6, C.R. 35 : 622. *Quand donc nous voyons que nostre Seigneur Jesus Christ a fait un tel eschange pour nous, et a voulu faire un payment entier de toutes nos dettes, afin que nous en fussions acquittez . . . voyla qui nous doit attirer a lui.*

[4]Serm. on 1 Tim. 2 : 5–6, C.R. 53 : 177.

[5]Inst. 4 : 17 : 2. Cf. serm. on Isa. 52 : 13 ff., C.R. 35 : 600. *Le Fils de Dieu n'a pas refusé d'estre comme desfiguré, luy qui est comme l'image de Dieu son Pere : et le tout afin que ceste image fust reparee en nous.* Cf. C.R. 35 : 602–3, C.R. 35 : 653.

instead of heirs of Hell, heirs of a heavenly kingdom. Who could do this unless the Son of God should also become the son of man, and so receive what is ours as to transfer to us what is His, making that which is His by nature to become ours by grace? . . . He declined not to take what was peculiar to us that He might in His turn extend to us what was peculiarly His own and thus might be in common with us both Son of God and son of man."[1]

Thus there is between Christ and ourselves, through His incarnation and death, what Calvin calls a "holy brotherhood (*fraternitas sancta*)".[2] All mankind have to a certain extent this "right to fraternal alliance (*ius fraternae coniunctionis*)"[3] set up through the relationship of the flesh (*carnis cognationis*)[4] which Christ has with us in the incarnation, nevertheless "the true enjoyment thereof belongs to genuine believers alone".[5] The exchange of properties between the Son of God and mankind is a covenant ratified by the sacrifice of the death of Christ, but it would not avail us without the addition of that "secret communication by which we are made one with Christ".[6] "No grace of the Holy Spirit can be communicated to us unless we are members of our Lord Jesus Christ. How can we become so unless He gives Himself to us, and shares our life so that we are truly united to Him? He must dwell within us so that everything that is His belongs to us, and we enjoy the benefits which have been given Him on our behalf. We read in the eleventh chapter of Isaiah that the Spirit of God rested upon Him, but it was not because He had need of it, nor for His private use; it was for the profit of His body, that is to say, of the whole Church."[7]

As it was through the influence of the Holy Spirit that the Father endowed the humanity of His son with those gifts which

---

[1]Inst. 2 : 12 : 2. *Quis hoc poterat nisi Filius Dei fieret idem filius hominis, et sic nostrum acciperet, ut transferret ad nos suum : et quod suum erat natura, nostrum faceret gratia? suscipere gravatus non est, ut vicissim ad nos pertineret quod proprium ipse habebat : atque ita in commune ipse nobiscum et Filius Dei esset et filius hominis.*

[2]Inst. 2 : 12 : 2.
[3]Comm. on Ps. 22 : 22, C.R. 31 : 231.
[4]Ibid.
[5]Ibid.
[6]Inst. 4 : 17 : 20.   *Arcana illa communicatio, qua in unum cum Christo coalescimus.*
[7]Serm. on Acts 2 : 1–4, C.R. 48 : 633.

He now makes ours, so it is the Holy Spirit who now effects the union between the humanity of Christ and ourselves essential for the further transfer of these gifts to us. "His whole strength, power and majesty, is here made to consist in gifts of the Spirit. Although Christ was not deficient in gifts of this kind, yet as He took upon Him our flesh, it was necessary that He should be enriched with them, that we might afterwards be made partakers of all the blessings of which otherwise we are destitute; for *out of* His fullness, as John says, *we must draw as from a fountain* (John 1 : 16 and 7 : 37–8). . . . This refers to Christ's human nature; because He could not be enriched with a gift . . . except in so far as He became man. Besides, as He came down to us, so He received the gifts of the Spirit, that He might bestow them upon us. This passage (i.e. Isa. 11 : 2) does not so much teach us what Christ is in Himself, as what He has received of the Father, that He might enrich us with His wealth."[1]

3. The reality of this union as sealed in the sacraments

Calvin speaks of both sacraments as being signs of our incorporation in the body of Christ. He speaks especially in this way of Baptism. When Paul in Romans 6 : 5, turning from the subject of Baptism, begins to speak of believers as being ingrafted into Christ, Calvin comments, "By plainer words he proves the argument already entered upon, for the similitude He brings in takes away all ambiguity, because grafting denotes not only conformity of example, but a secret conjunction, whereby we grow up together with Him."[2] The purpose of Baptism is to show us that we are members of the body of Christ, and that He has united us to Himself by an indissoluble union by which we partake of His blessings.[3] It is a "symbol of our implanting in Christ".[4] "Baptism is an engrafting into the body of Christ, for God in that ordinance does not represent anything but what He is prepared to accomplish, provided we are on our

---

[1]Comm. on Isa. 11 : 2, C.R. 36 : 235–6.
[2]Comm. on Rom. 6 : 5, C.R. 49 : 106. . . . *Insitio non exempli tantum confirmitatem designat, sed arcanam coniunctionem, per quam cum ipso coaluimus.*
[3]Cf. C.R. 46 : 578, 580.
[4]Comm. on Titus 3 : 5, C.R. 52 : 430. *Symbolum nostrae in Christum insitionis.*

part capable of it. The Apostle, also, observes here a most admirable medium in teaching that the nature of Baptism is—to connect us with Christ's body."[1]

The Lord's Supper is equally with Baptism a sign of this same mystical incorporation in the body of Christ. "The signs are bread and wine which represent the invisible food which we receive from the body and blood of Christ. For as God, regenerating us in Baptism, ingrafts us into the fellowship of the Church, and makes us His by adoption, so . . . He performs the office of a provident parent in continually supplying the food by which He may sustain and preserve us in the life to which He has begotten us by His Word."[2] "We do not less truly become participants in Christ's body in respect of spiritual efficacy than we partake of the bread."[3] In the Lord's Supper "we are ingrafted into the Lord's body".[4] The Lord's Supper "is a help by which we may be ingrafted into the body of Christ, or, already ingrafted, may be more and more united to Him, until the union is completed in heaven".[5] It should be noted that Calvin looks on both sacraments as having the same end— to testify, and to assist in effecting our union with the body of Christ.[6] Baptism, however, mainly bears witness to our initiation into this union, while the Lord's Supper is a sign of our continuation in this union. Baptism is "a kind of entrance into the Church, an initiation into the faith, and the Lord's Supper the constant aliment by which Christ spiritually feeds His family of believers".[7] The sacraments are thus complementary.[8]

[1]Comm. on 1 Cor. 12 : 13, C.R. 49 : 501–2. . . . *Hanc quidem Baptismi naturam esse docet, nos coadunare in Christi corpus.*
[2]Inst. 4 : 17 : 1.
[3]Comm. on 1 Cor. 11 : 24, C.R. 49 : 487. *Non minus vere nos, quantum ad vim spiritualem attinet, participes corporis Christi fieri, quam pane vescimur.*
[4]Comm. on 1 Cor. 10 : 15, C.R. 49 : 463; cf. Inst. 4 : 17 : 33.
[5]Inst. 4 : 17 : 33; cf. C.R. 48, 594.
[6]Cf. C.R. 45 : 710.
[7]Inst. 4 : 18 : 19. *Baptismus quidam quasi ingressus in ipsam esset et fidei initiatio Coena vero assiduum velut alimentum, quo Christus fidelium suorum familiam spiritualiter pascit.*
[8]Commenting on the issue of blood and water from the side of our Lord (John 19 : 34–5), Calvin points out that in the Law sacrifices of blood atoned for sins, while washings were remedies for taking away uncleanness, tokens of true holiness. Thus the fulfilment of both these graces is seen here to be in Christ. The sacraments have the same design, "for the purification and sanctification of the soul, which consist in newness of life, is pointed out in Baptism,

When Calvin thinks out the nature of this union between Christ and His people as figured forth in the sacraments, he finds it indeed shown forth in the sacraments to be a mystery. He insists that it is no mere spiritual connection between Christ and ourselves, as if the relation between us and Christ was merely that of believing in Him through our own mental apprehension of what He is and what He has done for us. Calvin cannot get away from the fact that our bodies as well as our souls are involved in this union, and that the sacrament of the Lord's Supper especially testifies that the flesh of Christ, the body in which He lived and died, is also involved in the mystery. Nor can Calvin put out of his mind the fact that in the sacrament of the Supper the elements of the bread and wine which represent the body and blood of Christ are not simply beheld and adored but really *eaten* by the participant.[1] All this, in spite of the intellectual difficulties involved, Calvin takes to signify the setting up of a real connection of being (he calls it a "substantial" connection) between Christ and the communicant. Christ "is *obtained*, I affirm, not only when we believe that he was made an offering for us, but when He dwells in us—when He is one with us— when we are *members of His flesh*—when, in fine, we are incorporated with Him (so to speak) into one·life and substance. . . . Christ does not simply present to us the benefit of His death and resurrection but the very body in which He suffered and rose again."[2] "In bidding us take, He intimates that it is ours: in bidding us eat, He intimates that it becomes one substance with us (*unam nobiscum substantiam*): in offering of His body that it was broken, and of His blood that it was shed for us, He shows that both were not so much His own as ours, because He took and laid down both, not for His own advantage, but for our

---

and the Lord's Supper is the pledge of a perfect atonement" (comm. in loc., C.R. 47 : 422). Cf. serm. on Deut. 7 : 19–24, C.R. 26 : 564. *Quand il nous souvient de nostre Baptesme, voila le Fils de Dieu qui nous testifie que nous l'avons vestu une fois. . . . Quand nous recevons la Cene, il nous monstre qu'il est nostre pasture.*

[1]Inst. 4 : 17 : 5.

[2]Comm. on 1 Cor. 11 : 24, C.R. 49 : 487. *Obtineri autem dico, non tantum quum pro nobis factum fuisse victimam credimus : sed dum in nos habitat, dum est unum nobiscum, dum eius sumus membra ex carne eius, dum in unam denique et vitam et substantiam (ut ita loquar) cum ipso coalescimus . . . neque enim mortis tantum ac resurrectionis suae beneficium nobis offert Christus, sed corpus ipsum, in quo passus est ac resurrexit.*

salvation."[1] The supper is given "first, that we might become one body with him; and secondly, that being made partakers of His substance, we might feel the result of this fact in the participation of all His blessings".[2]

4. The spiritual nature of this union effected by
the power of the Holy Spirit

The nature of the union indicated by Calvin in the foregoing discussion is beyond our power to conceive, especially when it is remembered that the flesh of Christ through which the Christian is united to Christ no longer exists in any form in the sphere of this earth but has been taken to heaven.[3] Nevertheless, this union is really and substantially brought about by the work of the Holy Spirit. "Though it seems an incredible thing that the flesh of Christ, while at such a distance from us in respect of space, should be food for us, let us remember how far the secret virtue (*virtus arcana*) of the Holy Spirit surpasses all our conceptions, and how foolish it is to wish to measure its immensity by our feeble capacity. Therefore what our mind does not comprehend let faith conceive, viz. that the Spirit really unites things separated by space."[4] "He it is who enlightens our minds by faith, who seals the adoption of God on our hearts, who regenerates us into newness of life, who grafts us into the body of Christ, that He may live in us and we in Him."[5] "Until our minds are intent on the Spirit, Christ is in a manner unemployed, because we view Him coldly without us, and so at a distance from us. Now we know that He is of no avail save only to those to whom He is a Head and the first born among the brethren, to those, in fine, who are clothed with Him. To this union alone it is owing that, in regard to us, the Spirit has not come in vain. To this is to be referred that sacred marriage by which we become bone of His bone, and flesh of His flesh, and so one with

---

[1]Inst. 4 : 17 : 3.
[2]Inst. 4 : 17 : 11. *Quo scilicet in unum corpus cum ipsum coalescimus, deinde participes substantia eius facti in bonorum omnium communicatione virtutem quoque sentiamus.*
[3]Cf. pp. 204 ff.
[4]Inst. 4 : 17 : 10.
[5]Comm. on Heb. 10 : 29, C.R. 55 : 136.

Him (Eph. 5 : 30), for it is by the Spirit alone that He unites Himself to us. By the same grace and energy of the Spirit we become His members, so that He keeps us under Him, and we in our turn possess Him."[1]

In thinking of the union thus achieved through the work of the Spirit between Christ and those united to Him, we must not imagine that some quality or substance is infused into the believer from Christ, nor must we imagine that there is any "gross mixture" of Christ and those who are His. Calvin opposed strongly the view of Osiander that there was "a substantial mixture, by which God, transfusing Himself into us, makes us, as it were, a part of Himself",[2] the essence of Christ being regarded as "mingled with us" (*nobis misceatur*) so that we become "substantially righteous in God by an infused essence (*essentia infusa*) as well as quality".[3] Calvin pours scorn on this view that "God by a gross mixture (*crassa mixtura*) transfuses Himself into us",[4] insisting that this is a "spiritual union" (*spiritualis coniunctio*). The analogy which Calvin often uses is that of the union of head and members of the body. Thus, though he insists on calling this union between Christ and His members a "substantial" union as against those who seem to dissolve its reality away into a mere mental act of remembering Christ in faith, Calvin is nevertheless equally emphatic, as against Osiander, in denying any infusion of substance from Christ to the believer. Indeed, he is willing to be counted as one who holds that in the Supper Christ is not eaten substantially.[5]

Calvin is obviously anxious to preserve the idea that grace is

[1]Inst. 3 : 1 : 3. . . . *Quo spectat sacrum illud coniugium, quo efficimur caro de carne eius, et ossa ex ossibus, adeoque unum cum ipso, solo autem spiritu unit se nobiscum. . . .* Cf. Inst. 4 : 17 : 24. W. Niesel points out that it was under the influence of a sermon by Chrysostom that Calvin formulated this doctrine. In the 1537 "*Confessio Fidei de Eucharistia,*" he writes. "*Spiritum eius vinculum esse nostrae cum ipso participationis agnoscimus,*" and speaks of the "*spiritus efficacia quin vere copulare et in unum colligere possit, quae locorum spatiis sunt disiuncta.* Later on he adds the thought of the Spirit as not only the "*vinculum*" but also the "*canalis per quem quicquid Christus ipse et est et habet, ad nos derivatur* (Inst. 4 : 17 : 12) and describes the effected union as "*non solum coniungi sed uniri ut, alimentum percipiant animae ex carne Christi*". (Cf. *Calvins Lehre von Abendmahl,* p. 92.)

[2]Inst. 3 : 11 : 5. *Substantialem mixtionem ingerit, qua Deus se in nos transfundens quasi partem sui faciat.*

[3]Inst. 3 : 11 : 5.

[4]Inst. 3 : 11 : 10. Cf. French = *mixtion telle que les viandes que nous mangeons.*

[5]Inst. 3 : 11 : 10.

not a substance but the personal presence of Christ offering men a personal relationship even in uniting them to Himself. In one passage, after defining grace as the mere goodness of God, he says, "We see how sottishly the schoolmen define grace, while they will have it to be nothing else than a quality infused into the hearts of men. For grace properly is in God, the effect of grace in us. And he says that the same grace was of one man Christ because the Father has made Him the fountain, of whose fullness all men must draw. And so He teaches that there cannot one drop be found out of Christ."[1] Thus while Calvin often insists that substantial union is nevertheless a spiritual union, at the same time, in the next sentence, he is equally anxious to remind us that it is a spiritual union effected with the flesh of Christ and through the flesh of Christ. "Paul in the Epistle to the Romans (Rom. 8 : 9–11) shows that the only way in which Christ dwells in us is by His Spirit. By this, however, He does not take away that communion with flesh and blood of which we now speak but shows that it is owing to the Spirit alone that we possess Christ wholly and have Him abiding in us."[2]

5. This union the basis of the Church

We have seen how, in many passages where Calvin speaks of our being ingrafted into the body of Christ, he is thinking of a substantial yet spiritual union created through the mysterious operation of the Holy Spirit between ourselves and the actual body in which Christ worked out our salvation and which is now glorified and in heaven. It must now be pointed out that there are many passages in Calvin's writings where he uses the phrase about our being "ingrafted into the body of Christ" to refer simply to our admission into the Church and our union with the life of the Church. And there are passages where it is difficult to decide whether Calvin, when he speaks of the body of Christ, means the actual glorified body now in heaven or the Church. "God hath saved us by His mercy, the symbol and pledge of which He gave us in Baptism, by admitting us into His

[1] Comm. on Rom. 5 : 15, C.R. 49 : 98–9, i.e. grace not a "*qualitatem hominum cordibus infusam*".
[2] Inst. 4 : 17 : 12.

Church and ingrafting us into the body of His Son.''[1] Calvin can thus speak of admission into the Church and ingrafting into the body of Christ as the same thing.[2] In one passage he can speak of Christ as imparting vigour ''to the flesh which He assumed, that a communication of life to us might thence emanate'';[3] there the reference is obviously to the corporeal frame in which Christ lived on earth. But in other passages Calvin can speak in similar terms of Christ as breathing life into the body of the Church[4] and of communicating what He possesses to His own body, where the context denotes this as the Church. Calvin can also speak of our being ingrafted into the body of the Church, and of our being ''ingrafted into the Church''[5] so that we ''belong to the body of the Church''.[6]

These quotations may serve to show how close, in Calvin's thought, is the relationship between Christ and the Church. It is natural that there should be this confusion of language, for we cannot be united to the Head without at the same time being united to the members of Christ. Moreover, as has been shown,[7] before Christ took on Himself a physical body from the Virgin Mary, He united Himself to Israel, His Church, and fore-shadowed in Israel's history the form of the historical life He was to live in that body. We cannot admit the assertion that for Calvin the body of Christ is no more than the Church.[8] But we can take many passages which have a primary reference to our connection with the heavenly body of Christ as also having a valid reference to the Church, since it is the mystical incorporation of each member in Christ that is the basis of the Church which is His body.

6. This union the pledge of eternal redemption

Calvin recognises that what we experience of this union with Christ now is but a small pledge of something far greater yet to

[1]Comm. on Titus 3 : 5, C.R. 52 : 430. Cf. C.R. 9 : 114. *Proprium esse Baptismi munus nos in Christi corpus inserere.*
[2]Cf. comm. on Isa. 42 : 1, C.R. 37 : 58.
[3]Inst. 4 : 17 : 8.
[4]Comm. on Isa. 54 : 1, C.R. 37 : 269.
[5]C.R. 9 : 114. *In ecclesiam inseri.*
[6]C.R. 9 : 115. *Ad corpus ecclesiae pertinere.*
[7]See pp. 43 ff.
[8]Cf. Beckmann: *Vom Sakrament bei Calvin*, p. 64.

come. Indeed it is precisely because we have it now only so faintly and dimly that we need the sacraments to show to us what it will be one day in reality. The sacraments are thus eschatological signs. They bear witness to a union that is begun, and more and more moving on to completion, but which can only be completed in heaven.[1]

The true goal of all human life is union with God. The use of the law in the Old Testament was to invite men to enter this union, for "indeed their true happiness lies in being united to God, and the sacred bond of union is faith and sincere piety".[2] "The chief good of man is to be united to God, with whom is the fountain of life and all blessing."[3] But this perfect union of man with God is now accomplished only in the person of Christ, who has entered the kingdom of heaven in our flesh and in whom there is set up a perfect and complete union between God and a human nature. Christ has, moreover, entered the kingdom of heaven not only in our flesh "but as it were in our name," says Calvin, and it follows that "we are in a manner now seated in heavenly places, not entertaining a mere hope of heaven, but possessing it in our head".[4] When Paul speaks of himself as not yet having attained, Calvin puts the rhetorical question, "What is it that Paul says he has not yet attained? For unquestionably as soon as we are by faith ingrafted into the body of Christ, we have already entered into the kingdom of God, and, as it is stated in Ephesians 2 : 6, we already in hope *sit in heavenly places.*" Calvin's answer to his own question is that our salvation is meantime "in hope", and "we have it not yet in possession".[5] This union between ourselves and the body of Christ is therefore eschatologically completed, the sacraments being a pledge of its present yet hidden fullness.

Moreover, Calvin bids us note the fact that this union is a pledge not only of the redemption of our souls but also of our bodies, which through the sacraments have the sign engraven on

[1]Inst. 4 : 17 : 33.
[2]Comm. on Isa. 45 : 19, C.R. 37 : 145.
[3]Comm. on Heb. 7 : 25, C.R. 55 : 94; cf. on Heb. 4 : 10, C.R. 55 : 48. *Summum ergo hominis bonum nihil aliud est quam cum Deo coniunctio.*
[4]Inst. 2 : 16 : 16. *Quando enim in carne nostra quasi nostro nomine eo ingressus est, inde sequitur nos quodammodo in coelestibus iam in ipso considere, utpote qui coelum non spe nuda exspectemus, sed in capite nostro possideamus.*
[5]Comm. on Phil. 3 : 12, C.R. 52 : 51.

them that they also, as well as our souls, are united to the body
of Christ. "Observe, that the spiritual connection which we
have with Christ belongs not merely to the soul, but also to the
body, so that we are *flesh of His flesh* etc. (Eph. 5 : 30). Otherwise the hope of a resurrection were weak, if the connection
were not of that nature—full and complete."[1] In the Geneva
Catechism it is taught that in the Lord's Supper the resurrection
is "confirmed to us by a kind of pledge, since the body also
shares in the symbol of life".[2] In the 1537 Catechism it is stated
that the virtue of the sacraments not only assures our spirits of
their immortality "but it also renders our flesh certain of the
same. For it is vivifying. Our flesh is vivified by His immortal
flesh, and shares in some manner in its immortality."[3] In the
Institutes Calvin speaks of the blessing of becoming one with
Christ "in body, soul, and spirit".[4] In one passage he does not
deny the view of Tertullian and Hilary that our flesh is nourished
by the flesh of Christ, only pointing out that these two writers
do not think of this as happening in such a way as some people
imagine.[5] It must be noted that Calvin consistently looks on
this connection which our bodies have with Christ and which
our souls have with the body of Christ as a "spiritual connection".[6] "We acknowledge Christ as man and as our brother in
His flesh—not in a fleshly manner (*in carne sua ; non carnaliter*);
because we rest solely in the consideration of His spiritual gifts.
Hence He is spiritual to us, not as if He laid aside His body, and
became a spirit, but because He regenerates and governs His
own people by the influence of His Spirit."[7]

Finally, it may be added here that we are meant to find
confidence in the hope of immortality by considering the nature
and reality of this union which is so vividly depicted in the

[1]Comm. on 1 Cor. 6 : 15, C.R. 49 : 398. *Nota, unitatem spiritualem, quae
nobis cum Christo est, non animae tantum esse, sed pertinere etiam ad corpus : ut
caro simus de carne eius etc. Alioqui infirma esset spes resurrectionis, nisi talis esset
nostra coniunctio, hoc est plena et solida.*
[2]C.R. 6 : 129.
[3]O.S., 1 : 413.
[4]Inst. 4 : 17 : 12; cf. C.R. 9 : 208. "We have communion with Christ in
the hope of a blessed resurrection, and therefore we must be one with Him not
only in soul but in flesh; just as each of us in respect of the flesh is said to be a
member of Christ, and the body of each a temple of the Holy Spirit."
[5]C.R. 9 : 493.
[6]Comm. on 1 Cor. 6 : 15, C.R. 49 : 398.
[7]Comm. on 2 Cor. 5 : 16, C.R. 50 : 69.

sacraments. "How could a most merciful prince destroy his own people? How could the head disperse its own members? How could the advocate condemn his clients? Scripture proclaims throughout, that Christ does now as certainly lead a glorious life in our flesh, as He once suffered in it. Nay more, take away this foundation, and our whole faith falls to the ground; from whence comes the hope of immortality, except from this, that we already have a pattern (*specimen*) of it in the person of Christ?"[1]

[1]Comm. on 2 Cor. 5 : 16, C.R. 50 : 68.

Chapter XIII

The Mystery of Sacramental Union

1. The sacraments effectual through the mystery of sacramental union

WE have seen, especially in our study of the use of sign and word in Old Testament revelation, that in revealing Himself God takes up into His activity an earthly action or event, and unites with Himself, for a moment, a human element. We may call this activity of God His sacramental action. In such sacramental action a union takes place between the divine element—the Spirit or action of God—and the human activity, so that the whole event is effectual in conveying the very grace depicted in its outward form. What God, therefore, depicts in the sacraments, He actually brings to pass through their agency.[1] "In the sacraments the reality is given along with the sign."[2] "The true effect is conjoined with the external sign."[3] In the Supper we are "effectually and in reality" invited to communion with Christ, "for we say that the reality which the promise contains is here exhibited and that the effect is annexed to the external symbol".[4] Christ "does the very thing which He shows, and ratifies what He does".[5] He "effectually uses this instrument to dwell in us".[6]

Were all this not so, the whole instituting of sacraments on the part of God would be mockery and a lie. "Unless we would charge God with deceit, we will never presume to say that He

[1]Cf. Inst. 4 : 17 : 3.
[2]Comm. on Isa. 6 : 7, C.R. 36 : 133. *Unde colligere possumus, in sacramentis rem nobis cum signo exhiberi.*
[3]C.R. 9 : 19. *Externae eorum figurae verum effectum esse coniunctum.*
[4]C.R. 9 : 68. *Dicimus enim veritatem quam continet promissio, illic exhiberi, et effectum externo symbolo annexum esse.* It is to be noted in this and subsequent discussion that Calvin uses the verb *exhibere* (often translated "to exhibit") more in the sense of "to present in reality", or even "to convey", rather than in the sense of "to show".
[5]C.R. 9 : 184. *Hoc ipsum agere Christum quod verbis ostendit, et sancire quod agit.*
[6]C.R. 9 : 77. *Assero efficaciter hoc organo Christum uti, ut in nos habitet.*

holds forth an empty symbol."[1] "If He gave us only the bread and wine, leaving the spiritual reality behind, would it not be under false colours that this ordinance had been instituted?"[2] Thus in the sacraments we have no bare figure but the giving of the thing itself.[3] Thus the function of the sacraments is not merely to produce a healthy psychological effect by depicting to the eyes doctrines and facts that must not be forgotten, but to be the instruments of a gracious divine action whereby what is represented to us is also presented to us. Calvin calls the elements of the Supper "instruments"[4] by which the Lord distributes His body and blood, as well as "representations" of them to us. "Christ in instituting the mystery of the Supper promises nothing falsely."[5] "The bread is called the body since it not only represents but also presents it to us."[6] Baptism likewise is no empty sign. "We are not in vain baptised with water by men, because Christ, who commanded the same to be done, will fulfil His office, and baptise us with the Spirit."[7] The sacraments are therefore not merely "speaking symbols" (to repeat a phrase of Bishop Gore's); they are signs not merely of something that happened once in the past but of a present activity of God which is taking place in the midst of, and alongside, the human action.

The sacraments thus deserve to be ranked along with the Word as true means of grace, and along with the Word of the Gospel can be called the *power of God unto salvation*. "We are not so raw as not to know that the sacraments, inasmuch as they are helps of faith, also offer us righteousness in Christ. Nay, as we are perfectly agreed that the sacraments are to be ranked in the same place as the Word, so while the Gospel is called the power of God unto salvation to every one that believeth, we hesitate not to transfer the same title to the sacraments."[8] To

[1]Inst. 4 : 17 : 10. *Inane symbolum propone.* Cf. C.R. 12 : 728.
[2]O.S. 1 : 509.
[3]Cf. comm. on Acts 22 : 16, C.R. 48 : 497. *Non proponi in baptismo nudam figuram, sed rei quoque exhibitionem simul annexam esse.*
[4]O.S. 1 : 508.
[5]C.R. 20 : 73.
[6]O.S. 1 : 509. *Le pain est nommé corps, puis que non seulement il le nous represente, mais aussi nous le presente.*
[7]Comm. on Acts 1 : 5, C.R. 48 : 7.
[8]C.R. 9 : 182. Cf. serm. on Acts 1 : 4–5, C.R. 48 : 601. *Tout ainsi que ie pren de l'eau pour baptizer, voyla Jesus Christ qui accomplit ce que ie signifie, et*

those men whose formal practice is daily to cry, "The Word of the Lord, the Word of the Lord" in their anxiety that the Scripture shall have first place of honour in the Church Calvin says, "They will find nothing applicable to the Word which we do not also give to the sacraments."[1]

In what follows in this chapter an attempt will be made to indicate from Calvin's writings the nature of the mystery of this union between the divine and human actions in the sacraments by which they become effective.

2. This union so close and intimate that the thing signified can be identified with the sign

In the ordinary affairs of human life a symbol can sometimes be addressed and thought of as if it were identical with what it stands for. Thus a mother can refer to "John" as being put up on the mantelpiece, when what she means is that John's photograph is being put there. Calvin points out, too, that even those who use "humanly devised symbols" to represent things which are sometimes quite unlike the symbol and quite apart from the symbol sometimes honour the symbol by giving it the name of the thing it represents. But in the sacraments we have such a close connection between the symbol and the spiritual gift which it represents that we can "easily pass from the one to the other"[2] in our speech and refer to the bread as being indeed the body of Christ, and Baptism as being the "laver of regeneration" (Tit. 3 : 5) and as an act that washes our sins away (1 Pet. 3 : 21).[3] "Although the sign differs essentially from the thing signified, the latter being spiritual and heavenly, the former corporeal and visible—yet, as it not only figures the thing which it is employed to represent as a naked and empty badge, but also truly exhibits it, why should not its name be justly applied to the thing?"[4] This manner of speaking Calvin calls a "sacramental mode of

l'accomplit par sa propre vertu. Cf. also C.R. 12 : 728. *In coena quum nobis signa carnis et sanguinis Christi porrigantur, dicimus non frustra porrigi quin res quoque ipsa nobis constet.*
[1] C.R. 9 : 20–1.
[2] Inst. 4 : 17 : 21.
[3] Cf. comm. on John 1 : 26, C.R. 47 : 23–4.
[4] Inst. 4 : 17 : 21.

speaking", and he often points out its use in Scripture. When, for example, he wants to describe the cloud as preceding the Children of Israel in their journey, Moses does not say "the cloud went before them" but "the Lord went before them", seeming to include the Lord in the cloud, since the cloud was no deceitful sign of God's presence but a truly sacramental object.[1] Likewise, when the clouds descended upon the tabernacle, the Lord is said to descend, the sacred name being applied to the visible symbol.[2]   Likewise, when the Ark with the sound of trumpets ascends into the temple, the sacred writer says, "God is gone up with a shout."[3]   Likewise, the dove, representing the Holy Ghost, is called "the Spirit" (John 1 : 32).   Likewise, the rock which represents Christ is called Christ (1 Cor. 10).   Thus "the name of the thing signified is aptly transferred to the sign".[4] The elements in the earthly action are spoken of as being identical with the heavenly realities which they represent, and what is done by man in figure is spoken of as being simultaneously done by God in reality.

This manner of speaking arises from the fact that the union formed between the divine and human activity in the event of God's action in the sacrament is so close as, practically speaking, to become one of identity.   Calvin, referring to the preaching of the word in which this same close sacramental union holds good, can speak of "such a connection between Christ's grace and man's effort, that in many cases *that* is ascribed to the minister which belongs exclusively to the Lord".[5]   We know that in preaching it is not the human effort of the preacher which saves and regenerates men, but so close is the union between man's speaking and God's Word that we can legitimately speak as if it were the word of the minister which accomplished that which is God's prerogative alone.   Calvin points out that Paul, in view of the similar close union between the divine grace and the human

---

[1]Cf. comm. on Exod. 13 : 21, C.R. 24 : 145.   *Etsi autem videntur Mosis verba Deum quodammodo in nube includere, notanda nobis sacramentalis loquendi ratio, qua Deus nomen suum ad visibiles figuras transfert.*
[2]Comm. on Exod. 34 : 5, C.R. 25 : 113.
[3]Comm. on Ps. 47 : 6 f., C.R. 31 : 469.
[4]Comm. on John 1 : 32, C.R. 47 : 27.   *Rei nomen apte ad signum transfertur.* Cf. on Matt. 26 : 26, C.R. 45 : 706; and Inst. 4 : 17 : 21.
[5]Comm. on 2 Cor. 3 : 6, C.R. 50 : 40.   *Eiusmodo coniunctio et nexus Christi gratiae cum labore hominis facit ut saepe ministro adscribatur quod solius Domini est.* Cf. comm. on 1 Cor. 3 : 7, C.R. 49 : 350–1.

action in the sacraments, uses the same mode of speaking in referring to Baptism. "Paul . . . because he speaks to the faithful conjoins the substance and effect with the external sign. For we know that by their faith is established and ratified whatever the Lord offers by the visible pledge. . . . Thus in Galatians it is affirmed that anyone whosoever is baptized in Christ has put on Christ. This way of speaking must be used so long as the institution of the Lord and the faith of the godly agree together."[1]

The close sacramental union which Christ sets up between Himself and the signs which testify of Him gives us a right to speak of the elements of the sacraments in the terms of identity with that which they represent. Because Christ was "connected" (*annexum*) with the Old Testament emblems of His presence "not locally, nor by a natural or substantial union, but sacramentally",[2] therefore the Apostle can say that *the rock was Christ*, for "nothing," adds Calvin, "is more common than metonymy in speaking of sacraments. The name of the thing, therefore, is transferred here to the sign—not as if it were strictly applicable, but figuratively on the ground of that connection which I have mentioned."[3]

3. This union so transcendent and freely personal that the thing signified must be regarded as distinct from the sign

Though this sacramental union here under discussion is so close as at times to justify our regarding it almost as a relation of identity, it is nevertheless so transcendent and freely personal that even in the event of the sacrament becoming effectual we must always in our thinking hold the grace and action of God as being quite distinct from our human activity. "God truly performs whatever He promises and figures by signs; nor are signs without effect, for they prove that He is their true and faithful author. The only question here is, whether the Lord works by proper and intrinsic virtue (as it is called) or resigns His office to external symbols. We maintain, that whatever

[1]Comm. on Rom. 6 : 4, C.R. 49 : 106.
[2]*Non localiter quidem, nec naturali, aut substantiali unione, sed sacramentali modo.*
[3]Comm. on 1 Cor. 10 : 4, C.R. 49 : 455.

organs He employs detract nothing from His primary operation."[1] "God alone performs whatever we obtain by the sacraments and that by His secret and as it is called intrinsic virtue.
But lest anyone should object, that the signs too have their
office ... we hasten to say ... that God uses their instrumentality, and yet in such a manner that He neither infuses His
virtue into them, nor derogates in any respect from the efficacy
of His spirit."[2] It will be noted in the foregoing quotations that
Calvin is concerned to allow for the complete sovereignty of
God's action in the sacraments over the human action, and in
the free personal nature of the grace conferred. He is anxious
to guard against any view that would suggest that the grace of
God is somehow included (*inclusa*) in or bound up with (*alligata*)
the sacraments, that here careless human initiative could cause
divine action, or mechanical operation could produce divine
grace. The truth for Calvin is simply that here God graciously
bestows His gift along with the sign. "Not that such graces are
included and bound in the sacrament so as to be conferred by
its efficacy, but only that by this badge the Lord declares to us
that He is pleased to bestow all these things upon us."[3]

Calvin sees what may be called a "parallel relationship"
between the sign and the thing signified, between the human
action and the divine grace. As indicated in the previous section,
there is a close and intimate connection, so that the one is not
separate from the other, but there is always maintained a sharp
and clear distinction so that the one is never merged into the
other to bring about any loss of continuity on either side. "The
truth is never to be separated from the signs, though it ought to
be distinguished from them. We perceive and feel a sign, such
as the bread which is put into our hands by the minister at the

---

[1]Inst. 4 : 14 : 7. ... *Tantum hic quaeritur, propriane et instrinseca (ut
loquuntur) virtute operetur Deus, an externis symbolis resignet suas vices. Nos vero
contendimus, quaecunque adhibeat organa, primariae eius operationi nihil decedere.*
[2]C.R. 9 : 22–3. ... *Sic Deum illorum uti ministerio, ut aeque vim ipsis suam
infundat, nec quidquam deroget spiritus sui efficaciae.*
[3]Inst. 4 : 15 : 14. *Non quia Sacramento tales gratiae alligatae inclusaeque
sint, quo eius virtute nobis conferantur : sed duntaxat quia hac tessera voluntatem
suam nobis Dominus testificatur nempe se haec omnia nobis velle largire.*
Beckmann points out, however (*Vom Sacrament bei Calvin*, p. 37), that in his
letter to Bullinger (C.R. 12 : 483) Calvin raises no objection to the phrase
contineri gratiam in sacramentis and with certain safeguards is willing to accept
gratiam conferre as applying to them.

Lord's Supper; and because we ought to seek Christ in heaven, our thoughts ought to be carried thither."[1] "The signs and the things signified are not disjoined but distinct."[2] "The sacrament is one thing, the virtue (*virtus*) of the sacrament is another."[3] Calvin is thus concerned to maintain a middle course between Papists who confound the reality and the sign, and profane men who separate the signs from the realities.[4] "The efficacy and use of the sacraments will be properly understood by him who shall connect the sign and the thing signified, in such a manner as not to make the sign unmeaning and inefficacious, and who nevertheless shall not, for the sake of adorning the sign, take away from the Holy Spirit what belongs to him."[5]

4. No natural analogy for this union

Calvin frankly calls this sacramental union a "mystery". "When our Lord instituted the Supper He spoke briefly, as is usually done in federal acts, whereas in the 6th chapter of John He discourses copiously and professedly on that mystery of sacred conjunction of which He afterwards held forth a mirror in the sacraments."[6] He can describe the relation between the earthly ceremony and the heavenly act as "a sacred union incomprehensible to carnal sense".[7] This means that the nature of this union is as unique and unparalleled as the incarnation itself is a unique and unparalleled event; and that there is no true analogy to this relationship under consideration, outside the events of the Bible and indeed outside of Jesus Christ. Calvin sees no "natural sacramental principle" running through the world of nature from the study of which we might begin our thinking about the sacraments.

[1]Comm. on Isa. 6 : 7, C.R. 36 : 133.
[2]C.R. 9 : 18. *A rebus signatis distincta sunt signa, non tamen disiungi nec separari.* Cf. C.R. 7 : 738.
[3]Inst. 4 : 17 : 34 (quoting Augustine).
[4]Cf. comm. on 1 Cor. 10 : 3, C.R. 49 : 454. *Confundunt papistae rem et signum : divellunt signa a rebus profani homines : nos mediocritatem servemus.*
[5]Comm. on Titus 3 : 5, C.R. 52 : 431.
[6]C.R. 9 : 200.
[7]C.R. 9 : 31. *Sacram unitatem . . . sensui carnis incomprehensibilem.*

There are no such things as sacraments apart from the events recorded in the Bible, for the sacrament is something God does in Christ with any earthly element He cares to lay hold of in His free and sovereign grace. Unless God acts in this way, nothing can possibly have any sacramental value. "I do not allow the force of those comparisons which some borrow from profane and earthly things; for there is a material difference between them and the sacraments of the Lord."[1] If God "had impressed memorials of this description on the sun, the stars, the earth, and stones they would all have been to us as sacraments. For why is the shapeless and the coined silver not of the same value seeing they are the same metal? Just because the former has nothing but its own nature, whereas the latter impressed with the public stamp, becomes money and receives a new value. And shall not the Lord be able to stamp His creatures with His word; that things which were formerly bare elements may become sacraments?"[2] For Calvin the institution of a sacrament is an act of God which "makes . . . divine mysteries lurk under things that are in themselves quite abject".[3] It is certainly not by nature that this takes place. Calvin brings out this point well in his comment on the healing of the man born blind. "Unquestionably there was not either in the clay or in the water of Siloam any power or fitness for curing the eyes; but Christ freely made use of those outward symbols on various occasions, for adorning His miracles, either to accustom believers to the use of signs, or to show that all things were at His disposal, or to testify that every one of the creatures has as much power as He chooses to give them."[4] Thus Calvin disallows natural analogies as being unable to cast for us any light on this great mystery, the only analogies from which he seeks to draw light on this mystery being those of God's parallel action in the events of Biblical history.

[1]Comm. on 1 Cor. 11 : 24, C.R. 49 : 486. Cf. C.R. 9 : 214–5, where Calvin agrees with Westphal that sacramental actions ought not to be compared with nature.
[2]Inst. 4 : 14 : 18.
[3]Inst. 4 : 19 : 2.
[4]Comm. on John 9 : 7, C.R. 47 : 221.

5. The mystery of sacramental union paralleled by the mystery of the incarnation

There is no doubt that Calvin sees an analogy which at least serves to regulate his thinking on this mystery of sacramental union, in the mystery of the union between God and man in Jesus Christ.   Calvin refers to this latter union as a "hidden and incomprehensible mystery"[1] but he himself had such definite views on the nature of this mystery of the incarnation that, though in another place he calls it "that unparalleled mystery",[2] his views on it serve largely to determine his thinking on the sacraments.

This "unparalleled mystery" of the union of the divine and human natures in the God-man Calvin calls a "union of person".[3]   In spite of its unparalleled nature, and in spite of his refusal to admit sacramental analogies from nature, Calvin does hazard very tentatively one illustration from nature to try to illuminate the subject.   "If, in human affairs, anything analogous to this great mystery can be found, the most apposite similitude seems to be that of man, who obviously consists of two substances, neither of which, however, is so intermingled with the other as that both do not retain their own properties.   For neither is soul body, nor is body soul."[4]

It will be seen that Calvin from the start chooses this illustration of the relation between body and soul in man to drive home the point that he is constantly out to safeguard, namely that the two natures do not become one through any "intermingling" or "confusion of substance".   This was the heresy of Servetus, with whom Calvin links Eutyches and the Anabaptists.[5]   These taught that God was made man "not by union but by confusion",[6] the humanity of Christ becoming deified and thus no

---

[1]Comm. on Exod. 26 : 31, C.R. 24 : 417.   *Reconditum et incomprehensibile mysterium.*

[2]Comm. on Isa. 7 : 14, C.R. 36 : 158.   *Incomparabile illud arcanum.*

[3]Inst. 2 : 14 : 1.   *Unitate personae*; cf. comm. on Isa. 7 : 14, C.R. 36 : 157 (*coniunctio personae*); on John 1 : 14, C.R. 47 : 14.

[4]Inst. 2 : 14 : 1.   Augustine employs the same simile, Ep. 102.   Cf. also Calvin, serm. on 1 Tim. 3 : 16, C.R. 53 : 326–7.

[5]Cf. Inst. 4 : 17 : 30, comm. on John 1 : 14, C.R. 47 : 14.

[6]Comm. on Ezek. 1 : 26 C.R. 40 : 54.

longer remaining true humanity,[1] the resultant Christ being confusedly compounded of two natures[2] and having no true humanity. Calvin condemns this "confusion of heaven and earth" and insists on asserting a union such that, in spite of the real unity achieved, each nature retains its own properties distinct and entire, without change, there being no fusion or blending of the one nature in the other.[3] This is what Calvin means by "personal union". "The unity of Person does not hinder the two natures from remaining distinct, so that His divinity retains all that is peculiar to itself, and His humanity holds separately whatever belongs to it."[4] Calvin hints at another analogy for the mystery of this union in mentioning in this connection the divine seed implanted in the Virgin's womb as in a temple in which He might dwell. "When it is said that the Word was made flesh, we must not understand it as if He were either changed into flesh, but that He made choice of the Virgin's womb as a temple in which He might dwell. He who was the son of God became the son of man, not by confusion of substance, but by unity of person (*non confusione substantiae sed unitate personae*)."[5]

Enough has now been said on this matter to show that though the union established between the grace of God and the human action in the sacraments cannot be called a "personal" union in the same sense of the word, and is but transitory, it nevertheless reflects characteristics of the deeper mystery, and for Calvin the one relation illuminated the other. It is because of his Christology that Calvin denies on the one hand any fusion of the heavenly and earthly elements of the sacrament, and yet on the other hand is equally emphatic in denying any view that would divorce the reality of divine grace from the human sacramental action and thus make the sacraments nothing but empty signs. It was no doubt with the Chalcedonian formula in mind that Calvin wrote: "The sacraments of the Word should not and cannot be at all separated from their reality and substance. To distinguish, in order to guard against confounding them, is not

[1]Comm. on 1 John 1 : 1, C.R. 55 : 300–1.
[2]Comm. on John 1 : 14, C.R. 47 : 14.
[3]Cf. serm. on Luke 1 : 39–44, C.R. 46 : 109–10.
[4]Comm. on John 1 : 14, C.R. 47 : 14.
[5]Inst. 2 : 14 : 1.

only good and reasonable, but altogether necessary; but to divide them, so as to make the one exist without the other is absurd."[1] And it was as an attack against a Christological heresy that he wrote: "The body with the bread is a thing of heaven with a thing of earth; to hold that the bread is the body is nothing else than to confound heaven and earth together."[2]

6. The sacraments effectual only through the working of the Holy Spirit

Since our incorporation in Christ is effected only by the secret and wonderful operation of the Holy Spirit, it follows that the efficacy of the sacraments depends entirely on the Spirit of God. "God acts by the sign in such a manner, that its whole efficacy depends on His Spirit."[3] "Whatever God offers in the sacraments, depends on the secret operation of His Spirit."[4] "The Holy Spirit . . . brings the gifts of God along with Him, makes way for the sacraments, and causes them to bear fruit."[5] It must be carefully noticed that the *whole efficacy* of the sacraments depends on the Spirit, who is sovereign and free in His operation through the sacraments and not in any way constrained by the human action or will. "So far, then, is God from resigning the grace of His Spirit to the sacraments, that all their efficacy and utility are lodged in the Spirit alone."[6] Thus the sacraments are effectual only "where and whenever God is so pleased."[7] God "uses the creatures thus freely and at His own will acts by means of them so far as He pleases".[8] God's grace is no more tied to the elements or the action of the sacraments than it is to preaching. "As the outward voice of man cannot at all penetrate

---

[1] O.S. 1 : 509.
[2] C.R. 9 : 209–10.
[3] Comm. on Eph. 5 : 26, C.R. 51 : 223. *Nam ita Deus per signum agit, ut tota signi efficacia nihilominus a spiritu suo pendeat.*
[4] Comm. on Deut. 30 : 6, C.R. 25 : 54.
[5] Inst. 4 : 14 : 17. *Spiritus sanctus . . . is est qui Dei gratias secum affert, qui dat sacramentis in nobis locum, qui efficit ut fructificent.*
[6] Comm. on Deut. 30 : 6, C.R. 25 : 54. *Tantum ergo abest quin spiritus sui gratiam resignet Deus sacramentis, ut tota eorum efficacia et utilitas nonnisi, penes spiritum resideat.*
[7] Inst. 4 : 14 : 7. *Ubi et quoties Deo placet.*
[8] C.R. 9 : 23.

the heart, it is in the free and sovereign determination of God
to give the profitable use of the signs to whom He pleases."[1]
"The external administration of Baptism profits nothing, save
only where God pleases it shall."[2]

The power of salvation is thus not "included in" the sacraments. God can use them or refuse to use them as He wills.
Calvin, when speaking in this strain, frequently uses the illustration of an "instrument",[3] for in the use of an instrument the
efficacy depends on the one who uses it, and the simile expresses
the inferiority of the sacrament to Him who uses it. He can call
Baptism and the Lord's Supper "these instruments of the Spirit
(*spiritus organa*) whereby God sanctifies us",[4] and he can use the
similitude in the following way: "Therefore, when the question
is concerning remission of sins, we must seek no other author
thereof but the heavenly Father, we must imagine no other
material cause but the blood of Christ; and when we come to the
formal cause, the Holy Ghost is the chief. But there is an inferior
instrument (*inferius organum*), and that is the preaching of the
Word and Baptism itself. But though God alone works by the
inward power of His Spirit, yet that does not hinder but that He
may use, at His pleasure, such instruments and means (*instrumenta et media*) as He knows to be convenient."[5] The illustration, of course, must never be so pressed as to give rise to the
inference that God is in any way dependent on this instrument
to fulfil even the work for which He has fashioned it. He can do
without an instrument if He wills, or He can do the same work

---

[1]C.R. 9 : 25. Cf. C.R. 12 : 727. *Nam quod ad sacramenta in genere spectat,
neque illis gratiam Dei alligamus, neque ad ea transferimus spiritus sancti officium
aut virtutem, neque in ipsis locamus salutis fiduciam. Diserte enim profitemur
solum Deum esse qui agit per sacramenta, et tam efficaciam spiritui sancto ferimus
acceptam.*

[2]Comm. on Acts 22 : 16, C.R. 48 : 497. There is thus no necessary temporal
simultaneity between the action of the Holy Spirit in making effective the sacraments and the action of the Church. "The advantage which we receive from
the sacraments ought by no means to be restricted to the time at which they
are administered to us" (C.R. 7 : 741; cf. C.R. 9 : 29). "Whenever He sees fit,
God fulfils and exhibits in immediate effect that which He figures in the sacrament. But no necessity must be imagined so as to prevent His grace from
sometimes proceeding, sometimes following, the use of the sign" (C.R. 9 :
118).

[3]*Instrumentum or organum.* Cf. O.S. 1 : 508; C.R. 12 : 727.

[4]Comm. on Lev. 16 : 16, C.R. 24 : 504.

[5]Comm. on Acts 22 : 16, C.R. 48 : 496.

by other means. "The grace of God is not confined (*affixa*) to the sign: so that God may not, if He pleases, bestow it without the aid of the sign."[1]

7. The grace of the sacraments withheld from human arrogance

What has been said in the previous section about the freedom of the Holy Spirit in the operation of the sacraments must not be taken to mean that God will fulfil the promise of His power in the sacraments in an arbitrary and spasmodic manner. We must always bear in mind that God will not mock us by holding forth empty signs. Calvin's aim in reminding us so forcibly of the sovereignty of the action of God in alone making the sacraments effective is to guard against the superstition, pride and presumption that always tend to arise in the perverse heart of man when he deals with the grace of God, and that lead him to imagine that in the means of grace he has acquired some power and mastery over God whereby he can automatically bring God down into the sphere of his need. It is not through God's unwillingness but through this pride that the "ungodly and hypocrites . . . by their perverseness (*perversitas*) either suppress or obscure or impede the effect of divine grace in the sacraments".[2] Though He seeks always to fulfil the promises of His Word, God does not put Himself at the disposal of those who presume upon His grace, and thus at times He causes the sacraments to remain nothing but empty and worthless symbols.

Calvin, moreover, wishes to guard against that ministerial pride whereby man can arrogate to himself the office of God, and can come to imagine that through the office assigned to him in the dispensation of the sacraments he himself is worthy of some honour and has the power to give or withhold the grace of God in the presence of His people. "As there is a strong tendency to fall into superstition, and as men through the pride which is natural to them take from God the honour due to him . . . so Scripture, in order to restrain the blasphemous arrogance, some-

[1]Comm. on Eph. 5 : 26, C.R. 51 : 223.
[2]Inst. 4 : 14 : 7.

times distinguishes ministers from Christ . . . that we may learn that ministers are nothing and can do nothing."[1] "When I baptise, is it as if I had the Holy Ghost up my sleeve to produce at any time? or the body and blood of the Lord to offer to whom I please? It would be sheer presumption to seek to attribute to mortal creatures what belongs to Jesus Christ."[2]

Here, again, we are forced, this time for reasons other than Christological ones, to make a clear distinction in all our thinking on the sacraments between the divine and human actions therein. Calvin in discussing the Baptism of John gives reasons why it was the same as Christian Baptism, and then, pointing out that John could baptise *only with water*, makes the comment: "Hence we deduce the general doctrine, as to what is done in Baptism by men, and what is accomplished in it by the Son of God. To men has been committed nothing more than the administration of an outward and visible sign: the reality dwells with Christ alone."[3] "We maintain that the internal grace of the Spirit, as it is distinct from the external ministration, ought to be viewed and considered separately."[4]

It was earlier pointed out that, owing to the reliability of the promises attached to the sacraments and to the closeness of the relation between the divine grace and the human action, the signs are sometimes justly called by the name of the thing they signify and the heavenly action is spoken of as automatically taking place when the sacrament is administered on earth. This mode of speaking Calvin finds abundantly justified, but at the same time he points out that, owing to the necessity of continually distinguishing the action of God from that of man, Scripture in many places speaks quite differently about the sacraments. It depends upon the potential attitude of those addressed. "Paul, addressing believers, includes communion with Christ in the sacraments. . . . But when he speaks of a preposterous use of the sacraments he attributes nothing more to them than frigid empty figures."[5]

[1]Comm. on John 1 : 26, C.R. 47 : 24.
[2]Serm. on Acts 1 : 4–5, C.R. 48 : 600.
[3]Comm. on Matt. 3 : 11, C.R. 45 : 122. *Hominibus sola externi et visibilis signi administratio commissa est : veritas autem ipsa penes Christum unum residet.*
[4]Inst. 4 : 14 : 17.
[5]Inst. 4 : 14 : 7.

Calvin thus notes a "twofold way of speaking (*duplex loquendi modus*) in Scripture about the sacraments".[1] "It is customary with Paul to treat of the sacraments in two points of view. When he is dealing with hypocrites, in whom the mere symbol awakens pride, he then proclaims loudly the emptiness and worthlessness of the outward symbol, and denounces, in strong terms, their foolish confidence. . . . When, on the other hand, he addresses believers, who make a proper use of the symbols, he then views them in connection with the truth which they represent."[2] We must always therefore be on our guard against over-confidence in sacramental efficacy. This is what destroys their efficacy more than anything else. And even when we read the great and confident language of the New Testament in reference to the sacraments, telling us that Baptism is indeed the "washing away of sins" and the "laver of regeneration", we must remember that "it is not declared what man being minister to the outward sign does; but rather what Christ does. . . . We must always hold fast this distinction lest whilst we deck man too much we take from Christ."[3] "Man cannot deck the earthly elements with the spoils of God."[4]

What has been said in this section has, of course, a very direct bearing on the relation of the faith of the recipient to the effectiveness of the sacrament. Faith alone can create within man the true attitude of fear and trembling which is alone safe and fitting when man is dealing with God. Faith alone can deliver man from that arrogance and presumption into the power of which God refuses to entrust His grace. A fuller discussion of the place of faith in the reception of the sacrament will be undertaken in dealing with the sacraments individually.

8. The effect of the sacraments independent of the *nature of the* presiding minister

It must here, however, be clearly stated that Calvin holds that the efficacy of the sacrament for the faithful cannot be hindered

[1] Comm. on John 1 : 26, C.R. 47 : 24.
[2] Comm. on Gal. 3 : 27, C.R. 50 : 222.
[3] Comm. on Acts 1 : 5, C.R. 48 : 7.
[4] C.R. 9 : 24.

by the unworthiness of the presiding minister. "We hold the ordinance of God to be too sacred to depend for its efficacy on man. Be it then that Judas, or any other epicurean contemner of everything sacred, is the administrator, the spiritual nourishment of the body and blood of Christ are conferred through His hand just as if He were an angel come down from heaven."[1] Jesus, according to Calvin, abstained purposely from administering Baptism to testify to all ages "that Baptism loses nothing of its value when it is administered by a mortal man".[2] Baptism is a "sacred and immutable testimony of the grace of God, though it were administered by the devil, though all who partake of it were ungodly and polluted as to their own persons. Baptism ever retains its own character and is never contaminated by the vices of men."[3]

[1]C.R. 9 : 26.
[2]Comm. on John 4 : 2, C.R. 47 : 78.
[3]Comm. on Amos 5 : 25–6, C.R. 43 : 98.

Chapter XIV

Baptism as Ingrafting into Christ

No single phrase could sum up the meaning which Calvin finds in the sacrament of Baptism. He sees it as a sign of the forgiveness of sins, mortification, renewal, adoption of entrance into the Church and separation from the world. He sees in it a sign of our participation in the victory of Christ over all the powers of evil. His interpretation of the sign is enriched through the parallels he is able to draw between Christian Baptism and circumcision, between the Baptism of the Church and the Baptism of Israel at the Red Sea, between the flood in the days of Noah and the water of the Baptismal font. If a simple definition has to be made, however, his view of Baptism could be best summed up by calling Baptism "the sign of ingrafting into Christ". This certainly makes the best starting point for a study of Calvin's views on this matter.

1. Baptism as a sign of introduction into a new sphere of common life in the body of Christ

In Baptism the baptised individual, as a member of Christ, is uprooted and separated from every corrupt source of life and introduced into a new sphere of common life which the members of Christ share with their exalted Head. Indeed, for Calvin each individual Christian's Baptism is merely the sharing of one common Baptism, which the whole Church shares in common with Christ, Himself baptised in the Jordan, a common Baptism in which the whole Church is made one body and soul in union with Christ. The Baptism of the individual Christian is merely one more act towards the completion of the one Baptism which the Church shares with Jesus Christ. *"One Baptism.* This does not mean that Christian Baptism is not to be ministered more than once, but that one Baptism is common to all; so that by means of it we begin to form one body and soul."[1] Jesus "consecrated and sanctified Baptism in His own body that He might have it in common with us as the foremost bond of union and fellowship which he deigned to form with us; and hence Paul proves us to be the sons of God from the fact that we have put on Christ in Baptism (Gal. 3 : 27)."[2] "For what purpose did the Son of God wish to be baptised? He received Baptism with us, in order to assure believers that they are ingrafted into His body, and that they are *buried with Him in Baptism*, that they may rise to *newness of life* (Rom. 6 : 4). But the end which He here proposes is more extensive *for thus it became him to fulfil all righteousness*. The general reason why Christ received Baptism was, that He might render full obedience to the Father; and the special reason was, that He might consecrate Baptism in his own body, that we might have it in common with Him."[3] As Israel through its Baptism in the Red Sea became the redeemed community sharing one great deliverance, so the Church through its Baptism becomes the one redeemed body that shares not only a great experience of redemption but the one life of the redeemer. Baptism is thus rightly made the sign of initiation by which a Christian is received into the visible Church. "As Baptism is a solemn recognition by which God introduces His children into the possession of life, a true and effectual sealing of the promise, a pledge of sacred union with Christ, it is justly said to be the entrance and reception into the Church."[4] "While I acknowledge that we become members of the Church by Baptism, I deny that they are duly baptised, if they do not belong to the body of the Church."[5]

[1]Comm. on Eph. 4 : 5, C.R. 51 : 191. *Unum baptisma perperam ex hoc loco quidam colligunt, non iterandum esse baptisma inter Christianos . . . sed idem esse omnibus commune, ideoque per ipsum initiari nos in unam animam et unum corpus.*
[2]Inst. 4 : 15 : 6. *Ideo enim baptismum in suo corpore dedicavit et sanctificavit, ut communem eum nobis cum haberat, ceu firmissimum unionis ac'societatis, quam nobiscum inire dignatus est, vinculum. . . .*
[3]Comm. on Matt. 3 : 13, C.R. 45 : 125. . . . *ut baptismum consecrare in suo ipsius corpore, ut nobis communis cum eo esset.*
[4]C.R. 9 : 116. . . . *Merito ingressus et receptio in ecclesiam esse dicitur.*
[5]C.R. 9 : 115.

2. Baptism as a sign of the mortification of the flesh and the forgiveness of sins

"In Baptism the sign is water, but the thing is the washing of the soul by the blood of Christ and the mortifying of the flesh."[1] Nothing is more needful, if the Christian is to receive new life, than that the old life should die, and that all its sources and impulses should be mortified. Baptism is a sign that we enter into life in Christ only through death, that there is a gulf between the realm of nature and the realm of grace, that what is new in Christ is indeed a new creation, and not simply a reshaping and improving, and heightening of the old. "The whole nature which we bring out of our mother's womb . . . is so incapable of the Kingdom of God, that it must needs perish, so far forth as we may be restored to new life."[2] Union with God, according to Calvin, implies continual self-mortification. "The chief good of man is nothing else but union with God; this is attained when we are formed according to Him as our exemplar. . . . Now this confirmation, the Apostle teaches us, takes place when we rest from our works. It hence at length follows that man becomes happy by self-denial. For what else is it to cease from our works, but to mortify our flesh, when a man renounces himself that he may live to God?"[3]

Baptism is, however, more than a mere *sign* of the necessity of mortification. This mortification, so necessary to the enjoyment of newness of life, is a gift of Christ given along with the sign of Baptism. Mortification is the effect of union with Christ. It is not simply something that we do to ourselves, stirred up to self-denying action by the sign of Baptism. It is something that is given us and done for us within our hearts as part of the grace

[1]Comm. on 1 Pet. 3 : 21, C.R. 55 : 268. *In baptismum signum est aqua ; res autem ablutio animae per sanguinem Christi, et carnis mortificatio.*
Cf. 1537 Cat. O.S. 1 : 412. *Le baptesme peculierement represente deux choses : la premiere est la purgation . . . l'autre est la mortification.*
[2]Comm. on Rom. 6 : 6, C.R. 49 : 107. Cf. C.R. 6 : 186. "If our nature requires to be renewed in order to gain admission to the Kingdom of God, it is a sign that it is altogether perverted and cursed. . . . For we are not capable of receiving grace unless we be first divested of all trust in our own virtue, wisdom, and righteousness, so as to condemn everything we possess." Cf. serm. on Deut. 6 : 20–5, C.R. 26 : 487–8.
[3]Comm. on Heb. 4 : 10, C.R. 55 : 48.

of Baptism. Baptism is union with Christ in His death[1] as well
as in His resurrection, and the power by which He died is the
power that enables us also to die. "Christ is not simply viewed
as our example when we speak of the mortification of the flesh;
but it is by His Spirit that we are really made conformable to
His death, so that it becomes effectual to the crucifying of our
flesh."[2] "Christ kills sin in His, by the effect of Baptism,
whereby we are incorporated into His faith. For it is out of
question that we put on Christ in Baptism. Now Paul takes
another principle, namely that we do then indeed grow up into
the body of Christ when His death brings forth fruit in us. Yea
he teaches that this participation of death is principally to be
respected in Baptism[3] . . . whereby it is manifest after we are
received into the grace of Christ, the efficacy of His death appears
straightway."[4] "Christ by Baptism has made us partakers of His
death, ingrafting us into it."[5] "Christ at the same time accom-
plishes efficaciously that mortification, which He there represents,
that the reality may be conjoined with the sign."[6] We have to
receive Baptism, says Calvin, fully persuaded that it is Christ
Himself "who makes us partakers of His death, destroys the
Kingdom of Satan, subdues the power of concupiscence, nay
makes us one with Himself".[7]

The purging out of the old life in mortification is accompanied
by the forgiveness of sins. "When Paul says that we are washed
by Baptism, his meaning is, that God employs it for declaring
to us that we are washed, and at the same time performs what it
represents."[8] "When he says, *wash away thy sins*, by his speech

---

[1]Cf. O.S. 1 : 412. *La mortification de nostre chair, laquelle nous avons eu par
sa mort.*

[2]Comm. on 1 Pet. 4 : 1, C.R. 55 : 270. *Tametsi non simpliciter considerandus
est nobis Christus tanquam exemplum, ubi de carnis mortificatione agitur : sed
spiritu eius vere inserimur in eius mortem, ut ipsa in nobis sit efficax ad cruci-
figendam carnem nostram.*

[3]*Nos in Christi corpus tunc vere coalescere, ubi mors eius fructum in nobis suum
profert. Imo docet hanc mortis societatem praecipue in baptismo spectandam esse.*

[4]Comm. on Rom 6 : 3, C.R. 49 : 105.

[5]Inst. 4 : 15 : 5. *Per baptismum Christus nos mortis suae fecerit participes,
ut in eam inseramur.*

[6]Comm. on Col. 2 : 12, C.R. 52 : 106. *Per baptismum ergo sepelimur cum
Christo, quia mortificationem, quam illic figurat Christus, efficaciter simul peragit ;
ut res signo sit coniuncta.*

[7]Inst . 4 : 15 : 14.

[8]Comm. on Eph. 5 : 26, C.R. 51 : 223. *Quod Baptismo nos ablui docet Paulus,
ideo est, quod illic nobis ablutionem nostram testatur Deus, et simul efficit quod figurat.*

he expresses the force and fruit (*vim fructumque*) of Baptism, as
if he had said *Wash away thy sins by Baptism.*"[1]   "Because
Baptism is the seal by which he confirms to us this benefit . . .
it is worthily said to be given us for the remission of sins."[2]
"We are to receive it as from the hand of its author, being firmly
persuaded that it is Himself who washes and purifies us, and
effaces the remembrance of our faults; that it is Himself who
makes us partakers of His death."[3]   It should be noted here that
forgiveness is accompanied by mortification, by the very power
that subdues within man the very sins from which he is pronounced absolved.   It therefore cannot be said that for Calvin
forgiveness is merely the non-imputation of a man's sins to himself in a verdict that leaves him completely unchanged.[4]

3. Baptism as a sign of renewal and adoption

Union with Christ in Baptism means union with His resurrection as well as with His death.   The sign figures our rising up
out of the water as well as our immersion in its depths.   Ingrafting
into the body of Christ means the gift of new life.   Calvin,
commenting on Paul's discussion of Baptism in Romans 6, says,
"From the participation of His death, He passes conveniently
into the participation of life; because these two hang together in
an inseparable connection; viz. that the old man is to be abolished
by the death of Christ; that His resurrection might restore
righteousness and make us new creatures."[5]   "As a graft has the

---

[1]Comm. on Acts 22 : 16, C.R. 48 : 496. Cf. C.R. 6 : 187. "He has ordained
the symbol of water to figure to us that as by this element bodily defilements are
cleansed, so He is pleased to wash and purify our souls." Cf. C.R. 12 : 728.

[2]Comm. on Acts 2 : 38, C.R. 48 : 53.

[3]Inst. 4 : 15 : 14.

[4]For Calvin the Old Testament sacrament of circumcision pointed to
exactly the same grace as Baptism, viz. forgiveness and mortification. "We
have therefore a spiritual promise given to the fathers in circumcision, similar
to that which is given to us in Baptism, since it figured to them both the forgiveness of sins and mortification of the flesh" (Inst. 4 : 14 : 3 and 4).   By the
coming of Christ what was figured in circumcision was "substantially confirmed" and made permanent; but in the outward ceremony which figured it,
Baptism was substituted for circumcision (comm. on Gen. 17 : 13, C.R. 23 :
243). "Baptism, therefore, is a sign of the thing that is presented (*exhibitae*) to
us which while absent (*absentam*) was prefigured by circumcision" (comm. on
Col. 2 : 12, C.R. 52 : 106; cf. C.R. 6 : 188).

[5]Comm. on Rom. 6 : 4, C.R. 49 : 105. *Nam a mortis societate transitum
merito facit ad vitae participationem : quia haec duo inter se individuo nexu
cohaerent, veterem hominem Christi morte aboleri, ut eius resurrectio iustitiam
instauret, nosque efficiat novas creaturas.* Cf. C.R. 6 : 186.

condition of life and death common together with the tree in which it is grafted, so it is reason we should no less be partakers of the life than the death of Christ."[1] Mortification is a necessary beginning to the Christian life, and indeed for Calvin the Christian life consists mainly of self-denial. But mortification, if it is true mortification in Christ, is always accompanied by a positive renewal of life in Christ. "Here he sets forth the way of ceasing from sin, that renouncing the covetings of men we should study to form our life according to the will of God. And thus he includes here the two ways in which renovation consists, the destruction of the flesh and the vivification of the Spirit. The cause of good living is thus to begin with the former, but we are to advance to the latter."[2]

This new life is the life of sonship of the Father in union with Christ, who was declared the son of God by the resurrection from the dead. Baptism is thus a sign of adoption into the family of God. "In Baptism, the *first* thing to be considered is, that God the Father, by planting us in His Church in unmerited goodness, receives us by adoption into the number of His sons. *Secondly*, as we cannot have any connection with Him except by means of reconciliation, we have need of Christ to restore us to the Father's favour by His blood. *Thirdly*, as we are by Baptism consecrated to God, we need also the interposition of the Holy Spirit whose office it is to make us new creatures."[3]   "In Baptism, we have to do with God, who, not only by testifying His paternal love, pledges His faith to us, so as to give us a sure persuasion of salvation, but also inwardly ratifies by His divine agency that which He figures by the hand of the minister."[4] "By what title can He be their Father if they in no way belong to the Church?"[5] The Church is for Calvin the sphere of the Fatherhood of God, and entrance into it is an entrance into the family of God, Baptism being the sign of adoption.[6] "When we are baptised in the name of our Lord Jesus Christ, we are

[1]Comm. on Rom. 6 : 5, C.R. 49 : 106.
[2]Comm. on 1 Pet. 4 : 2, C.R. 55 : 271.
[3]Comm. on 1 Cor. 1 : 13, C.R. 49 : 318.
[4]C.R. 9 : 116. *Nobis in baptismo cum Deo esse negotium, qui non modo paternum amorem testando fidem nobis suam obligat, ut de salute nostra certo simus persuasi, sed etiam quod per ministri manum figurat, ipse intus sua virtute sancit.*
[5]C.R. 9 : 115.
[6]Cf. Inst. 4 : 15 : 14.

brought into God's household: it is the mark of our adoption. Now, He cannot be our Father, unless we are under His divine protection and governed by His Holy Spirit: as we have an evident witness in Baptism and a greater in the Lord's Supper."[1]

4. Baptism as a sign of our separation from the world to God

Calvin sees clearly the implication of the fact that the Baptismal font stands as a sign of division between the Church and the world, separating those within from those without. The Church is differentiated from the world by the sign of Baptism. Baptism is *burial* with Christ. "We ought not to be led away by wicked examples . . . to mix with the world. This is made evident in Baptism, in which we are buried together with Christ, so that being dead to the world, and to the flesh, we may live to God. On this account, he says that our Baptism is an antitype . . . to the Baptism of Noah . . . so at this day the death which is set forth in Baptism is an entrance into life, nor can salvation be hoped for, except we be separated from the world (*a mundo segregati*)."[2] His use of the flood as a type of Baptism shows that Calvin recognised the eschatological significance of Baptism as denoting participation in the age to come. The fact that we share at present in the resurrection as well as in the death of Christ is a sign that even in this life there is for the Christian a measure of participation in the new age, but for Calvin the unfolding of the resurrection side of the Baptismal action is reserved mainly for the next world. "We will have to observe that our old man must be crucified, if we will be partakers of the

[1]Serm. on 1 Tim. 3 : 14–18, C.R. 53 : 313–4. *Les Sacremens tendent à ceste fin que nous cognoissions que l'Eglise est la maison de Dieu en laquelle il reside* (ibid.).
[2]Comm. on 1 Pet. 3 : 21, C.R. 55 : 267–8. Cf. comm. on Gen. 7 : 17, C.R. 23 : 133. "The method of salvation which we receive through Baptism, agrees with this deliverance of Noah. Since at this time also the world is full of unbelievers as it was then: therefore it is necessary for us to separate ourselves from the greater multitude, that the Lord may snatch us from destruction. It is fitting that we should renounce the world and die, in order that the Lord may quicken us by His Word."
This separation follows naturally from union with Christ. Cf. serm. on 1 Tim. 3 : 14–15, C.R. 53 : 314. *Dieu nous a tellement unis à nostre Seigneur Jesus Christ, qu'il ne veut point que nous soyons separez en façon que ce soit d'avec luy, ni distraits. Quand donc nous avons cela, n'est-il point question d'estre ravis en cest honneur inestimable et que nous apprenions de plus en plus de nous retirer des corruptions de ce monde.*

glory of our Lord Jesus Christ, and rise again with Him . . . we must walk in death before we can come to life. How long will this death continue? As long as we are in this world. Therefore St. Peter says, Baptism is, as it were, a figure of the ark of Noah. For we must be enclosed, as it were, in a grave, being dead to the world, if we will be quickened by the mark of our Lord Jesus Christ. They that would have a resurrection midway, do they not pervert the nature of Baptism, and consequently all the order that God hath set among us? Let us learn that until God shall take us out of this world, we must be as pilgrims in a strange country; and that our salvation shall not be shown us until the coming of our Lord Jesus Christ, for He has become the first fruits of them that slept."[1]

This separation signified in Baptism involves the forsaking of all false lords and the confession of allegiance henceforth to Christ alone as Lord. It is in this context that Calvin thinks of Baptism as our confession of faith before men in his infrequent references to this aspect of the matter. "Observe that the nature of Baptism resembles a contract of mutual obligation; for as the Lord by that symbol receives us into His household, and introduces us among His people, so we pledge our fidelity to Him, that we will never afterwards have any other spiritual Lord. Hence it is on God's part a covenant of grace that He contracts with us, in which He promises forgiveness of sins and a new life, so on our part it is an oath of spiritual warfare (*sacramentum spiritualis militiae*), in which we promise perpetual subjection to Him."[2] "To this Paul referred when he asked the Corinthians whether or not they had been baptised in the name of Christ (1 Cor. 1 : 13), intimating that by the very circumstances of having been baptised in His name they had devoted themselves to Him, had sworn and bound themselves in allegiance to Him before men."[3] "We must be separated from sin and uncleanliness. It is true that all those who are baptised, all who are par-

---

[1]Serm. on 2 Tim. 2 : 16–18, C.R. 54 : 162–3.

[2]Comm. on 1 Cor. 1 : 13, C.R. 49 : 317. *Hic baptismi naturam syngraphae mutui contractus similem esse observa : nam sicut eo symbolo nos Dominus in familiam suam recipit, ac populo suo accenset, ita fidem illi nostram obligamus, neque posthac habeamus alium dominum spiritualem.*

[3]Inst. 4 : 15 : 13. Cf. O.S. 1 : 412. *Il (Baptesme) sert pareillement a nostre confession envers les hommes, car il est une marque par laquelle publiquement nous faisons profession que nous voullons estre anombres au peuple de Dieu.*

takers of the supper of our Lord Jesus Christ, and joined with the faithful, are already separate from unbelievers: no man will say that they are Turks or Heathens. Yet notwithstanding ... we must not have the outward mark only, and boast of our Baptism and profession to serve God, but our life must witness."[1]

[1]Serm. on 2 Tim. 2 : 20 f., C.R. 54 : 183.

Chapter XV
Baptism and Faith

CALVIN, in his treatment of Baptism in the *Institutes*, considers the subject at first quite independently of any later intention of justifying the practice of baptising infants. It is only after having clearly stated his doctrine as to the meaning of the sign when it is applied to those who have faith and maturity that he proceeds to justify the application of the sign to the children of believers. The importance of this subject justifies our devoting a separate chapter to Calvin's views on Baptism and faith.

1. Baptism inefficacious without faith

Calvin is quite clear in stating that Baptism has no efficacy where there is no faith in the recipient and no discernment of the meaning of the sign. "From this sacrament we gain nothing, unless in so far as we receive in faith."[1] "Baptism is an appurtenance of faith, and therefore it is later in order, . . . if it be given without faith whose seal it is, it is both a wicked and exceedingly gross sacrilege."[2] Commenting on the fact that Simon Magus was baptised, Calvin says, "It appears plainly, by this example of Simon, that all men have not that grace given them in Baptism, which is there figured."[3] Calvin appeals for the most diligent

[1] Inst. 4 : 15 : 15.
[2] Comm. on Acts 8 : 37, C.R. 48 : 196. *Est enim baptismus quasi fidei appendix, ideoque ordine posterior est. Deinde si datur sine fide, cuius est sigillum, et impia et nimis crassa est profanatio.*
[3] Comm. on Acts 8 : 13, C.R. 48 : 180. If our Baptism is to be more than a mere empty sign, we must, as it were, baptise ourselves inwardly through continual self-mortification. In his sermon on Deut. 10 : 15–17, C.R. 27 : 49 —where Moses calls on the people who had the outward sign of Circumcision to circumcise also their hearts—Calvin gives the parallel exhortation: *Nous avons desia touché la similitude qui est entre ces deux Sacremens : c'est autant comme si auiourd'huy on nous disoit : que vous soyez baptisez en vos ames. . . . Et comment? . . . L'eau n'est rien, sinon que nous ayons la verité, c'est assavoir que nous soyons tellement plongez sous l'eau, que nous soyons comme en un sepulchre, c'est à dire, que cela nous face mourir en nous-mesmes, tellement que nos affections*

care in bestowing the sacrament only on those from whom there are clear signs either that they have faith or that they are likely to come to full faith. "While I acknowledge that we become members of the Church by Baptism, I deny that they are duly baptised if they do not belong to the body of the Church. It is not ours to confer the sacraments on all and sundry; but we must dispense them according to the rule prescribed by God.[1] Who authorised you Westphal to bestow the pledge of eternal life, the symbol of righteousness and renovation, on a profane person lying under a curse?"[2] "If we do not wish to annihilate Holy Baptism, we must prove its efficacy by newness of life."[3]

2. Where there is no faith present, the sign of Baptism can retain its latent efficacy till it becomes profitable

The absence of faith in the person being baptised does not take away from the fact that through the very administration of Baptism grace may be offered, even though it is not accepted, and the validity of that offer is kept open before the one who has been baptised unless it is deliberately renounced. Calvin admits the ultimate validity of a Baptism that has lain neglected, or whose significance has not been perceived, when later on the baptised person comes to realise the meaning of the sign and claims the grace contained in it. "We acknowledge therefore that at that time Baptism profited us nothing since in us the offered promise, without which Baptism is nothing, lay neglected."[4] "Although by Baptism wicked men are neither washed nor renewed, yet it retains that power so far as related to God, because, although they reject the grace of God, still it is offered to them. But here Paul addresses believers in whom Baptism is always efficacious, in whom, therefore, it is properly connected

ne dominent plus en nous . . . mais que nous souffrions d'estre gouvernez de Dieu, que toutes nos cupiditez charnelles soyent assuietties sous luy. . . . Advisez d'estre baptisez au dedans.

[1]Neque enim nostrum est quibuslibet promiscue largiri sacramenta: sed ad praescriptum Dei exigenda est eorum dispensatio.

[2]C.R. 9 : 115.

[3]Comm. on Titus 3 : 5, C.R. 52 : 431. Nisi velimus exinanire sacrum baptismum, virtutem eius novitate vitae esse comprobandam.

[4]Inst. 4 : 15 : 17. . . . Ablata promissio sine qua baptismus nihil est, neglecta iacebat.

with its truth and efficacy."[1] "We must hold that there is a mutual relation between faith and the sacraments, and hence that the sacraments are effective through faith. Man's unworthiness does not detract anything from them, for they always retain their nature. Baptism is the laver of regeneration, although the whole world should be incredulous (Titus 3 : 5); the supper of Christ is the communication of His body and blood (1 Cor. 10 : 16) although there were not a spark of faith in the world: but we do not perceive that grace which is offered to us."[2]

3. Baptism used by faith a powerful and practical means of grace

Where there is faith Baptism can become in the life of the believer a powerful means of grace, assisting faith, and directing and inspiring Christian living.

Calvin has many helpful remarks to make on the practical use to which the fact of having been baptised can be put by the Christian man. The chief practical use of Baptism is to give us the full assurance of salvation, carrying with it all the effects of renewed and confident Christian living that such an assurance inspires. Baptism saves us by assuring us that we are indeed saved. "*Peter says that Baptism also doth now save us* . . . nor does he mean that it is the cause of salvation, but only that the knowledge and certainty of such gifts are perceived in this sacrament."[3] "Because Baptism is the seal whereby He confirms to us this benefit (i.e. forgiveness of sins) . . . it is worthily said to be given us for the remission of sins. For because we receive Christ's gifts by faith, and Baptism is a help to confirm and increase our faith, remission of sins which is an effect of faith is annexed unto it as unto the inferior means."[4] "Baptism seals to us the salvation obtained by Christ."[5] On the case of Cornelius being baptised Calvin says that he sought in the sacrament "not

---

[1]Comm. on Titus 3 : 5, C.R. 52 : 431. *Tametsi autem neque abluuntur Baptismo impii, neque renovatur, nihilominus vim istam quod ad Deum retinet; quia, utcunque Dei gratiam respuant, illis tamen offertur.* . . .

[2]Comm. on Ezek. 20 : 20, C.R. 40 : 492.

[3]Inst. 4 : 16 : 2.

[4]Comm. on Acts 2 : 38, C.R. 48 : 53. . . . *Fidei autem confirmandae et augendae baptismus adminiculum est, illi, tanquam inferiori medio, remissio peccatorum, quae fidei est effectus, annectitur.*

[5]Comm. on Titus 3 : 5, C.R. 52 : 430.

a fuller forgiveness, but a surer exercise of faith; nay an argument of assurance from a pledge."[1]

Such assurance, obtained by constantly looking at the sign of Baptism set between us and our past and all our enemies, can be a powerful incentive to us to start anew in the effort of the Christian life, and to face all the evils of life with the confidence that will enable us to overcome. "In this way also He promises us in Baptism and shows us a given sign that we are led by His might and delivered from the captivity of Egypt, i.e. from the bondage of sin, that our Pharaoh is drowned; in other words the devil, although he ceases not to try and harass us. But as the Egyptian was not plunged into the depth of the sea, but, cast out upon the shore, still alarmed the Israelites by the terror of his look, though he could not hurt them, so our enemy still threatens, shows his arms and is felt, but cannot conquer."[2] "He declares what is the design of Baptism and of our being washed. It is that we may live in a holy and unblameable manner before God. We are washed by Christ, not that we may return to our pollution, but that we may retain through our life the purity which we have once received."[3] Calvin can urge his hearers to use the power of the grace given to them in Baptism, to restrain them to a life of self-denial even when such a faculty as that of curiosity tends to go out of bounds. "By this we can reprimand these curious folk who ask idle questions, and we can say to them, 'My friend, since you put such useless questions, it is obvious that you have not yet understood what your Baptism means. For then you would know that it means self-denial. But now, instead, you want God to allow your mind to stray everywhere it pleases you.' "[4]

4. Baptism rightly used can cover the whole life of
the Christian from infancy to death

Baptism is never repeated. It is a sign given once to each believer. But the sign given on that one occasion can in later

[1]Inst. 4 : 15 : 15. *Non largiorem remissionem e baptismo petens, sed certiorem fidei exercitationem : imo fiduciae argumentum ex pignore.*
[2]Inst. 4 : 15 : 9.
[3]Comm. on Eph. 5 : 27, C.R. 51 : 224.
[4]Serm. on Acts 1 : 6–8, C.R. 48 : 613.

years still remain continually efficacious if it is properly used
and continually "connected with its truth and efficacy".[1] "The
Papists are much deceived therein who restrain Baptism unto
the nativity and former life, as if the signification and force
thereof did not reach even unto death."[2] The power of Baptism
never "becomes obsolete" (*obsoleta*) in a believer.[3] Thus even
though the believer cannot with any vividness remember the
occasion of his Baptism, nevertheless in remembering the simple
fact that at one time he was baptised his Baptism can in his
time of need yield all the efficacy attached to the sacrament by
the promises of God. "Though the visible figure immediately
passes away, the grace which it testifies still remains."[4] Calvin
points out that "even the use of the Holy Supper which, from
thoughtlessness or slowness of heart, does little good at the time
afterwards bears its fruit".[5] Much more does this apply to
Baptism. "The advantage received from the sacrament ought
not to be restricted to the time of external partaking."[6] He
points out, moreover, that the spiritual grace of which Baptism
is a sign, namely mortification, is not given simply in one great
crisis but is "a continued process" taking place throughout all
the length of the Christian life.[7]

It is true of both the sacraments of the New Testament that
the grace which they confer is not temporally confined to the
moment of their administration.[8] Calvin notes that the Psalmist
in exile, deprived of the privilege of being present in the temple,
nevertheless found grace in remembering the sanctuary, and he
makes the comment: "We may learn by this, when deprived at
any time of the outward means of grace, to direct the eye of our
faith to God in the worst circumstances, and not to forget Him
whenever the symbols of holy things are taken out of our sight.
The great truth, for example, of our spiritual regeneration,
though but once represented to us in Baptism, should remain

---

[1]Comm. on Titus 3 : 5, C.R. 52 : 430–1.
[2]Comm. on Acts 2 : 38, C.R. 48 : 53.
[3]Inst. 4 : 15 : 3.
[4]C.R. 9 : 30.
[5]C.R. 7 : 720.
[6]C.R. 7 : 720; cf. C.R. 9 : 30.
[7]Comm. on Col. 2 : 12, C.R. 52 : 105–6. *Consepulti cum ipso : sepultura enim continuum mortificationis progressum exprimit.*
[8]Cf. pp. 169 f.

fixed in our minds throughout our whole life. The mystical union subsisting between Christ and His members should be a matter of reflection not only when we sit at the Lord's table, but at all other times."[1]

All this has an important bearing on the Baptism of infants. For it shows that, whether or not infant Baptism is justifiable on other grounds, there is humanly speaking nothing to hinder Baptism undergone in the days of infancy, and not remembered in any of its respects, from nevertheless becoming a completely effective means of grace in later life. "We ought to consider that at whatever time we are baptised, we are washed and purified once for the whole of life. Wherefore as often as we fall, we must recall the remembrance of our Baptism, and thus fortify our minds so as to feel certain and secure of the remission of sins."[2] Thus Baptism is bestowed not only with reference to the past but also with reference to the future.[3] It is a sign through which "infants begotten of believers may grow up the more into communion with Christ".[4]

5. A baptised person may be said to carry the seeds of future faith

On the Baptism of Simon (Acts 8 : 13) Calvin comments, "Although the receiving of Baptism profited him nothing then, yet if conversion followed afterward, as some men suppose, the profit was not extinguished nor abolished. For it comes to pass often that the spirit of God works afterwards, after a long time, that the sacraments may begin to show forth their force."[5] The sacraments thus "do good just as a seed when thrown into the ground, though it may not take root and germinate at the very moment, is not without its use. Had it not been sown in this manner it would not in the process of time have sent forth its

---

[1]Comm. on Ps. 63 : 3, C.R. 31 : 594.
[2]Inst. 4 : 15 : 3. Calvin adds that this doctrine is intended only for those who, when they have sinned, groan under their sins.
[3]Inst. 4 : 16 : 3.
[4]C.R. 9 : 114.
[5]Comm. on Acts 8 : 13, C.R. 48 : 180. *Saepe enim fit, ut post longum tempus demum operetur spiritus Dei, quo efficaciam suam sacramenta proferre incipiant.* Cf. C.R. 9 : 117.

shoot. Baptism becomes at last effectual, though it does not work effectually at the same moment at which it is performed."[1] This latent power, which lies in the fact of the sacrament having been given to one who as yet shows no sign of actively profiting from it, may later on through a change of attitude burst forth in living faith, as the latent life from a seed that has long lain hidden in the ground.

It must be carefully noted that in this illustration of Calvin's there is no thought of Baptism as implanting a small seed of eternal life in the heart of a child which might later burst forth and increase. It is the *Baptism* that is the seed. It is in the fact of having been baptised that the future potentiality lies, and not in the heart of the baptised person. It is in the grace of the Holy Spirit that the seed lies, and not in the recipient of what has been an empty sign. In the *Institutes* Calvin calls the Spirit "the seed and root of heavenly life within us".[2] It is most important that all this should be remembered in the interpretation of another passage in the *Institutes*. "Children are baptised for future repentance and faith. Though these are not yet formed in them, yet the seed of both lies hid in them by the secret operation of the Spirit."[3] It is obvious that here Calvin is thinking of the seed of future repentance and faith in the same way as in those other passages under discussion, not as a present possession of the child but as held over the child transcendently and eschatologically through the potentiality of Baptism and the Spirit. To interpret the passage otherwise seems quite absurd. In this sense, however, a baptised person may confidently be said to carry in him the seeds of future faith. Commenting on the Baptism of the eunuch by Philip, Calvin says, "He confesses that Jesus Christ is that redeemer of the world and the *Son of God*. This is the perfect faith whereof Philip spake. . . . Whoever has not this when he is grown up, in vain does he boast of the Baptism of his infancy. For to this end Christ admits infants by Baptism, that so soon as the capacity of their age shall suffer, they may addict themselves to be His disciples, that being

---

[1]C.R. 9 : 118. . . . *Efficax tandem est baptismus, licet non eodem quo peragitur momento efficaciam suam proferat.*

[2]Inst. 3 : 1 : 2. *Spiritus . . . radix ac semen est coelestis vitae in nobis.*

[3]Inst. 4 : 16 : 20. . . . *in futuram poenitentiam et fidem : quae etsi nondum in illis formatae sunt, arcana tamen spiritus operatione utriusque semen in illis latet.*

baptised by the Holy Ghost, they may comprehend, with the understanding of faith, His power which Baptism prefigures."[1]

All this, however, does not justify the application of Baptism to all and sundry in the hope that thereby they may be brought to the faith. The application of Baptism to an adult unbeliever is, of course, with Calvin quite inadmissible; and the application of Baptism to the children of believers must be justified on yet other grounds. Such considerations as have already been brought forward are, however, of weight as practical considerations, in arguing towards a justification of infant Baptism.

6. Infant Baptism justified through the significance of being born within the Church

(i) Before anything else is said under this section, it is important, in order to guard against misunderstanding, that some quotations should be given from Calvin to the effect that *by nature we have no share in the Kingdom of God*. When Calvin speaks of the children of the Church he regards these as being born into the Kingdom of God not by a natural process of propagation but, each generation in its turn, by the free and gracious action of the Spirit of God. "We know that the children of God are not born of flesh and blood, but of the Spirit through faith. Therefore, flesh alone does not constitute the union of brotherhood (i.e. with Christ) . . . the intervention of faith being necessary to our being spiritually ingrafted into the body of Christ."[2] "As a new offspring grows up among men every day, by which the human race is propagated, so the children of God and of the Church are born, who *not from flesh and blood* but by the secret power of God are formed again to be new creatures. By nature we have no share in the Kingdom of God."[3] "We know, therefore, that this promise was not common to all the sons of Abraham who were His offspring according to the flesh, but it was peculiar to the elect alone."[4]

[1]Comm. on Acts 8 : 37, C.R. 48 : 197.
[2]Inst. 2 : 13 : 12. . . . *Fraternam coniunctionem non facit sola caro fides media interponitur, quae nos in Christi corpus spiritualiter inserit.*
[3]Comm. on Isa. 49 : 21, C.R. 37 : 208. . . . *Natura enim a regno Dei alieni sumus.*
[4]Comm. on Ezek. 16 : 60, C.R. 40 : 392.

(ii) With this safeguard in mind we can now go on to show that, in Calvin's view, it is a *most significant matter for a child to be born within the sphere of the Church.*

Calvin regards the children of believers as under the covenant of grace, which in their case allows us to consider the curse of nature as removed, and to bestow on them the sign of Baptism with confidence. Calvin, commenting on the statement of Paul that the children of believers are holy (1 Cor. 7 : 14), asks how this can be reconciled with the statement that we are by nature all the children of wrath (Eph. 2 : 3), and with our being all conceived in sin (Ps. 51 : 3). He answers his own question. "There is a universal propagation of sin and damnation through the seed of Adam, and all, therefore, to a man are included in this curse, whether they are the offspring of believers or of the ungodly; for it is not as regenerated by the spirit that believers beget children after the flesh. The natural condition, therefore, of all is alike, so that they are liable equally to sin and to eternal death. As to the Apostle's assigning here a peculiar privilege to the children of believers, this flows from the blessing of the covenant, by the intervention of which the curse of nature is removed; and those who were by nature unholy are consecrated to God by grace (cf. Rom. 11 : 16). Paul argues that the whole of Abraham's posterity are holy, because God had made a covenant of life with him—if the root be holy, the branches also are holy. Now that the partition is broken down, the same covenant of salvation . . . is communicated to us. But if the children of believers are exempted from the common lot of mankind, so as to be set apart to the Lord, why should we keep them back from the sign? If the Lord admits them into the Church by His Word, why should we refuse them the sign?"[1] "Let it be without controversy that God is good and liberal to His people, that He is pleased, as a mark of His favour, to extend their privileges to the children born to them."[2] "The children of the godly are born

[1]Comm. on 1 Cor. 7 : 14, C.R. 49 : 412. *Omnes igitur ad unum sub hac maledictione includi, sive ex fidelibus sive ex impiis descendant : neque enim fideles liberos generant secundum carnem, quatenus spiritu sunt regenerati. Aequalis est igitur in omnibus naturae conditio, ut sint tam peccato quam aeternae morti obnoxii. Quod autem hic tribuit liberis fidelium speciale privilegium apostolus, id fluit ex beneficio foederis, quo superveniente deletur naturae maledictio : et Deo per gratiam consecrantur qui natura profani erant. . . .*
[2]Inst. 4 : 16 : 15.

the children of the Church, and they are accounted members of Christ from the womb."[1]

Under the Old Covenant, to be born an Israelite by birth meant an entrance into the privileges of the covenant God made with Abraham and his children to a thousand generations. A sign that the child came under these special privileges was given in circumcision. For Calvin, the replacement of the Old Covenant by the New does not overturn this process of transmitting spiritual privilege graciously through natural propagation.[2] Indeed, the New Covenant heightens the privileges granted to the children of the Church under the promise made to Abraham, and widens the sphere of their application. "Did not God transmit his grace from parents to children, to admit new born infants into the Church would be a mere profanation of Baptism. But if the promise of God under the law caused holy branches to proceed from a holy root, will you restrict the grace of God under the Gospel, or diminish its efficacy by withholding the testimony of adoption by which God distinguishes infants?"[3] The gracious promises of the New Covenant, held out therefore to the children of the Church, may be sacramentally sealed by bestowing Baptism upon them. "Since the Lord, immediately after the covenant was made with Abraham, ordered it to be sealed in infants by an outward sacrament, how can it be said that Christians are not to attest it in the present day, and seal it in their children?"[4] It is therefore, according to Calvin, "of some value to descend from saints and men beloved of God",[5] though this value arises, not from any natural cause, but only from a gracious ordinance of God. Indeed it almost seems as if Calvin is attributing a sacramental value to natural propagation within the Church, basing his authority for this on the promise given to Abraham. He can speak of a "hereditary right, as it were", of children to partake of the religious privileges of their

---

[1]Comm. on Acts 8 : 37, C.R. 48 : 197. *Piorum liberos dico ecclesiae filios nasci, et ab utero reputari in Christi membris.*

[2]Cf. comm. on Matt. 28 : 19, C.R. 45 : 823, and serm. on Deut. 7 : 7–10, C.R. 26 : 526. *Quand Dieu a une fois planté sa parolle, qu'il continue ceste grace-la, non seulement iusques à la mort de ceux auxquels il a parlé, mais en leurs enfans, et en leur lignage.*

[3]C.R. 9 : 115.

[4]Inst. 4 : 16 : 6.

[5]Comm. on Rom. 9 : 5, C.R. 49 : 173.

parents, for God "not only receives each of us individually into His favour, but also herein associates with us our offspring".[1] At the same time he is careful to point out that the holiness of the fathers "flowed exclusively from God's election and not from their own nature".[2]

Calvin admits the practical difficulties in his position. Many under this arrangement are baptised and do not come to faith. "I grant, indeed, that many which are the children of the faithful, according to the flesh, are counted bastards, and not legitimate, because they thrust themselves out of the holy progeny through their unbelief."[3] Indeed, Calvin says that the "greater part is without the covenant through their own unbelief".[4] There was, however, a remnant in Israel, and there is a "special elect" among the children of the elect, and the door of Baptism must not be closed to them through the offence that others cause. "This in no way hinders the Lord calling and admitting the seed of the godly into the fellowship of grace. And although the common election be not effectual in all, yet may it set open a gate for the special elect."[5] Those born of the holy seed have at least to give a decision about the Baptism which has been bestowed on them, and thus it is that even in them Baptism is efficacious in bringing them to decision. If their decision is a rejection of grace, it brings judgment and condemnation upon themselves.

Calvin points out that it was a very high honour to be born in Israel. For Christ, though He honoured all mankind when He "connected Himself to us by a community of nature",[6] nevertheless bound Himself by a closer tie to the chosen race.[7] But in many of the Jews "the blessing of kindred was separated from

---

[1]Comm. on Ps. 103 : 17, C.R. 32 : 82. *Non tantum singulos in gratiam recipit, sed quasi hereditario iure posteros associat, ut eiusdem sint adoptionis consortes.* No doubt Calvin lived at a time when such arguments had even greater force than to-day. Cf. comm. on Deut. 29 : 10, C.R. 25 : 48. "Surely since slavery passes on by inheritance, it ought not to appear absurd that the same right should be assigned to God which mortal men claim for themselves."

[2]Comm. on Ps. 105 : 6, C.R. 32 : 100. Cf. on Rom. 11 : 16, C.R. 49 : 221.

[3]Comm. on Acts 3 : 25, C.R. 48 : 76.

[4]Comm. on Ezek. 16 : 21, C.R. 40 : 355.

[5]Comm. on Acts 3 : 25, C.R. 48 : 76.

[6]Comm. on Rom. 9 : 5, C.R. 49 : 174. *Quum se naturae communione nobis copulavit.*

[7]Ibid. Calvin speaks of this as, *Arctum coniunctionis vinculum.*

piety", and instead of profiting them it turned to their greater condemnation.[1] To be born in the sphere of the Church brings us into this specially close relation to Christ which can either profit us or turn to our greater condemnation. Calvin makes the sad comment that "many . . . become degenerate".[2] Indeed it is only those "who do not turn aside from the faith of the parents" who inherit the blessings of the covenant made with the fathers.[3] The solemn word of Moses to the children of Israel applies with no less relevance to the children of Christian parents. *Ye stand this day all of you before the Lord your God* (Deut. 29 : 10). "Though they did not receive by faith the promised salvation, nor, on the other hand, renounce the flesh so as to dedicate themselves to God, still they were bound to God under the same obligations under which their parents laid themselves."[4]

The arguments set forth in this section are Calvin's main arguments for infant Baptism. Speaking of the promise to Abraham, *I will be the God of thy seed,* Calvin can say, "If God do not ingraft into the body of His people those on whom He bestows this high privilege, not only is injury done to His Word, but infants ought to be denied the external sign."[5]

7. The possibility of early regeneration in children

Calvin's views on infant Baptism are to an extent influenced by his very strong views on the likelihood of early regeneration of Christian children. That some are saved in the earliest infancy is to him "without question".[6] Calvin can express great wonder over the care of God for an unborn child.[7] That John was filled with the Holy Ghost from his mother's womb is "a proof of what He might do in others". "Christ was sanctified from the earliest infancy that He might sanctify His elect in Himself at any age without distinction."[8] "It were dangerous to

[1] Ibid.
[2] Comm. on 1 Cor. 7 : 14, C.R. 49 : 413; cf. on Ps. 102 : 28, C.R. 32 : 74.
[3] Comm. on Ps. 102 : 28, C.R. 32 : 74.
[4] Comm. on Deut. 29 : 10, C.R. 25 : 48. . . . *Eodem iure Deo fuisse devinctos quo se patres obligabant.*
[5] C.R. 9 : 102.
[6] See e.g. Inst. 4 : 16 : 16–17.
[7] Cf. comm. on Ps. 22 : 10, C.R. 31 : 226.
[8] Cf. Inst. 4 : 16 : 17–18.

deny that the Lord is able to furnish them (i.e. infants) with knowledge of Himself in any way He pleases."[1] In his comments on Jesus' blessing of the children by laying on them His hands, Calvin insists that this could not have been a "trifling and empty sign" nor could the prayers of Jesus on that occasion have been "idly wasted in air". He argues that the children must have been given "purity", and renewed by the Spirit. But he denies that this was given through faith. Here is an exception to the rule that men become reconciled to God by faith alone. He makes the speculation that "*Infants* are renewed by the Spirit of God according to the capacity of their age, till the power which was concealed in them grows by degrees and becomes fully manifest at the proper time".[2] Calvin can go even further. He grants to Westphal the possibility that God might regenerate some infants when they are baptised. At the same time he is emphatic that this cannot be a "universal rule".[3] "We hold that Baptism, instead of regenerating them or saving them, only seals the salvation of which they were previously partakers",[4] for "infants may obtain salvation without Baptism".[5] This regeneration and salvation is given to infants outside the usual dispensation, which requires faith. "Though faith be requisite in those who are grown up, yet this is falsely transferred to infants whose condition is quite different."[6]

[1]Inst. 4 : 16 : 18.
[2]Comm. on Matt. 19 : 14, C.R. 45 : 535. *Renovari Dei spiritu pro aetatis modulo, donec per gradus suo tempore quae in illis occulta est virtus augescat, et palam refulgeat.* In view of accusations sometimes made against Calvin that he would consign helpless infants to eternal damnation, his further comment should be noted: "To exclude from the grace of redemption those of that age would be too cruel."
[3]C.R. 9 : 118. *Catholicum theorema.*
[4]C.R. 9 : 101.
[5]Ibid.
[6]Comm. on Acts 8 : 37, C.R. 48 : 197. Beckmann (*Vom Sakrament bei Calvin*, p. 97) notes that in the 1st Edition of the *Institutes* Calvin asserted, with Luther, faith in the child as an element in Baptism, but later dropped the idea.

Chapter XVI

The Lord's Supper as Communion with Christ

1. The Words of institution to be interpreted
according to sacramental usage

THE word of Jesus in instituting the Supper must be interpreted, according to Calvin, not literally but sacramentally, according to the normal usage of Scripture, whereby the sign is given the name of the thing signified. As against the Lutherans who interpreted the "is" in *this is my body* literally, Calvin insists on the validity of an analogical interpretation. "This . . . is our wall of brass—as Christ instituted a sacrament, His words ought to be expounded sacramentally (*sacramentaliter*) according to the common usage of scripture. For a kind of perpetual rule in regard to all sacraments is that the sign receives the name of the thing signified."[1] "To give a literal meaning to the words, *this is my body,* we hold to be contrary to the analogy of faith, and we at the same time maintain that it is remote from the common usage of scripture where sacraments are spoken of."[2] With a sigh of exasperation he utters against his opponents, "I wish they were as literary as they long to be literal!"[3]

But Calvin with equal insistence rejects any purely figurative interpretation of the words of institution, which might make the sacrament nothing more than an empty symbolic action. Jesus was not speaking in a purely figurative way when He instituted the Supper. There is a mystery of sacramental union here indicated that lifts His language far above being legitimately called "figurative" without any qualification. "Let our opponents, therefore, cease to indulge their mirth in calling us Tropists, when we explain the sacramental mode of expression according

---

[1] C.R. 9 : 195; cf. pp. 161 ff.

[2] C.R. 9 : 514. *Literalem sensum in his verbis : Hoc est corpus meum, negamus fidei analogon esse : et simul asserimus a communi scripturae usu remotum, quoties de sacramentis agitur.*

[3] C.R. 9 : 198. *Utinam tam literati essent, quam literales esse appetunt.*

to the common use of scripture."[1] He reminds us that "on account of the affinity which the things signified have with their signs, the name of the thing signified is given to the sign figuratively indeed but very appropriately".[2] "When the cup is called a *participation*, the expression, I acknowledge, is figurative, provided that the truth held forth in the figure is not taken away, or, in other words, provided that the reality itself is also present."[3] Thus the word "is" in the words of institution denotes not a relation of identity, such as would hold in the proposition "Christ *is* the Son of God", but a sacramental union.[4] The bread is called body "in a sacramental manner (*sacramentali modo*)".

The account of the institution of the Lord's Supper is thus one of the "obscure passages" of Scripture which must be interpreted according to the rule of faith, derived from the study of the clearer parts of Scripture. "Brevity is obscure," says Calvin. The longer sentences dealing with this mystery better elucidate the meaning than the shorter sentences.[5] Therefore, to understand the sacrament, we do not begin with a minute study of the words of institution. It is better to begin with such a passage as the sixth chapter of John, where Jesus had it in mind to give a body of teaching which would afterwards illuminate what He meant in instituting the Lord's Supper. "When our Lord instituted the supper, He spoke briefly, as is usually done in federal acts, whereas in the sixth chapter of John, He discourses copiously and professedly on that mystery of sacred conjunction of which He afterwards held forth a mirror in the sacraments."[6] Therefore we must not lay too much stress on what a grammarian might have to say concerning the exact meaning of the sentences of institution. This is rather the field of the theologian. "The

---

[1]Inst. 4 : 17 : 21. Cf. C.R. 9 : 184. *Neque ubicunque de sacramentis agitur, dicimus referri parabolas, sed modos discendi esse sacramentales, quibus exprimi debet inter rem et signum analogia.* Calvin here insists that there is a "*mysterium, cui conveniant sacramentales loquendi formae*".

[2]Inst. 4 : 17 : 21. *Propter affinitatem, quam habent cum suis symbolis res signatae, nomen ipsum rei fateamur attributum fuisse symbolo : figurate id quidem, sed non sine aptissima analogia.*

[3]Comm. on 1 Cor. 10 : 16, C.R. 49 : 464. *Iam vero quod vocatur calix communicatio, figuratam loquutionem esse fateor : modo non tollatur figurae veritas, hoc est ; modo res quoque ipsa adsit.*

[4]Inst. 4 : 17 : 20.

[5]Inst. 4 : 17 : 20.

[6]C.R. 9 : 200.

words of Christ are not subject to the common rule and ought not to be tested grammatically."[1] A too literal interpretation would actually lead to a statement of doctrine which would endanger the real presence of Christ in the sacrament.

2. The gift communicated

Calvin freely and frequently admits that his answer to the question What is given in the sacraments? is exactly the same as those of the Lutherans and the Roman Church. He agrees with his opponents that the flesh of Christ is given in the sacrament. "Westphal insists on the presence of the flesh in the supper. We do not deny it."[2] "The controversy with us is not as to reception but only the mode of reception."[3] "That we really feed in the Holy Supper on the flesh and blood of Christ, no otherwise than as bread and wine are the aliments of our bodies, I freely confess."[4] Calvin can also say that the *materia* or *substantia* of the Supper is the flesh, or the body of Christ; or he can say that the *materia* or *substantia* of the sacrament is "Christ with His death and resurrection".[5] Or he can define the gift simply as "Christ".[6] He frequently speaks of the Lord's Supper as leading us by the hand to Christ. He can also say that in the gift is the "substance of Christ's flesh". "I confess that our souls are truly fed by the substance of Christ's flesh."[7] "Those who exclude the substance of vivifying flesh and blood from the communion defraud themselves of the use of the supper."[8] "When, therefore, we speak of the communion which believers have with Christ, we mean that they communicate with His flesh and blood not less than with His Spirit, so as to possess thus the whole Christ."[9]

[1]Inst. 4 : 17 : 20. *Christi verba non subiici communi regulae, nec debere ad grammaticam exigi.*
[2]C.R. 9 : 73.
[3]C.R. 9 : 74. *Non de sumptione sed tantum de sumptionis modo.*
[4]C.R. 20 : 73.
[5]Inst. 4 : 17 : 11. *Christum cum sua morte et resurrectione.*
[6]Inst. 4 : 17 : 33, 4 : 14 : 16.
[7]C.R. 9 : 70. *Substantia carnis Christi.*
[8]C.R. 9 : 76.
[9]O.S. 1 : 435. *Itaque quum de communione quam cum Christo fideles habent, loquimur non minus carni et sanguini eius communicare ipsos intelligimus quam spiritui ut ita totum Christum possideant.*

Calvin, by using such terms, seems anxious to assert both the reality and the wholeness of the gift of Christ in the Lord's Supper. The whole of Christ is given in the sacrament. It is not only His Spirit and His divine nature that are mediated to us but also His humanity, and indeed the whole humanity which was centred in His earthly body, including that body which was such a necessary part of Him. "The sacraments direct our faith to the whole, not to a part of Christ."[1] Union with Christ, for Calvin, means a participation in the whole Christ. It means union with His human nature as well as His divine nature. "He is both God and man in us," says Calvin, "for, in the first place, He makes us alive by the power of His Holy Spirit: then He is man within us, for He makes us participate in the sacrifice He offered for our salvation, and declares to us that it is not without cause that He has appointed His flesh to be our food indeed, and His blood our drink indeed."[2] The communion which we have with Christ in the Lord's Supper is thus communion with the whole Christ in both His natures—divine and human.

This communion can be ours only through participation in His flesh. For the flesh is the "channel which conveys to us that life, which dwells intrinsically, as we say, in His divinity, and in this sense it is called life-giving because it conveys to us that life which it borrows from another quarter".[3] "Two things are to be sought for in Christ, that we may find salvation in Him: His divinity and His humanity. His divinity contains in itself His power, righteousness and life which are communicated to us by His humanity."[4] Thus everything we need for our sanctification and righteousness is to be found near to us, in our own nature, in the humanity of the Son of God, "in our own flesh".[5] Where the humanity of Christ is, there is the divinity; but apart from the humanity we cannot communicate with the divinity. What is therefore effected in the Lord's Supper is communion

---

[1]Inst. 3 : 11 : 9. *Fidem nostram ad totum Christum non dimidium dirigunt.*

[2]Serm. on Luke 2 : 1-14, C.R. 46 : 966. *Mesmes il est et Dieu et homme en nous.* Cf. O.S. 1 : 508. *Il n'est pas seulement question que nous soyons participans de son Esprit : mais il nous fault aussi participer à son humanité, en laquelle il a rendu toute obeissance à Dieu.*

[3]Comm on John 6 : 51, C.R. 47 : 152; cf. pp. 145 ff.

[4]Comm. on Rom. 1 : 3, C.R. 49 : 9. *Duo sunt in Christi quaerenda, quo salutem in ipso reperiamus : divinitas et humanitas. Divinitas in se continet potentiam, iustitiam, vitam, quae per humanitatem nobis communicantur.*

[5]Comm. on Heb. 2 : 11, C.R. 55 : 28.

with the whole Christ, with all His gifts, so that He becomes wholly ours, and we are pledged as wholly His. But since this communion cannot take place without participation in His flesh, it is necessary in the definition of the gift given in the Supper to stress this aspect of the communion. "There is no other way in which He can become ours than by our faith being directed to His flesh. For no man will ever come to Christ as God who despises Him as man; and therefore, if you wish to have any interest in Christ, you must take care, above all things, that you do not disdain His flesh."[1]

The whole Christ is *really given* in the sacrament. "We say that the substance of Christ's flesh and blood is our spiritual life, and that it is communicated to us under the symbols of bread and wine: for Christ, in instituting the Supper, promises nothing falsely, nor mocks us with a vain show, but represented by external signs what He has really given us."[2] "The truth of God, therefore, in which I can safely rest, I embrace without controversy. He declares that His flesh is the meat, His blood the drink, of my soul. I give my soul to Him to be fed with such food. In His sacred Supper He bids me take, eat and drink His body and blood under the symbols of bread and wine. I have no doubt that He will truly give, and I receive."[3]

· Since the gift in the sacrament is the whole Christ, there is given along with Him those benefits that He has won for His people through His death and resurrection.[4] Thus through our participation in the body of Christ through the Supper there flows to us righteousness, forgiveness, sanctification, indeed all the blessings that are the fruit of His death, for the Lord's Supper is in figure not only a participation in His body but also in His death. It is "a mirror in which we may contemplate Jesus Christ crucified to take away our offences and raised again to deliver us from corruption".[5] "The body which was once offered for our

[1]Comm. on John 6 : 56, C.R. 47 : 156. *Negaret se aliter nostrum fieri, nisi quum fides nostra in eius carnem dirigitur. Neque enim ad Christum Deum unquam perveniet qui hominem negligit. Quare si tibi vis aliquid cum Christo esse commune, cavendum imprimis est ne carnem eius fastidias.*

[2]C.R. 20 : 73.

[3]Inst. 4 : 17 : 32.·

[4]Cf. pp. 145 f.

[5]O.S. 1 : 506–7. *Un miroir auquel nous contemplions nostre Seigneur Jesus crucifié pour abolir noz faultes et offences, et resuscité pour nous delivrer de corruption.*

salvation we are enjoined to take and eat, that while we see ourselves made partakers of it, we may safely conclude that the
virtue of that death will be efficacious in us."[1] Here again it
must be remembered that just as we cannot communicate in the
divinity of Christ apart from His humanity, so neither can we
participate in the blessings won for us through His death apart
from real communion with the whole human nature in which He
won for us these benefits. "Christ," says Calvin, "does not
simply present to us the benefit of His death and resurrection,
but the very body in which He suffered and rose again."[2]

We have seen that Calvin often calls the whole Christ the
"matter" or "substance" of the sacrament. He sometimes, in
addition, uses other distinct terms to describe what is given in
the sacrament.[3] He can speak in various contexts of the "virtue",
or "fruit", or "efficacy", or "effect" of the Sacrament,[4] and he
can use these terms *as if* they signified something that is different
from the matter or substance of the Sacrament. "Christ descends
to us by His virtue."[5] "A life-giving virtue from Christ's flesh
(*vim ex Christi carne vivificam*) is poured into us by the Spirit."[6]
He speaks of "the spiritual efficacy which emanates from the
body of Christ".[7] In a similar way, and referring to the same
gift given in the Supper, he can call it the "efficacy and fruit"
(*efficacia et fructus*) of Christ's nativity, death and resurrection.[8]

Immediately Calvin uses such terms and phrases, however, he
usually adds some kind of qualification or parallel statement
which shows clearly that this *virtus* or *efficacia* is not something
different or separate from the substance of the body of Christ.

---

[1]Inst. 4 : 17 : 1. *Corpus ergo, quod oblatum semel est in salutem nostram,
iubemur accipere et comedere, ut dum huius fieri nos videmus participes, vivificae
illius mortis virtutem certo statuamus in nobis efficacem fore.*

[2]Comm. on 1 Cor. 11 : 24, C.R. 49 : 487.

[3]Cf. O.S. 1 : 507, Inst. 4 : 17 : 11.

[4]Cf. Inst. 4 : 17 : 11. "When attempting familiarly to explain its nature,
I am accustomed to set down three things—the thing meant, the matter which
depends on it, and the virtue or efficacy consequent upon both. The thing
meant (*significatio*) consists in the promises which are in a manner included in
the sign. By the matter or substance I mean Christ, with His death and resurrection. By the effect (*effectum*), I understand redemption, justification, sanctification, eternal life, and all the other benefits which Christ bestows upon us."

[5]C.R. 9 : 72. *Christum ad nos sua virtute descendere.*

[6]Comm. on 1 Cor. 11 : 24, C.R. 49 : 487.

[7]Comm. on Heb. 9 : 11, C.R. 55 : 110. *De virtute spirituali quae inde ad nos
manat.*

[8]Inst. 4 : 17 : 5. Cf. 4 : 17 : 11, 4 : 17 : 33.

To say that a life-giving virtue from Christ's flesh is poured into us by the Spirit, is the same thing as saying that our souls are nourished by the substance of the body of Christ.[1] "Because I say . . . that Christ, while remaining in heaven, descends to us by His virtue . . . I deny that I am substituting something different (i.e. from the body) which is to have the effect of abolishing the gift of the body."[2] The "substance" and the "virtue" or "efficacy" are not disjoined in reality[3] and can merely be distinguished in thought for the sake of giving expression to a mystery that is inexpressible. Having given this warning, however, Calvin can go as far as to say, "This power and faculty of vivifying might not improperly be said to be something abstracted from the substance."[4]

Calvin's purpose in using such language is to express the fact that the "substance" of the flesh is not to be thought of as "material" substance. In his use of these additional terms he is seeking to avoid the impression that there is "anything earthly or material"[5] in the body and blood of Christ as given in the Sacrament. He also seeks by their use to avoid the impression of any "carnal mixture" (carnalis mixtura)[6] of the flesh of Christ with the recipient, emphasising that the flesh of Christ, though we feed on it, actually "remains at a great distance from us and is not mixed with us".[7] Calvin has, however, no doubt about the reality and concreteness of the gift of the body and blood of Christ. His paradoxical statements are due to the necessity of giving an explanation where silence and wonder are more fitting attitudes.

3. The communication of the gift

It is when he enters into a discussion upon the mode of communication and reception of Christ's body that Calvin finds

[1]Cf. comm. on 1 Cor. 11 : 24, C.R. 49 : 487.
[2]C.R. 9 : 72. *Nego me substituere aliquid diversum, quod donationem corporis aboleat, quia modum donationis simpliciter explico.*
[3]Cf. O.S. 1 : 507. *Il faut donc que la substance soit conioncte avec (i.e. avec l'efficace), ou aultrement il n'y auroit rien de ferme ne certain.*
[4]C.R. 9 : 522. *Vis et facultas vivificandi non incommode abstractum aliquid a substantia dici posset.*
[5]Comm. on Heb. 9 : 11, C.R. 55 : 110. *Nihil in illis terrenum velel ementale.*
[6]C.R. 9 : 521.
[7]Comm. on 1 Cor. 11 : 24, C.R. 49 : 487. Cf. C.R. 16 : 430. *Nomen vero efficaciae in hunc finem usurpo, non ut confundam quae distingui debent, sed ut transfusionem substantiae excludam.*

himself in decided opposition to the Lutherans and Romanists. "No one of us denies that the body and blood of Christ are communicated to us. But the question is, what is the nature of this communication?"[1]

(i) *The body of Christ,* in which He wrought our redemption and apart from which we cannot be saved, in being communicated to us in the sacrament *remains,* throughout the participation, *in heaven,* beyond this world, *and retains all its human properties.*

The body of Christ can no longer be thought of as present on this earth in any form or condition. The testimony of the Scripture is quite final. Christ, according to Peter, is contained in heaven till He appears to judge the world.[2] The logic of the angels is incontrovertible. "He is not here," they said. "He is risen." "The assigning of one place is the denial of any other."[3] His body cannot be present in two places at once. When Christ said, *Me ye have not always,* He spoke of His bodily presence. It is true that He also said *Lo I am with you alway,* but these latter words refer to His divinity and majesty, and not to His humanity or flesh. With regard to that which was born of a virgin, apprehended by the Jews and nailed to the cross, wrapped in linen clothes, laid in the tomb and manifested in the resurrection, the final word is *Me ye have not always.* The body of Christ which is the "substance" of the sacrament is in heaven, remains there throughout the sacramental action, and will remain there till the end of the world.[4]

For Calvin, heaven must at least be spoken of as a place quite distinct from this earth. We must not "quibble" with him about "heaven" being merely a state of "boundless glory" or an "invisible habitation".[5] The cloud was interposed at the ascension as a sign that He had really been removed from this world and not merely been made invisible. "When it is said that Christ is taken up into heaven; here is plainly noted the distance of place. . . . It is evident that the heaven whereunto Christ was received is opposite from the frame of the world; therefore it

[1]C.R. 9 : 31–2.
[2]C.R. 9 : 72.
[3]C.R. 9 : 221. This Calvin calls, *dialectica angelica.*
[4]Inst. 4 : 17 : 26. Cf. serm. on 1 Cor. 10 : 15–18, C.R. 49 : 667.
[5]C.R. 9 : 77.

necessarily follows that if He be in heaven, He is beyond the world."[1] "Heaven we regard as the magnificent palace of God, far outstripping all this world's fabric."[2] In thinking of Christ as dwelling in heaven we must not, therefore, imagine Him "as dwelling among the spheres and numbering the stars", for Heaven is "beyond this created world".[3]

But though we must speak in this way of "heaven", as a word which "denotes a place higher than all the spheres",[4] Calvin admits that this is an inappropriate way of speaking about something for which we have no better language. "Not that it is literally a place beyond the world, but we cannot speak of the Kingdom of God without using our ordinary language."[5] Calvin, moreover, admits that "philosophically speaking" there is no place above the skies, but it is quite obvious that he refuses to have his views on this matter determined by philosophy, and in the same passage in which he makes this philosophical concession he insists that heaven is "a place . . . distant . . . in point of space . . . from earth".[6]

In heaven the body of Christ retains all its human properties unimpaired. The body of Christ in heaven is still flesh, without having the attributes of divinity so transform it that its true nature as flesh is destroyed. "Flesh must therefore be flesh, and spirit spirit; each under the law and condition in which God has created them. Now the condition of flesh is, that it should have one certain place, its own dimensions, its own form."[7] Christ, even in giving incorruption and glory to the flesh which He assumed and has now taken to heaven, has not, as Augustine

---

[1]Comm. on Acts 1 : 11, C.R. 48 : 13. *Nam quum assumptus in coelum dicitur Christus, certe aperte notatur locorum distantia. . . . Coelum quo sublatus est Christus, universae mundi machinae opponi, planum est. Ergo ut in coelo sit, extra mundum esse oportet.*

[2]C.R. 9 : 79. *Coelum est magnificum Dei palatium, toto mundi opificio superius.*

[3]Comm. on Eph. 4 : 10, C.R. 51 : 195. *Extra mundum hunc creatum.* Cf. C.R. 20 : 75. *Ex communi scripturae usu coelum nomino, quidquid extra mundum est.*

[4]Ibid. *Illic coelum significat locum sphaeris omnibus superiorem.*

[5]Ibid. *Non quod proprie locus sit extra mundum : sed quia de regno Dei loqui nisi more nostro non possumus.*

[6]C.R. 7 : 743. *Corpus Christi . . . finitum est, et coelo, ut loco, continetur : necesse est a nobis tanto locorum intervallo distare, quantum coelum abest a terra.* Cf. C.R. 12 : 728.

[7]Inst. 4 : 17 : 24. *Carnem igitur carnem esse oportet : spiritum spiritum : unumquodque qua a Deo lege et conditione creatum est. Ea vero est carnis conditio, ut unocertoque loco, ut sua dimensione, ut sua forma constet.*

says, destroyed its nature and reality.[1] Therefore we cannot doubt that Christ's heavenly body is bounded according to the invariable rule,[2] "in the dimensions of a human body".[3]

It follows from what has been said in this section that there can be no physical descent[4] of the body of Christ in any way into the elements, since it remains in heaven; nor can the body become invisibly present on earth, since visibility is a "proper and inseparable quality of body".[5] The body of Christ, throughout the action of the Supper, remains "contained in heaven where it was once received", and it is "altogether unlawful to bring it back under those corruptible elements or to imagine it everywhere present".[6] Therefore in our formulation of the doctrine of the Supper we must allow Christ to remain in His heavenly glory,[7] and seek His body "in heaven which has received Him till He appear to judgment".[8]

(ii) *Communion with the body of Christ is effected through the descent of the Holy Spirit, by whom our souls are lifted up to heaven,* there to partake of the life transfused into us from the flesh of Christ.

"The Lord by His Spirit bestows upon us the blessing of being one with Him in soul, body, and spirit. The bond of connection is therefore the Spirit of Christ, who unites us to Him and is a kind of channel by which everything which Christ has and is, is derived to us."[9] "Christ, then, is absent from us in respect of His body, but dwelling in us by His Spirit, He raises us to heaven to Himself, transfusing into us the vivifying vigour of His flesh just as the rays of the sun invigorate us by His vital warmth."[10] "No extent of space interferes with the boundless energy of the Spirit, which transfuses life into us from the flesh of Christ."[11] "It is not necessary that He should descend from heaven in order

---

[1]Ibid. *Naturam et veritatem non abstulit.*
[2]Cf. Inst. 4 : 17 : 12.
[3]Inst. 4 : 17 : 30. *Circumscribi humani corporis mensura.*
[4]But cf. § iv infra.
[5]C.R. 9 : 230.
[6]Inst. 4 : 17 : 12.
[7]C.R. 49 : 488.
[8]C.R. 9 : 33.
[9]Inst. 4 : 17 : 12; cf. pp. 152. f.
[10]C.R. 9 : 33. *Spiritu autem suo in nobis habitans, in coelum ad se ita nos attollit ut vivificum carnis suae vigorem in nos transfundat, non secus ac vitali solis calore per radios vegetamur.*
[11]C.R. 37 : 48.

to assist us, since He can assist us by the grace of His spirit as if He stretched out His hand from heaven. For He who, in respect of His body, is at a great distance from us not only diffuses the efficacy of His Holy Spirit through the whole world but actually dwells in us."[1] "By the virtue of His spirit and His own divine essence, He . . . unites us with Himself in one body so that that flesh, although it remain in heaven, is our food."[2] "Christ, though absent in the body, is nevertheless not only present with us by divine energy which is everywhere diffused, but also makes His flesh give life to us."[3]

Calvin does not expect us fully to understand this. He does not fully understand it himself. What he claims to happen is incomprehensible to human reason. "It is certainly a proof of truly divine and incomprehensible power that how remote so ever He may be from us, He infuses life from the substance of His flesh and blood into our souls so that no distance of place can impede the union of head and members."[4] In another place, stating the same doctrine, Calvin says, "He who feels not that in these few words are many miracles is more than stupid."[5] We may not understand how all this happens, but if we are to begin to understand the sacrament we must believe it. "No slight insult is offered to the Spirit if we refuse to believe that it is by His incomprehensible power that we communicate in the body and blood of Christ."[6]

(iii) Partaking of the flesh of Christ in the supper is thus a *heavenly action*, in which the flesh is *eaten in a spiritual manner*.

"The supper being a heavenly action (*coelestis actio*)," says Calvin, "there is no absurdity in saying that Christ, while remaining in heaven, is received by us."[7] This heavenly action involves the receiving of life from the substance of Christ's flesh

---

[1]Comm. on Matt. 28 : 20, C.R. 45 : 826. *Modus autem praesentiae, quam Dominus suis promittit, spiritualiter intelligi debet : quia ut nobis auxilietur, non opus est e coelo descendere, quum spiritus sui gratia, quasi extenta manu e coelo, iuvare nos possit. Nam qui secundum corpus immensu locorum spatio a nobis distat, non modo per totum mundum spiritus sui efficaciam diffundit, sed in nobis quoque vere habitat.*

[2]C.R. 9 : 76.

[3]C.R. 9 : 76.

[4]C.R. 9 : 193.

[5]Inst. 4 : 17 : 24.

[6]Inst. 4 : 17 : 33. *Incomprehensibili eius virtute, ut cum carne et sanguine Christi communicemus.*

[7]Comm. on 1 Cor. 11 : 24, C.R. 49 : 488.

into our souls.[1] But this participation in the flesh of Christ is a spiritual participation. We must not imagine any "transfusion of substance".[2] "Although Christ breathes life into us from His flesh and blood we deny that there is any mingling of substance, because while we receive life from the substance of the flesh and blood, still the entire man Christ remains in heaven."[3] This manner of participation, in which there is a real communication and a real gift substantially given without any mingling or transfusion of substance, Calvin can call a spiritual participation as opposed to participation in a natural or carnal manner. "Spiritual then is opposed to carnal eating. By carnal is meant that by which some suppose that the very substance of Christ is transfused into us. . . . In opposition to this it is said that the body of Christ is given to us in the Supper spiritually."[4] "We must not dream that His substance passes in a natural manner into our souls; but we eat His flesh when, by means of it, we receive life."[5] "The flesh . . . gives life because the Holy Spirit pours into us the life which dwells in it."[6]

(iv) The presence of the body of Christ in the Supper, though it may be called a *real presence* and a *descent of Christ* by the Spirit, is nevertheless also a *"celestial mode of presence"* and leads to no localisation of the body of Christ on earth, no inclusion of it in the elements, no attachment of it to the elements.

Calvin appears at times to be inconsistent in his statements about the Supper. He can in one place deny that Christ "descends to the earth" in the Supper. "Christ ceases not to offer Himself to be enjoyed by His faithful followers though He descend not to the earth;"[7] and yet in other places he speaks freely about Christ as descending through the Supper. His meaning depends on the context and the course taken by the argument which has led up to the making of his statement. It

---

[1]C.R. 9 : 47.
[2]Ibid. *Substantiae transfusio*, cf. C.R. 9 : 70.
[3]C.R. 9 : 182. *Etsi autem vitam ex carne sua et sanguine nobis inspirat Christus, negamus tamen fieri commixtionem substantiae : quia dum vitam ex substantia carnis et sanguinis percipimus, manet tamen integer homo Christus in coelo.*
[4]C.R. 9 : 522.
[5]Comm. on Matt. 26 : 26–8, C.R. 45 : 708. *Neque enim somniandum est, naturalem fieri substantiae eius transitum in animas nostras, sed comeditur a nobis eius caro, dum ex ea vitam percipimus.*
[6]Ibid. *Vitam quae in ea residet, Spiritus sanctus in nos diffundit.*
[7]C.R. 9 : 68.

must be noted that whenever he allows the statement to be made that Christ "descends" he always insists on adding an almost paradoxical qualification to it. Indeed, he will admit that Christ descends only after he has made it clear that Christ remains entire in heaven, and even then he insists that it is always a spiritual and heavenly descent. "Christ descends by His Spirit."[1] "In no other way than a celestial mode of presence may His flesh descend to us."[2] The same paradoxical way of speaking occurs, it is to be noted, in his statements about the presence of Christ in the Supper. It is a real presence of the flesh of Christ, for Calvin does not think of the real presence as apart from His body. But it is also a "celestial" mode of presence, and, for Calvin, the "celestial" is that which is removed from this earth. "Westphal insists on the presence of the flesh of Christ in the Supper; we do not deny it *provided He will rise upwards with us by faith*."[3]

Calvin denies the "substantial presence", as affirmed by Westphal, because he thinks that such a phrase implies "transfusion of substance".[4] "Though I have classed among the opinions to be rejected the idea that the body of Christ is really and substantially present in the Supper, this is not at all repugnant to a true and real communion, which consists in our ascent to heaven, and requires no other descent of Christ than that of spiritual grace."[5] Calvin also denies any local presence. "Participation . . . does not require a local presence."[6] "Let there be . . . no local enclosing or carnal infusing."[7] Calvin will not "place Christ in the bread."[8] Nor does he approve of the Lutheran attempt, based on the doctrine of ubiquity, to

[1] Cf. C.R. 16 : 677. *Christum secundum corpus suum in coelo manens, admirabili spiritus sui virtute ad nos descendit, et simul nos ad se sursum attollit.*

[2] C.R. 9 : 172. *Non nisi coelestem esse praesentiae modum, ut minime ad nos caro ipsa descendat.* Cf. serm. on Luke 1 : 31–5, C.R. 46 : 82. Where Calvin, speaking of the reign of Christ without special reference to the Sacrament, says, *Il faut donc qu'il regne, c'est à dire, qu'estant au ciel, neantmoins il descende à nous, non point en chair, mais par la puissance inestimable de son Esprit.*

[3] C.R. 9 : 73.

[4] C.R. 9 : 70. *Substantialem praesentiam.* But he adds, "*The fiction of transfusion being taken out of the way,* it never came into my mind to raise a debate about the term substance."

[5] C.R. 9 : 73.

[6] Comm. on 1 Cor. 11 : 24, C.R. 49 : 488. *Commuinicatio localem praesentiam non flagitat.*

[7] C.R. 9 : 34. *Modo ne qua localis fingatur inclusio, vel carnalis infusio misceatur.*

[8] Inst. 4 : 17 : 31. *In pane.*

"include Christ under the bread."[1] He insists that we can have the gift of the body of Christ really given to us otherwise than by such a process. "To the giving of the body, its presence (i.e. locally and substantially) is not at all requisite",[2] for we "equally gain His presence when He raises us to Himself".[3] This means then a "local absence", but even in using such a phrase Calvin hastens to add that it "does not exclude the mystical and incomprehensible operation of the flesh".[4]

Thus, for Calvin, there is a descent of Christ, but it is a "mode of descent by which He raises us up to Himself".[5] It is by the Holy Spirit that He descends, but it is Christ who descends and not the Holy Spirit alone. "We say that Christ descends to us, as well by the external symbol as by His Spirit."[6] The descent of Christ to be present in the Supper is an event of grace, in which the Lord really presents Himself as an objective reality, yet never in such a way that man, holding Him "there", can treat Him simply as a part of this world under his own power.

It may be noted that when Calvin has been insisting on the substantial nature of the gift he stresses that it is given in a spiritual manner. In the mystery of the Supper it is "the very flesh of Christ"[7] that is given, the body which He once offered to the Father",[8] for Christ has not outlived the days of His flesh in the sense that He has not put off the reality of His manhood.[9] But this "very flesh of Christ" in the mystery of the Supper is "no less a spiritual matter than eternal salvation".[10] The flesh of Christ is "a living and spiritual temple", a "heavenly food to nourish souls".[11]

---

[1]Inst. 4 : 17 : 30. *Sub pane includere*, though with qualification Calvin allows the use of "sub", e.g. body and blood of Christ are "offered and exhibited" (O.S. 1 : 435) and "represented" (Inst. 4 : 17 : 3) *sub pane et vino.* Cf. C.R. 9 : 34 and C.R. 20 : 73.

[2]C.R. 9 : 80–1.

[3]Inst. 4 : 17 : 31.

[4]C.R. 9 : 509.

[5]Inst. 4 : 17 : 16. *Modum descensus, quo nos ad se sursum evehit.*

[6]Inst. 4 : 17 : 24. *Tam externo symbolo, quam spiritu suo, ad nos descendere.*

[7]Inst. 4 : 17 : 33.

[8]C.R. 9 : 48.

[9]Cf. comm. on Heb. 5 : 7, C.R. 55 : 61–3.

[10]Inst. 4 : 17 : 33. *Ipsa Christi caro in mysterio coenae non minus spiritualis res est, quam aeterna salus.*

[11]Comm. on Heb. 9 : 11, C.R. 55 : 110.

4. The reception of the gift

In the Lord's Supper the body of Christ is received by *faith*.
"I deny that men carry away more from the sacrament than they
collect in the vessel of faith."[1] But the body of Christ is really
received by faith.

No one can deny that the Lord's Supper in an impressive
Christian act which, apart from any supernatural mystery, must
have the effect, as a mere spectacle contemplated by the participant, of making the meaning and reality of the Cross so vivid
that faith is strengthened merely by beholding the action. Calvin
admits the power of this aspect of the Lord's Supper. "We
deny not that in the Supper the sacrifice of Christ is so vividly
exhibited (*monstretur*) as almost to set the spectacle of the Cross
before our eyes."[2] "The Supper is a mirror which represents to
us Christ crucified."[3] But he could not agree with those who
found in this aspect of the Supper its main significance, and who
equated the action of eating and drinking in the Supper to this
mental process. Some, for example, held that the main effect
of the Supper was that the believing man had his mind turned
towards the death of Christ and its meaning, in thankfulness and
wonder, his "intellect and imagination"[4] being stimulated by the
"sight" (*aspectus*) set before his eyes. Thus no gift is given in
the sacrament other than a mental picture as a stimulus to a
faith that is already the perfect possession of the believer. Thus
"to eat is merely to believe". Calvin opposes such a view. He
denies "that the life which we obtain from Him is obtained by
simple knowledge (*simplici cognitione*)"[5] or that "we stop short
at the sight or mere knowledge (*nuda notita*) of Him".[6]

Calvin, moreover, insists that there is a difference between
eating and believing, since the mere act of believing does not
necessarily imply any real spiritual event as taking place through

---

[1] Inst. 4 : 17 : 33. *Nego, plus referre homines ex Sacramento, quam vase fide
colligunt.*
[2] Inst. 4 : 18 : 11.
[3] Comm. on 1 Cor. 11 : 24, C.R. 49 : 489. *Coena speculum est quod Christum
crucifixum nobis repraesentat.* Cf. comm. on 1 Cor. 11 : 23.
[4] Inst. 4 : 17 : 11.
[5] Inst. 4 : 17 : 5.
[6] Inst. 4 : 17 : 11.

the sacrament, or any real breaking in upon the sphere of this world of a heavenly reality. Faith is like a vessel which receives something other than itself.[1] It is an attitude of soul which by the grace of God enables a transaction to take place between Christ and the soul whereby something else is effected besides the giving of faith. In participating in the Supper faith connects itself with something outside of itself and other than a mere idea, and, in so doing, effects in the spiritual realm a real communication between itself and the earthly reality such as that figured in the act of eating the bread. Thus Calvin says that the eating is more than simply believing. Eating is for him the effect or fruit of faith. Faith can receive Christ, and this is more than having faith.[2] "According to them, to eat is merely to believe; while I maintain that the flesh of Christ is eaten by believing, because it is made ours by faith, and that eating is the effect and fruit of faith."[3] "Though the act of eating the flesh of Christ is different from believing in Him; yet we ought to know that it is impossible to feed on Christ in any other way than by faith because the eating itself is the consequence of faith."[4] "My writings everywhere proclaim that eating differs from faith inasmuch as it is an effect of faith."[5] "I distinctly affirm that those who receive the promise by faith become truly partakers of Christ, and are fed by His flesh. Therefore the eating of Christ is something else than the receiving of the promise."[6] "Although the Apostle teaches that Christ dwells in our hearts by faith (Eph. 3 : 17), no one will interpret that dwelling to be faith."[7]

In the controversy whether or not the unbelieving participant in the Lord's Supper receives the body of Christ Calvin denies the possibility of such a reception. "That Christ is received without faith is no less monstrous than that a seed should germinate in the fire."[8] "Christ cannot be disjoined from His Spirit. Hence . . . His body is not received as dead or even

[1]Inst. 3 : 11 : 7.
[2]Cf. Inst. 3 : 11 : 7.
[3]Inst. 4 : 17 : 5.
[4]Comm. on Matt. 26 : 26 ff., C.R. 45 : 708.
[5]C.R. 9 : 75.
[6]C.R. 9 : 75.
[7]Inst. 4 : 17 : 5.
[8]C.R. 9 : 27.

inactive, disjoined from the grace and power of His Spirit."[1]
But this does not mean that the body of Christ is not present to
unbelievers and indeed offered to unbelievers in the sacrament,
though they are incapable of receiving the gift. "God ceases
not to send rain from heaven though the moisture is not received
by stones and rocks."[2] Calvin holds that "the body of Christ
is given indiscriminately to good or bad"[3] but there is no receiving except by faith. "The body of Christ is offered and given to
unbelievers as well as believers, and . . . the obstacle which prevents enjoyment is in themselves."[4] The view stated by Westphal was that unbelievers receive the body of Christ but are
not nourished by it, receiving it rather to their own damnation. Calvin rejects this view as degrading to the dignity of
Christ.

Calvin approves quotations from Augustine to the effect that
"a sacrament is separated from the reality by the unworthiness
of the partaker, so that nothing remains but an empty and useless
figure",[5] but this does not mean that Christ has not been chal-
lenging the unbeliever in the very sacrament which has become
thus emptied of its meaning. A decision has been made by one
who was confronted with a heavenly reality, and the unbeliever
becomes guilty of the body and blood of Christ in this very
decision that has made the sacrament an unmeaning sign. He is
guilty not because he has eaten unworthily but because he has
refused and despised the grace of God which was there. This
Calvin regards as a much more serious matter than had there
been a real communication of Christ to the unworthy in the
Supper. As against those who complained that if Christ were
not actually eaten by the unworthy in the sacrament, they could
not really be condemned for despising His grace, Calvin replies:
"It will be said that Paul would not charge those who eat
unworthily with being guilty of the body and blood of the Lord
were they not also made partakers of Christ—Nay, I should
rather say, that if access was given them to Christ, it would

[1]Comm. on 1 Cor. 11 : 27, C.R. 49 : 491.
[2]C.R. 9 : 89.
[3]C.R. 9 : 157.
[4]C.R. 9 : 90.
[5]Inst. 4 : 14 : 15. *Sacramentum sic a sua veritate separari indignitate sumentis
ut nihil maneat praeter inanem et inutilam figuram.*

exempt them from all guilt. But now as they foully trample upon
the pledge of sacred communion, which they ought to receive
with reverence, it is not strange that they are counted guilty of
His body and blood."[1]

5. The Eucharistic sacrifice

Calvin denies that in the Lord's Supper man offers anything
to God by way of a propitiatory sacrifice. Man's part is to
receive with thanksgiving all that is offered in the one completed
sacrifice on the Cross. "Christ did not offer Himself once, in
the view that His sacrifice should be daily ratified by new
oblations, but that by the preaching of the Gospel and the dispensation of the sacred Supper, the benefit of it should be communicated to us."[2] He rejects even the idea that the Supper is
"not a repetition but an application" of the once-given sacrifice.
The Supper is "a gift of God which was to be received with
thanksgiving", not a price paid to God. "As widely as giving
differs from receiving, does sacrifice differ from the sacrament of
the Supper."[3] Jesus in the words of institution said *take*, "hence
those that offer a sacrifice to God have some other than Christ as
their authority, for we are not instructed in these words to perform a sacrifice".[4] "In the Holy Supper there is not an offering
of bread and wine . . . but a mutual participation (*communicatio
inter fideles*) of it among the faithful."[5] "The Lord has given us a
table at which we may feast, not an altar on which a victim may
be offered; He has not consecrated priests to sacrifice, but ministers to distribute a sacred feast."[6]

But Calvin finds two types of sacrifices distinguished in the
Old Testament ritual. Firstly the propitiatory sacrifice, the

---

[1]C.R. 9 : 27.

[2]Inst. 4 : 18 : 3.

[3]Inst. 4 : 18 : 7. But in receiving the gift we apply the once-offered sacrifice
to ourselves. Cf. serm. on 1 Cor. 10 : 15–18, C.R. 49 : 665, where Calvin says
that the bread and wine are sanctified to their special use, *pour monstrer . . .
que nous soyons unis à luy, pour ce que la mort et passion qu'il a enduree nous
appartient, et que ce sacrifice-là . . . auiourd'huy nous est imputé et attribué, comme
si nous l'avions offert nous mesmes, en nos propres personnes.*

[4]Comm. on 1 Cor. 11 : 24, C.R. 49 : 485–6.

[5]Comm. on Ps. 110 : 4, C.R. 32 : 165; cf. also on Heb. 7 : 10.

[6]Inst. 4 : 18 : 12.

character of which he denies to the Sacrament; and secondly "another class of sacrifice", offered as "a symbol and attestation of religion and divine worship", such as gifts offered "by way of thanksgiving, to testify gratitude to God for benefits received".[1] Calvin saw that an essential aspect of the Lord's Supper was the presence of such a willing sacrifice of gratitude to God on the part of the communicants, and He expressed Himself willing, to give this sacrificial and spontaneous response of thanksgiving the name of "Eucharistic" sacrifice. Even in the first edition of the *Institutes* he suggests that the "Eucharist" is as suitable a name for the sacrament as the "Lord's Supper".[2]

Under the heading of this Eucharistic sacrifice, which Calvin sees as an "indispensable"[3] part of the Lord's Supper, "are included all the offices of charity, by which, while we embrace our brethren, we honour the Lord Himself in His members; in fine all the prayers, praises, thanksgiving, and every act of worship which we return to God".[4] It is to be noted that in this Eucharistic response Calvin insists on the presence not only of prayers and praises but also of the "faith and charity" which are stirred up within us by the grace given in the Sacrament.[5] "That worthiness which is commanded by God consists especially in faith, which places all things in Christ, nothing in ourselves, and in charity, which though imperfect, it may be sufficient to offer to God, that He may increase it, since it cannot be fully rendered."[6]

Thus, for Calvin, the sacrament is indeed an "agape" in which the members of Christ "cherish and testify" towards each other that mutual charity the bond of which they see in the unity of the body of Christ. "As often as we communicate in the symbol of our Saviour's body, as if a pledge were given and received, we mutually bind ourselves to all the offices of love, that none of us may do anything to offend his brother, or omit anything by which he can assist him when necessity demands, and oppor-

---

[1]Inst. 4 : 18 : 13.
[2]O.S. 1 : 136. *Vocamus autem vel coenam Domini, vel eucharistiam, quod in ipso et spiritualiter benignitate Domini pascimur et nos illi suae beneficentiae gratias agimus.*
[3]Inst. 4 : 18 : 17.
[4]Inst. 4 : 18 : 3.
[5]Inst. 4 : 17 : 42.
[6]Inst. 4 : 17 : 42.

tunity occurs."[1] While Calvin thus stresses the "love" aspect
of the Eucharistic offering,[2] he also names prayer as a truly
acceptable offering. "Though He can derive no benefit from us,
yet he regards prayer as a sacrifice and so much as the chief
sacrifice that it alone can supply the place of all the rest. . . . If
we wish to sacrifice to God, we must call on Him and acknowledge His goodness by thanksgiving, and further, we must do
good to our brethren; these are the true sacrifices."[3]

Calvin, with this in mind, can speak of the "necessity that
each of us should offer Christ to the Father. For although He
only, and that but once, has offered Himself, still a daily offering
of Him, which is effected by faith and prayers, is enjoined to
us."[4] This offering is, however, quite different from anything
accomplished through the elements of the sacrament, and is the
offering "whereby alone we apply to ourselves the virtue and
fruit of Christ's death".[5] Anything we offer to God in the
Supper comes not from ourselves but is His own gift, given to
us through that very grace that receives us into such blessed
communion. "Wherefore the best and only which we can bring
to God is to offer Him our own vileness, and, if I may so speak,
unworthiness, that His mercy may make us worthy; to despond
in ourselves that we may be consoled in Him; to humble ourselves that we may be elevated by Him; to accuse ourselves that
we may be justified by Him; to aspire, moreover, to the unity
which He recommends in the Supper; and, as He makes us all
one in Himself, to desire to have all one soul, one heart, one
tongue."[6]

[1]Inst. 4 : 17 : 44. Cf. serm. on 1 Cor. 10 : 15–18, C.R. 49 : 668. *Ainsi que de
plusieurs grains de blé, il y aura un pain faict, nous devons estre unis ensemble,
comme une personne et l'Esprit de Dieu nous doit tellement gouverner, qu'il y ait
et dilection, et humanité et sollicitude, et tout ce qui est requis à une droite et
parfaite amour.*

[2]Cf. esp. O.S. 1 : 146.

[3]Comm. on Heb. 13 : 16, C.R. 55 : 194.

[4]Comm. on Num. 19 : 2, C.R. 24 : 333. *Toti autem populo datur mandatum
offerendi : quia, ut ablutionis simus participes, necesse est ut Christum quisque Patri
offerat. Etsi enim ipse unus, et quidem semel, se ipsum obtulit, quotidiana tamen
oblatio, quae fit per fidem et preces, nobis mandatur.*

[5]Ibid. *Qua tantum nobis applicamus vim et fructum mortis Christi.*

[6]Inst. 4 : 17 : 42.

Chapter XVII

Calvin's Justification of his Doctrine of the Lord's Supper

1. Calvin's claims for his doctrine

THERE are many lines along which Calvin argues in order to justify his doctrine of the Lord's Supper against the other prevalent doctrines of his time, and fair assessment of the value of his doctrine can be made only after some study of the controversy which forced him to make his exact statements. In this chapter an attempt will be made not to outline the history of the controversy, or to give any close definitions of the views which Calvin opposed, but to indicate some of the main considerations that were in Calvin's mind in formulating his own doctrine.

(i) *Clarity achieved*

Calvin's aim, throughout the course of the controversy in which this subject involved him, was to achieve clarity of thought and expression on a matter which was to him of the utmost importance and in which he saw the majority of other men going hopelessly astray through inability to think things out to logical and consistent conclusions, and through a love for obscurity which arose from a Satanic fear of the truth. He laments, indeed, that controversy over this central matter should have shown the Church so tragically rent at the very place where her unity should be most openly shown, but the cure for such division does not, for Calvin, lie in avoiding frank and frequent discussion of points of controversy. Such controversy is a necessary step towards achieving that clarity of thought on this matter which alone can dispel the mists of obscurity by which Satan for centuries has sought to deprive the Church of a proper use of this inestimably valuable gift of God. "Knowledge of this great mystery is most necessary, and, in proportion to its importance, demands an accurate exposition."[1] The pastors of Zürich, with whom Calvin collaborated in framing the "Mutual Consent", were reflecting truly Calvin's own views in their prefatory letter to this document, in which they commend Calvin for his efforts to remove offences and to renew the tottering peace and tranquillity of the Church through endeavouring "by simple and accurate explanation to render Christian doctrine more and more plain and clear to men, and rid their minds of vague causes of discord".[2] "We see no more convenient way and method of ending religious controversy or suppressing vague suspicions where no discrepancy exists, or, in fine, of removing offences which sometimes arise in the Church of God from contrariety of opinion in the teachers, than by mutually explaining their mind with the greatest openness both by speech and writing."[3]

Calvin expresses a certain amount of satisfaction with the clarity which he claims to have achieved on this matter. "In this doctrine of the sacraments, their dignity is highly extolled, their use plainly shown, their utility sufficiently proclaimed, and moderation in all things duly maintained; so that nothing is attributed to them which ought not to be attributed, and nothing denied them which they ought to possess."[4] He claims for himself that he never employed ambiguous forms of expression which might suggest anything other than the exact meaning he wished to convey.[5] He challenges his opponents to attain like clarity, and insinuates that they "dare not explain the matter clearly lest they be thought to subscribe to our view".[6]

(ii) *Mystery preserved*

Calvin's claim that his doctrine is clear does not imply that he has in any way sought to explain away the sacrament, or to diminish the mystery acknowledged in the sacrament by centuries of Christian worship. The clarity which he claims to have

[1]Inst. 4 : 17 : 1.
[2]C.R. 7 : 746.
[3]C.R. 7 : 745.
[4]Inst. 4 : 14 : 17. *Id quum docetur de sacramentis, et eorum dignitas praeclare commendatur, et usus aperte indicatur, et utilitas abunde praedicatur, et modus in iis omnibus optimus retinetur. . . .*
[5]C.R. 9 : 51. *Nunquam me ambigua loquendi forma captiose aliud prae me tulisse quam sentirem,* c.f. C.R. 9 : 71.
[6]C.R. 9 : 21.

achieved is a clarity in thinking *round* the sacrament but not in thinking *through* it. For at the heart of the sacrament Calvin freely recognises that there takes place a miracle which it is quite beyond human thought to understand. Here, in the sphere where God operates in the sacrament, we are standing before a mystery which man dare not try to explain, but at which man can only wonder. If clarity of thought is to be justified here, it must be indulged in only for the purpose of refuting the false views and false suggestions that would take away the mystery or obscure the true nature of the incomprehensible miracle. In his commentary on Matthew Calvin speaks of the amazement of the women, awed by the earthquake, standing gazing at the sign of the empty tomb and listening to the word of the angels proclaiming the miracle of the resurrection. Then he immediately draws a parallel between the attitude of mind shown in this scene by the women reverencing the mystery of this new and mighty work of God which surpassed all the expectations of men, and the attitude of mind that is alone fitting when the outward signs of the sacrament are exhibited before our eyes. For in this event too, according to Calvin, we are confronted, no less than the amazed spectators at the empty tomb, with the tokens of a hidden miracle of the power of God.[1] Calvin held that one of the main purposes of the thanksgiving prayer of Jesus before He distributed the supper amongst His disciples was to arouse their minds to the fact that they were in the presence of "so lofty a mystery". Calvin himself therefore seeks to approach the discussion of the theological problems connected with the sacrament with the reverence and humility due to such a mystery, regretting that such discussion is necessary, though acknowledging the necessity for it: "—if indeed it be lawful to put this great mystery into words, a mystery which I feel and therefore freely confess that I am unable to comprehend with my mind, so far am I from wishing anyone to measure its sublimity by my feeble capacity . . . and though the mind is more powerful in thought than the tongue in expression, it is too overcome and overwhelmed by the magnitude of the subject. All that remains is to break forth in admiration of the mystery . . . I will, however, give a summary of my view as best I can, not doubting its

[1]Comm. on Matt. 28 : 2, C.R. 45 : 795.

truth and therefore trusting that it will not be disapproved by pious breasts."[1]

Therefore Calvin repudiates with indignation the charge of Westphal that he is "wedded to human reason" and that his formulation of his doctrine on the sacrament is dictated by the demands of common sense and human philosophy seeking to "measure" the mysteries of God.[2] "Is it common sense that tells us to seek the immortal life of the soul from human flesh? Is it natural reason which declares that the living virtue of Christ's flesh penetrates from heaven to earth and is in a wondrous manner infused in our souls? Is it in accordance with philosophical speculation, that a lifeless earthly element should be the effectual organ of the Holy Spirit? Is it from natural principles we learn that whatever the minister pronounces with his lips according to the word of God, and figures by a sign, Christ inwardly performs? Certainly did we not regard the holy Supper as a heavenly mystery, we should not attribute to it effects so distinguished and incredible to carnal reason."[3] "It is not philosophy that dictates to us either that human flesh is endued with spiritual virtue so as to give life to our souls or that this life breathes from heaven, or that we gain effectual possession of the same life under the external symbol of bread. Nothing of this kind lies within the reach of common sense or can come forth from schools of philosophy. Hence it appears how careful we are to extol the mystery of the supper as transcending the reach of human intellect."[4]

Calvin claims, on the contrary, that his own doctrine of the Lord's Supper actually involves, on the part of God, a greater miracle of wonder and power than any of the doctrines he opposed. "That we detract in any way from the power of God, is so far from being true, that our doctrine is the loudest in extolling it."[5] He asserts that "nothing is more contrary to

[1]Inst. 4 : 17 : 7. *Si tamen ullis verbis complecti tantum mysterium liceat, quod ne animo quidem satis me comprehendere video et libenter ideo fateor, ne quis eius sublimitatem infantiae meae modulo metiatur. . . .*
[2]C.R. 9 : 194–5.
[3]C.R. 9 : 94.
[4]C.R. 9 : 78–9. . . . *Nihil tale vel communis sensus capiet, vel ex philosophicis scholis prodibit. Unde etiam apparet, quam magnifice supra humani ingenii captum coena mysterium extollere nobis curae sit.*
[5]Inst. 4 : 17 : 25.

nature", and "nothing more incredible",[1] than the doctrine he expounds. "It is too high a mystery either for my mind to comprehend or my words to express. I rather feel than understand it (*experior magis quam intelligam*)."[2]

(iii) *Absurdities avoided*

Though Calvin is so anxious to safeguard the mystery of God's action in the sacrament, he nevertheless refuses to admit any doctrine that might seem to assert on the part of God any miracle that is absurd or abhorrent to the moral sense or inconsistent with other aspects of the Christian faith. He will admit everything his opponents say in their desire to give as literal a meaning to the words of institution as possible and to magnify the supernatural power of God, up to the point where they begin to assert any doctrine savouring of such absurdity. He agrees with his opponents in extolling the supernatural character of God's gracious action in the Supper; "only", he adds, "I reject the absurdities which appear unworthy of the heavenly majesty of Christ."[3] Against Westphal he says, "I deny not that there is a mystery passing human comprehension in the fact that Christ in heaven feeds us on earth with His flesh, provided that He refuses not to obviate the absurdities which He carelessly passes by with His eyes shut."[4] "We declare that we reverently embrace what human reason repudiates. We only shun absurdities abhorrent to piety and faith."[5] At one point he brings forth this syllogism: "A doctrine carrying many absurdities with it is not true. The doctrine of the corporeal presence of Christ is involved in many absurdities; therefore it follows that it is not true."[6]

It is along this line that Calvin argues against the assertion that the body of Christ was locally present in the elements. Such a doctrine involves the idea that the body of Christ can exist without definite dimensions and without being confined to any one particular place, having indeed the ability to be in several

[1] Inst. 4 : 17 : 24. *Nihil magis praeter naturam—nihil magis incredibile.*
[2] Inst. 4 : 17 : 32. Cf. C.R. 9 : 471.
[3] Inst. 4 : 17 : 32.
[4] C.R. 9 : 81.
[5] C.R. 9 : 514. *Reverenter nos amplecti quod repudiat humana ratio. Tantum absurditates fugimus, a quibus abhorret sensus ipse pietatis et fidei.*
[6] C.R. 9 : 233.

different places at one time. Calvin replies that for the flesh of
Christ to assume such properties would mean that it had really
ceased to be flesh, and he points out the folly of expecting such an
absurd miracle. "Fool! why do you require the power of God
to make a thing at the same time flesh and not flesh? It is just
as if you were to insist on His making light to be at the same time
light and darkness."[1] In the same way he disposes of the suggestion of a twofold body, from one aspect visible and occupying
its place in heaven, and at the same time immortal, invisible and
immense.[2] This latter idea involves the ludicrous suggestion
that in the first celebration of the sacrament Christ had such a
twofold body. "We do not open our arms to embrace such a
monster,"[3] says Calvin, expressing his reaction to such doctrines. How could the Apostles, he asks, "have been so ready to
believe what is repugnant to all reason, viz. that Christ was
seated at table under the eye and yet was contained invisible
under the bread?"[4] Such views are as revolting to him as the
Roman doctrine of transubstantiation. "We deem it no less
absurd to place Christ under the bread or couple Him with the
bread, than to transubstantiate the bread into the body."[5]

The moral absurdity involved in the doctrine of the local
presence of Christ's body is no less abhorrent to Calvin than the
implied logical absurdities. According to those who held this
doctrine, the body of Christ is given with the bread even to
unbelievers. To Calvin this is one of the "absurdities abhorrent
to piety", to which he objects strongly. "Christ is shamefully
lacerated when His body as lifeless and without any vigour is
prostituted to unbelievers."[6] Such a doctrine is "derogatory to
the heavenly glory of Christ".[7]

It is to be noted in this connection that Calvin defends the use
of reason and common sense in judging, as above outlined,
whether a doctrine is to be accepted as part of the Christian
faith or not. In an interesting passage in his controversy with

[1] Inst. 4 : 17 : 24.
[2] C.R. 9 : 107; cf. 9 : 171, 72 f.
[3] C.R. 9 : 74. *Obviis ulnis tale monstrum non amplecti.*
[4] Inst. 4 : 17 : 23.
[5] C.R. 7 : 742–3.
[6] Inst. 4 : 17 : 33; cf. C.R. 9 : 89.
[7] Inst. 4 : 17 : 19; cf. O.S. 1 : 521–2. *Nous aneantissons la gloire de son
ascension.*

Westphal he writes: "Three kinds of reason are to be considered. There is a reason naturally implanted which cannot be condemned without insult to God, but it has its limits which it cannot overstep without being immediately lost. Of this we have sad proof in the fall of Adam. . . . There is another kind of reason which is vicious, especially in a corrupt nature, and is manifested when mortal man, instead of receiving divine things with reverence, would subject them to his own judgment. . . . In regard to the heavenly mysteries, we must adjure this reason. . . . But there is a third kind of reason which both the Spirit of God and the Scripture sanction."[1] It is this "third kind of reason" which should here be exercised to prove whether a statement of doctrine has passed beyond the limits of mystery into the realms of absurdity, and whether any statement of doctrine is in conformity with the rest of the Christian faith. It is with this kind of reason that we must interpret the words of institution of the sacrament, so that we do not through sheer literalism make nonsense of the sacred rite. "I admit it to be impious curiosity to scrutinise the mysteries of God, which lie beyond the reach of our reason; but we must prudently distinguish between different kinds of questions. For in what labyrinth shall we be involved if, without taking care to avoid absurdity, we seize at random on everything that is said."[2]

(iv) Conformity with the rule of faith observed

Calvin states that his aim in expounding the Lord's Supper as he does is "to make the sacred ordinance of the supper conformable to the rule of faith".[3] By this phrase he no doubt means to express his concern that no one doctrine should assert anything contradictory to any other part of the faith, and that the interpretation of any one part of Scripture should be partly determined by what the Scripture teaches as a whole, it being assumed that there is a unity of doctrine throughout the Scripture. It has already been shown how Calvin's view of the New Testament sacraments is largely determined by the use made of signs in

[1]C.R. 9 : 474.
[2]C.R. 9 : 86.
[3]C.R. 9 : 74. Cf. C.R. 9 : 514. *Literalem sensum in his verbis : Hoc est corpus meum, negamus fidei analogon esse.*

Old Testament revelation,[1] and how his views on Christology have also a determining influence in this direction.[2] His concern that the body of Christ should be thought of as remaining localised in heaven and, though glorified, as yet retaining all the normal properties of human nature is partly due to his similar concern to preserve the doctrines of the resurrection of the body and of the second coming of Jesus Christ. The Lutherans asserted that since the body of Christ was glorified the divine attributes of invisibility and omnipresence have been communicated to it, and thus it can be locally present in the sacrament. Calvin argued that, since the resurrection and glorification of the man Jesus was a pattern and first fruits of the resurrection and glorification of all His members, His endowment with a body now immense, invisible and omnipresent would imply such a change in all the redeemed and would make nonsense of the promise that the same Jesus who ascended to heaven shall come in like manner at the last day. "The question is . . . whether credit is to be given to the heavenly oracles which declare that we are to hope for a resurrection which shall make our mean and corruptible body like unto the glorious body of Christ—that the Son of Man shall come on the clouds of heaven to judge the world—that Jesus of Nazareth after ascending to heaven will come in like manner as He was seen to ascend. . . . Let Westphal say whether he thinks that anybody will be immense at the last day. For when Paul asks us to form an estimate of the power of Christ from the fact of His transfiguring our bodies into the same glory, either that power is reduced to nothing or we must believe that the body of Christ is not more immense now than ours will be then."[3] "The immensity which they imagine the flesh of Christ to possess is a monstrous phantom, which overturns the hope of a resurrection. To all the absurdities they advance concerning the heavenly life, I will always oppose the words of St. Paul that we wait for Christ from heaven who will transform our poor body and make it comfortable to His own glorious body. Need we say how absurd it were to fill the whole world with the single body of each believer?"[4]

[1]Cf. pp. 21 ff.
[2]Cf. pp. 167 ff.
[3]C.R. 9 : 79.
[4]C.R. 9 : 33–4. Calvin interprets the accounts of the resurrection appearances

Calvin further maintains, arguing along the same line of thought, that such inclusion of Christ's body in the elements is inconsistent with the doctrine that Christ is true man as well as true God. To maintain "local presence" implies "either that the body of Christ is without limit or that it may be in different places . . . that is, that it is a mere phantom". Calvin calls this "a damnable error . . . destructive of what we ought to hold in regard to His human nature".[1] "Let no property be assigned to the body inconsistent with His human nature."[2]

(v) *A true eschatological tension maintained*

One of the great merits of Calvin's doctrine in comparison with that of his Lutheran opponents is the fact that he leaves room for a more significant eschatology than would be possible on the assumptions of his opponents. For the Lutherans the ascension of Christ did not imply His removal from this earth to another place beyond this earth. The ascension was to them merely a symbol for the "majesty of empire" which He assumed.[3] It was merely a "change of mortal state"[4] through which Jesus became invisible and omnipresent but not removed from this earth. On this view, of course, the second coming is merely the re-assumption of a visible shape. "He will come in visible form" is the argument of the Lutherans, "though He never departed from the earth, but remained invisible among the people".[5] Calvin, on the other hand, following on his insistence that Heaven is a place removed from this earth,[6] sees the ascension more clearly as the judgment of this world, and as an event

of our Lord accordingly. He does not approve, for example, of that suggestion that Christ's resurrection body could become invisible, or penetrate closed doors, or assume a variety of forms, or resemble a spirit. The apparent invisibility was due to the eyes of the beholders being "holden". The risen Jesus was no less able to open the doors than he was to roll away the stone from the tomb. The body had not changed its nature so that it had ceased to be what it was. Cf. Inst. 4 : 17 : 29; comm on Luke 24 : 31, 39, C.R. 45 : 809, 813; comm. on John 20 : 19, C.R. 47 : 436; C.R. 9 : 214.

[1] O.S. 1 : 521. *Un erreur damnable . . . et detruisant ce que nous devons tenir de sa nature humaine.*

[2] Inst. 4 : 17 : 19. *Ne quid eius corpori affingatur humanae naturae minus consentaneum.*

[3] Inst. 4 : 17 : 27.

[4] Inst. 4 : 17 : 26. *Mutationem mortalis status.*

[5] Inst. 4 : 17 : 27.

[6] Cf. pp. 204 f.

pointing man to a destiny beyond and above this world. Henceforth the expectation of Christ's people must be set on a Kingdom that will come from beyond this world, as if the angels had said, "It remains for you to wait patiently until He again arrive to judge the world. He has not entered heaven to occupy it alone but to gather you and all the pious along with Him."[1] The ascension for Calvin is the assumption by Christ of a Kingdom that far transcends the limits of this earth and which yet includes this earth in its scope.[2] The second coming therefore means for Calvin a far more world-shattering and world-transcending event than merely the visible revelation of what has been present in this world all the time in a hidden way. It is the breaking into this world of a Kingdom that is indeed from beyond.

Therefore Calvin insists that Christ has indeed gone away from this earth, and His doctrine of the Supper is such as to safeguard the reality of the ascension and the true heavenly glory and dignity of the body of Christ. The gift of the Holy Spirit was poured out upon the Church as a substitute for the presence of Christ "to supply the defect of His absence".[3] Through the Holy Spirit the members of Christ are already introduced into the heavenly glory of His Kingdom in being ingrafted into His body, and a pledge is given of an inheritance which is beyond and which must be waited for continually in hope, though it is nevertheless being at present enjoyed. Thus Calvin, through his emphasis on the exalted state of the ascended Christ, and on the work of the Holy Spirit, preserved the eschatological emphasis which should undoubtedly be found in any true doctrine of the Lord's Supper.

2. Calvin's doctrine determined by his views on the nature of the sacraments

It has been pointed out[4] that when God, in revealing Himself, gives signs of His presence, it is always intended that the minds of the spectators should be directed away from the sign to the

[1]Inst. 4 : 17 : 27.
[2]Inst. 2 : 16 : 14; cf. Inst. 4 : 17 : 18.
[3]Inst. 4 : 17 : 26.
[4]See pp. 78 ff.

divine reality which is never to be thought of as in any way attached to the sign. Thus on the signs and wonders done by the Apostles Calvin comments, "For this cause are they called signs, because the Lord will not have men's minds stay there but to be lifted higher; as they are referred to another end."[1] Similarly, the sacraments are means by which God "comes down to us" in order to invite us into communion with Himself, and "aids which He holds out"[2] so that our minds may be led to seek Him aright. But the purpose of God in extending to us these aids is that we may raise our thoughts far above such aids, "that our minds may not grovel upon the earth",[3] and the purpose of God in "coming down" through the sacraments into the midst of our world is that we may be "raised up" spiritually to heaven for a communion that transcends our earthly existence. Thus the sacraments are signs that point to God as beyond themselves. They are ladders by which the soul of man is enabled to "mount upwards". "It is true that by them God comes down to us, but that is not to hold us still down below, but to make us fly up to Him."[4] "He holds out to us in the sacraments an image both of His grace and spiritual blessings, yet this is done with no other intention than to lead us upwards to Himself."[5] "By the corporeal things which are produced in the sacrament we are by a kind of analogy conducted to spiritual things."[6]

The ascension of Jesus is thus, for Calvin, decisive in illuminating the meaning of the sacraments. The ascension declared plainly that Christ is to be thought of by His people as dwelling above the earth, and that communion with Him is an event in which the soul of man is made to transcend supernaturally the limits of earthly existence. On the words of Jesus, *I ascend to my Father*, Calvin comments, "By using the word *ascend* he confirms the doctrine which I have lately explained; that He rose from the dead not for the purpose of remaining any longer on

---

[1]Comm. on Acts 2 : 22, C.R. 48 : 37–8. *Signa autem ideo vocantur, quia Dominus mentes hominum ibi fixas haerere non vult, sed altius attolli : sicuti in alium finem referuntur.*

[2]Cf. comm. on Isa. 37 : 16, C.R. 36 : 627.

[3]Ibid.

[4]Serm. on Deut. 4 : 15, C.R. 26 : 158.

[5]Comm. on Isa. 40 : 20, C.R. 37 : 20. *Quamvis autem et gratiae suae et bonorum spiritualium imaginem nobis obiiciat in sacramentis, non alio tamen spectat, quam ut sursum ad se nos invitet.*

[6]Inst. 4 : 17 : 3. . . . *Quadam analogia nos ad spirituales deduci.*

the earth but that He might enter into the heavenly life. There is great emphasis on the word *ascend*; for Christ stretches out His hand to His disciples that they may not seek their happiness anywhere else than in heaven; for *where our treasure is, there must also our heart be* (Matt. 6 : 21). Now Christ declares that He *ascends* on high; and therefore we must *ascend*, if we do not wish to be separated from Him."[1] The sacraments are instituted that we may be able to *ascend*, in order, by the grace of Christ, to attain this communion. "We teach that if believers would find Christ in heaven, they must begin with the Word and Sacraments. We turn their view to Baptism and the Supper that in this way they may rise to the full height of celestial glory. Thus Jacob called Bethel the gate of heaven, because aided by the vision he did not fix down his mind on earth, but learned to penetrate by faith to heaven."[2] "Our Lord in instituting the sacrament by no means surrounded us with impediments to confine us to the world. He rather set up ladders by which we might scale upwards to the heavens."[3] "God who helps our infirmity by these aids also gives faith which, elevated by proper ladders, may climb to Christ and obtain His grace."[4]

Hence any doctrine of the sacraments that fixes the attention of men on the elements, thus "withdrawing the minds of men from heaven" and preventing this lifting up of the hearts of the participants, is a triumph for the "wiles of Satan", who wishes nothing more than to tie the minds of men to earthly things and to prevent them from rising into true communion with God.[5] This consideration is decisive with Calvin, in making him reject the doctrines of his opponents which caused men to "stop short at the external sign" and thus stray from the right path of seeking Christ".[6] "Have done, then, with that foolish fiction which affixes the minds of men as well as Christ to bread."[7] The

[1]Comm. on John 20 : 18, C.R. 47 : 435.

[2]C.R. 9 : 84. . . . *Visione adiutus non in terra mentem defixit : sed didicit fide in coelum penetrare.*

[3]C.R. 9 : 22.

[4]C.R. 9 : 25. . . . *Fidem etiam dare, quae idoneis fulturis subnixa ad Christum conscendat, ut eius gratiis potiatur.*

[5]Inst. 4 : 17 : 12.

[6]Inst. 4 : 17 : 36. *Qui in signo externo detinentur, a recta quaerendi Christi via aberrant.*

[7]Inst. 4 : 17 : 29. *Facessat igitur stultum illud commentum, quod tam mentes hominum, quam Christum pane affigit.*

tragedy is that the mind of the natural man in its perversity
takes kindly to those Satanic doctrines which fix Christ to the
earthly elements.[1] "Those who call themselves Christians have
never left off looking for Him here below. And because of this,
people look for Jesus Christ inside the bread and wine. They
want to shut Him up in a box, and to carry Him here and there,
and to play with Him like a doll. How do such superstitions
arise, if not from the fact that our nature has a downward
tendency, like a stone? And when I say this, I mean that we
want to drag God down at the same time, with all that we know
of Him, and we want Him to be like ourselves."[2]

The minds of the participants in the Supper must be continually roused out of this fatal downward propensity. That is
why Calvin mentions with approval the custom of the ancient
Fathers previous to the consecration of the elements of calling
aloud upon the people to lift up their hearts—"Sursum Corda"[3]
—so that the minds of the people should not "stop at the visible
sign". "It is a foolish and destructive madness to draw Him down
from heaven by any carnal consideration, so as to seek Him upon
earth. Up, then, with our hearts, that they may be with the
Lord!"[4] It is obvious that Calvin feels that his doctrine is in
line with true Catholic practice as embodied in the central act
of the ancient liturgical custom.[5]

3. Calvin's view of the "communication of properties"
in relation to his doctrine of the Lord's Supper

Calvin, as we have seen, consistently denies that in the Person
of Christ there is any fusion of the two natures, insisting always
that each nature retains entire that which is proper to itself.
Nothing is more abhorrent to him than the idea that the man-

---

[1]Cf. pp. 69; 78.

[2]Serm. on Acts 1 : 9–11, C.R. 48 : 616.

[3]Inst. 4 : 17 : 36. Cf. O.S. 1 : 522. *Pour denoter qu'on ne se devoit arrester
au signe visible.*

[4]Comm. on Phil. 3 : 20, C.R. 52 : 56. Cf. C.R. 12 : 728. "What then is
the sum of our doctrine? It is this, that when we discern here on earth the bread
and wine, our minds must be raised to heaven in order to enjoy Christ, and that
Christ is there present with us (*ac tum praesentem nobis esse Christum*) while we
seek Him above the elements of this world."

[5]Cf. on p. 244.

hood of Christ should become absorbed in the divinity, or that the flesh of Christ should be thought to assume the attributes of divinity and thus become capable of infinite extension in order to be invisibly present everywhere. "No one except Eutyches," he writes in the dedicatory preface to his commentary on Jeremiah, "has hitherto taught that the two natures became so blended that when Christ became man, the attributes of deity were communicated to His human nature." The Lutherans with their "strange notion of ubiquity" have joined Servetus in reviving this mad heresy of confounding heaven and earth.[1]

At the same time, Calvin points out that the Lutheran use of this doctrine of the "communion of properties" from one nature to another is merely the abuse of a doctrine originally invented by the Holy fathers "not without reason",[2] and he cites Biblical passages to show that the Scripture speaks frequently of the one nature of the Person of Christ as being involved in activities and events that seem mainly the concern of the other nature. "There is a communication of *idiomata*, or properties, when Paul says that God purchased the Church *with His own blood* (Acts 20 : 28) and that the Jews *crucified the Lord of glory* (2 Cor. 2 : 8). In like manner, John says that the word of God was *handled*. God certainly has no blood, suffers not, cannot be touched with hands; but since that Christ who was true God and true man shed His blood on the cross for us, the acts which were performed in His human nature are transferred improperly, but not inappropriately, to His divinity. We have a similar example in the passage where John says that God laid down His life for us (1 John 3 : 16). Here a property of His humanity is communicated with His other nature."[3] This legitimate use of the "communicatio idiomatum" doctrine has some bearing on Calvin's doctrine of the Lord's Supper, and an understanding of it on our part can undoubtedly help us to understand His way of speaking about the sacrament. He himself was so influenced by his sense of the indivisible unity of the Person of Christ that

---

[1]Inst. 4 : 17 : 30.
[2]Inst. 4 : 17 : 30; cf. C.R. 20 : 72 ff.
[3]Inst. 2 : 14 : 2. *Quae in humana eius natura peracta sunt, ad divinitatem improprie, licet non sine ratio, transferuntur. Simile est exemplum, ubi Iohannes docet, Deum posuisse animam suam pro nobis. Ergo et illic humanitatis proprietas cum altera natura communicatur.*

in thought and in speech he is able without any difficulty to attribute to the human nature what belongs to the divine nature. Though insisting that the whole man Christ since His resurrection remains entire in heaven, Calvin can nevertheless at the same time speak of Him as being on earth, and indeed he can speak almost as if the body of Christ were present on earth, since wherever the divinity is present there the whole Christ can be spoken of as present. He quotes with approval the saying of Lombard, "Although the whole Christ is everywhere, yet everything which is in Him is not everywhere,"[1] and also the saying of Augustine, "One person is God and man, and both one Christ, everywhere inasmuch as He is God, and in heaven, inasmuch as He is man."[2]

It is obvious that in making such quotations he is justifying the assertion that the whole humanity of Christ, though now remaining in heaven, can nevertheless exert its virtue on earth and can indeed be spoken of as active upon the earth. "It is unlawful to dissever the flesh of Christ from His divinity. Wherever the divinity dwells, the flesh also dwells corporeally. But the deity of Christ always dwells in believers as well in life as in death; therefore so dwells the flesh. . . . I again repeat, as the divine majesty and essence of Christ fills heaven and earth, and this is extended to the flesh; therefore independently of the use of the Supper, the flesh of Christ dwells essentially in believers, because they possess the presence of His deity."[3] In connection with this argument Calvin can quote the saying of Jesus to Nicodemus, in which He called Himself *the Son of man who is in heaven.* "Certainly, regarded as man in the flesh which He had put on, He was not then in heaven, but inasmuch as He was both God and man, He, on account of the union of a twofold nature, attributed to the one what properly belonged to the

---

[1]Inst. 4 : 17 : 30. *Quamvis totus Christus ubique sit, non tamen totum, quod in eo est.* Cf. C.R. 9 : 195 and C.R. 20 : 75.

[2]Inst. 4 : 17 : 28. *Una enim persona Deus et homo est, et utrumque unus Christus, ubique per id quod est Deus, in coelo per id quod est homo* (Ep. ad Dardanum).

[3]C.R. 9 : 509. Cf. C.R. 20 : 75. "He, I say, God and man, is everywhere as to His authority and incomprehensible power, and infinite glory. It is not then without reason that Paul declares that He dwells in us. But to distort what is said of His infinite power . . . and to apply it to His flesh, is by no means reasonable."

other."[1] "I confess indeed that we may not conceive the Son of God in any other way than as clothed with flesh. But this did not prevent Him, while filling heaven and earth with His divine essence, from wearing His flesh in the womb of His mother, on the cross, in the sepulchre. Though then Son of God He was, nevertheless man in heaven as well as on earth."[2] It is quite obvious from such passages that Calvin would not have much difficulty in arguing further that Christ can be man on earth, even though His manhood is now confined in its entirety to heaven.

While arguing in this strain, however, Calvin is always ready to point out the significance of the other clauses of the two Patristic quotations which he gives with such warm approval. "Everything which is in Him is not everywhere," says Lombard. "He is in heaven inasmuch as He is man," says Augustine. "Therefore," comments Calvin, "while our whole mediator is everywhere, He is always present with His people, and in the Supper exhibits His presence in a special manner; yet so that while He is wholly present, not everything which is in Him is present because, as has been said, in His flesh He will remain in heaven till He comes in judgment."[3] The saying of Jesus, *Lo I am with you alway*, Calvin holds as referring to His divinity rather than to His humanity,[4] quoting again with approval from Augustine: "Christ in respect of His majesty is always present with believers, but . . . in respect of the presence of His flesh, it was rightly said to His disciples, *me ye have not always*."[5] "Who can be offended," he asks, "when we wish Christ to remain complete and entire in regard to both natures, and the mediator who joins us to God be not torn in pieces?"[6]

A study of such passages makes it easier to understand Calvin's doctrine of the Supper, especially His emphasis on the fact that the flesh of Christ can remain in heaven while exercising its virtue on the earth. The accomplishment of this miracle is the work of the Holy Spirit, but even this event is possible only

[1]Inst. 2 : 14 : 2. . . . *Propter duplicis naturae unionem, alteri dabat quod erat alterius.*
[2]C.R. 9 : 171.
[3]Inst. 4 : 17 : 30.
[4]Cf. Inst. 4 : 17 : 28.
[5]C.R. 9 : 77.
[6]C.R. 9 : 33.

because the divine essence of Christ is everywhere diffused. "By the virtue of His Spirit and His own divine essence, He not only fills heaven and earth, but also miraculously unites us with Himself in one body so that that flesh, although it remain in heaven, is our food. Thus I teach that Christ, though absent in the body, is nevertheless not only present with us by His divine energy, which is everywhere diffused, but also makes His flesh give life to us."[1] "Although all power is committed even to His human nature by the Father, He still would not truly sustain our faith, unless He were God manifested in the flesh. And the fact that the body of Christ is finite, does not prevent Him from filling heaven and earth, because His grace and power are everywhere diffused (*ubique diffusa est eius gratia et virtus*), whence also, Paul being witness, He *ascended into heaven that He might fill all things*."[2]

[1]C.R. 9 : 76.
[2]Comm. on Gen. 28 : 12, C.R. 23 : 391. Cf. O.S. 1 : 142. *Caeterum tametsi carnem suam a nobis sustulit et corpore in coelum ascendit, ad dexteram tamen patris sedet, hoc est, in potentia, maiestate et gloria patris regnat. Hoc regnum nec ullis locorum spatiis limitatum, nec ullis dimensionibus circumscriptum, quin Christus virtutem suam ubicunque placuerit, in coelo et in terra exerat, quin se praesentem potentia et virtute exhibeat, quin suis semper adsit, ut in iis vivat, eos sustineat, confirmet, vegetet, conservet, non secus ac si corpore adesset.*

Chapter XVIII

The Church as the Sphere of Sacramental Action

1. Word and sacraments committed to the Church

I T has already been shown how strongly Calvin held the view
that the Word of God is normally heard by the individual
through the preaching of the minister of the Word exercising
his function in the fellowship of the Church.[1] Calvin is equally
emphatic in stressing the more obvious point that it is to the
Church also that the individual must turn in order to receive the
grace of God which comes through the sacraments. Christ has
bound the Church to Himself organically as His body, and the
life of the Head flows to the members through the ministry of
the Word and Sacrament committed to the Church. To refuse
the gracious ministry of the Church is to refuse to come to the
one sure source of the grace of Christ. "Nothing is more for-
midable than to be rejected from God's flock. For no safety is
to be hoped for except as God collect us into one body under
one head. First, all safety resides in Christ alone; and then we
cannot be separated from Christ without falling away from all
hope of safety; but Christ will not and cannot be torn from His
Church with which He is joined by an indissoluble knot, as the
head of the body. Hence, unless we cultivate unity with the
faithful, we see that we are cut off from Christ."[2] Speaking on
Isaiah's description of the restored Jerusalem as a *quiet habitation*
in which *the people that dwell therein shall be forgiven their iniquity*,
Calvin says: "It is also worthy of observation that none but the
citizens of the Church enjoy this privilege; for, apart from the
body of Christ and the fellowship of the godly, there can be no
hope of reconciliation with God. Hence, in the creed we profess
to believe in *the Catholic Church and the forgiveness of sins*; for

[1]See Ch. VII.
[2]Comm. on Ezek. 13 : 9, C.R. 40 : 281. *Christus non vult nec potest divelli
a sua ecclèsia, cum qua coniunctus est nodo insolubili ut caput cum corpore. Ergo
nisi colamus unitatem cum fidelibus, videmus nos a Christo reiici.* Cf. comm. on
Isa. 54 : 1, C.R. 37 : 269.

God does not include among the objects of His love any but those whom He reckons among the members of His only begotten Son, and, in like manner, does not extend to any who do not belong to His body the free imputation of righteousness. Hence it follows that strangers who separate themselves from the Church have nothing left for them but to rot amidst their curse. Hence, also, an open departure from the Church is an open renouncement of eternal salvation."[1]

So closely does Calvin identify incorporation in Christ with incorporation in the Church that he regards the activity of the Church towards its individual members as being identical with the action of Christ towards the individual. The response of the individual to the ministry of the Church is thus identical with his response towards Christ. Under certain conditions the authority of the Church is nothing less than the authority of Christ Himself, and obedience to Christ involves obedience to the Church. Commenting on Isaiah 45 : 14, Calvin writes: "When he says that the Israelites shall be victorious over all the nations, this depends on the mutual relation between the head and the members. Because the only begotten Son of God unites to Himself those who believe in Him, so that they are one with Him. It frequently happens that what belongs to Him is transferred to the Church which is His body and fullness. In this sense, rule also is attributed to the Church, not so as to obscure by haughty domination the glory of her Head, or even to claim the authority which belongs to Him, or in a word, so as to have anything separate from her Head; but because the preaching of the Gospel which is committed to her is the spiritual sceptre of Christ, by which He displays His power. In this respect no man can bow down submissively before Christ, without also obeying the Church, so far as the obedience of faith is joined to the ministry of doctrine, yet so that Christ their Head alone reigns, and alone exercises His authority."[2]

---

[1]Comm. on Isa. 33 : 24, C.R. 36 : 578. . . . *Discessio ab ecclesia aperta est aeternae salutis abnegatio.*

[2]Comm. on Isa. 45 : 14, C.R. 37 : 140–1. *Quia enim unigenitus Dei filius sic fideles suos sibi associat, ut simul unum sint : saepius quod illius proprium est ad ecclesiam, quae eius corpus est ac complementum, transfertur. Hoc sensu et regimen tribuitur ecclesiae, non ut superba dominatione capitis gloriam obscuret, vel etiam arroget sibi proprium imperium : denique separatum quidquam habeat a suo capite : sed quia evangelii praedicatione, quae apud eam deposita est, spirituale est Christi*

It will be noted from this last quotation that the Church must never assume that Christ has in any way bound Himself to the Church or put Himself at its disposal. The Church can never in any self-confident way claim authority for its rule and efficacy for its sacramental action, for Christ has not bound Himself to the Church. Immediately the Church ceases to have a humble trembling attitude towards the Word of God it ceases to be united to its Head, and the Church has "nothing separate from her Head". But the fact that the Church can often "obscure by haughty rule the glory of her Head" does not alter the main issue. Christ has committed to the Church the ministry of His grace. He has, moreover, attached many of His promises to the Church so that the individual can have no certainty of obtaining salvation and the benefits of His death and resurrection apart from the Church. Understood in this sense, Calvin is ready on all occasions to state clearly his belief that outside of the Church there is no salvation. "They who wish to become partakers of so great a benefit must be a part of Israel, that is, of the Church, out of which there can be neither salvation nor truth."[1] "Such as forsake the Church ... wholly alienate themselves from Christ."[2] In his commentary on Hebrews 10 : 25 Calvin identifies departing from the Church with a "falling away from the living God". On the verse in Isaiah 54 : 13, *All thy children shall be taught of the Lord*, Calvin says, "We see that these two things, *children of the Church* and *taught by God*, are united in such a manner that they cannot be God's disciples who refuse to be taught in the Church."[3]

Calvin, of course, would warn us that as individuals we must not rest our confidence of salvation in the mere fact of belonging to the Church. It is vain to belong to the Church if we have of ourselves no living connection with Christ through faith and prayer. "We are called into the Church in order that we may call

---

sceptrum, quo potentiam suam exserit : hoc modo supplex coram Christo nemo se humiliare potest, quin ecclesiae quoque se addicat, quatenus fidei obedientia cum doctrinae ministerio coniuncta est, sic tamen ut ipsius caput Christus emineat solus, potestamque suam exerceat.

[1] Comm. on Isa. 49 : 7, C.R. 37 : 199. ... *extra quam nec salus nec veritas esse potest.*

[2] Comm. on Heb. 10 : 26, C.R. 55 : 133.

[3] Comm. on Isa. 54 : 13, C.R. 37 : 276. ... *'Nam ecclesiae filii esse non possunt, nisi in ea se educari sinant.*

on God; for in vain do they boast who neglect prayer and true calling upon God, and yet hold a place in the Church."[1] Moreover, Calvin recognises the fact that there might come a stage in the departure of the Church from the Word of God when it would be the duty of men, in order to adhere to the truth of God, to separate themselves from the Church that adhered to error. That Calvin, even while admitting the possible necessity of such a step, was also aware of its seriousness may be judged from the following passage: "Whosoever tears asunder the Church of God, disunites himself from Christ who is the Head, and who would have all His members to be united together. . . . We thus understand that God ought to be sought in order to be rightly worshipped by us; and also that He ought to be thus sought, not that each may have his own peculiar religion, but that we may be united together, and that everyone who sees his brethren going before, and excelling in gifts, may be able to follow them, and to seek benefit from their labours. It is indeed true that we ought to disregard the whole world, and to embrace only the truth of God; for it is a hundred times better to renounce the society of all mortals, and union with them, than to withdraw ourselves from God; but when God shows Himself our leader, the prophet teaches us that we ought mutually to stretch forth our hand, and unitedly to follow Him."[2]

2. The use of the sacraments necessary to the health of the Church and its individual members

How much Christ makes the life and health of the Church depend upon the preached Word has already been shown. As Christ called His Church into being by the Word,[3] continually governs it by the Word,[4] so Calvin refuses to "admit the existence of a Church where we cannot discover the Word of God. For this is the perpetual mark by which our Lord has characterised His people. *Everyone that is of the truth heareth my voice.*"[5]

[1]Comm. on Isa. 56 : 7, C.R. 37 : 300.
[2]Comm. on Zech. 8 : 23, C.R. 44 : 258.
[3]Cf. comm. on Isa. 2 : 3, C.R. 36 : 61 f.
[4]Cf. Inst. 4 : 2 : 4, comm. on John 5 : 24, C.R. 47 : 115.
[5]Inst. 4 : 2 : 4.

But the sacraments are equally essential as marks of a true Church. The Word that must rule and give life to the Church is the Word sealed by two sacraments, Baptism and the Lord's Supper.

Calvin brands it as a "gross error" to suppose, as some of the ancient fathers did, that participation in the sacraments is essential either to salvation, or to communion with the body of Christ. There is an "uninterrupted communication of the flesh of Christ" which we obtain apart from the use of the Lord's Supper.[1] Calvin calls this communion "the perpetual manducation of faith".[2] Jesus' discourse in the sixth chapter of John refers primarily to this ordinary state of communion with the flesh of Christ in which believers stand from day to day, and which the Lord's Supper seals and confirms.

What is given in the sacraments is thus no more than is given through the Word apart from the sacraments, and though it is a serious matter for anyone to be deprived of the use of the sacraments, nevertheless the believer so placed is not beyond the reach of the continual grace of God. "The grace of God is not so inseparably annexed to them (i.e. the sacraments) that we cannot obtain it by faith, according to His Word."[3] In one sense, the sacraments are but signs of a salvation that has already been obtained otherwise than through the sacraments. Thus even Baptism is not essential to salvation. "We must hold that it is not required as absolutely necessary to salvation, so that all who have not obtained it must perish; for it is not added to faith as if it were half the cause of our salvation, but as a testimony."[4]

Nevertheless, when faced with the question of how to use the sacraments, we have no choice but to use them diligently and thankfully[5], for we are "laid under the necessity of not despising

[1]Comm. on John 6 : 53, C.R. 47 : 154. *Perpetua communicatione, quae extra coenae usum nobis constat.*

[2]Comm. on John 6 : 54, C.R. 47 : 155. *Perpetua fidei manducatio.* Cf. Inst. 4 : 17 : 5. Cf. serm. on Isa. 53 : 11, C.R. 35 : 671. *Ainsi donc apprenons de priser la cognoissance de l'Evangile mieux que nous ne faisons pas : et cognoissons que c'est pour nous faire participans de la mort et passion de nostre Seigneur Jesus Christ. Car nous sommes entez en son corps, nous sommes faits ses membres, et tout ce qu'il ha nous est fait commun, et nous est approprié par l'Evangile.*

[3]Inst. 4 : 15 : 22. *Non sic illis alligata est Dei gratia quin eam fide ex verbo Domini consequamur.* Cf. C.R. 9 : 29.

[4]Comm. on Mark 16 : 16, C.R. 45 : 824. . . . *Neque enim hic fidei adiungitur tanquam dimidia salutis causa sed ut testimonium.*

[5]Cf. C.R. 9 : 29.

the sign of the grace of God",[1] and in this sense the observance of the sacraments is a necessary obligation laid upon us—an obligation for which there must be a corresponding need. Calvin's logic is irrefutable. God commands the use of the sacraments. He would command nothing that was superfluous or vain. Therefore the sacraments are necessary. God has promised His grace along with the use of the sacraments. No man dare neglect the offered grace of God without condemnation. Therefore, the diligent use of the sacraments is necessary. "If God chooses to add anything to His Word, it ought not to be regarded as a virtue to reject this addition as superfluous. It is no small insult offered to God, when His goodness is despised in such a manner as if His proceeding towards us were of no advantage, and as if He did not know what it is that we chiefly need. . . . We ought indeed to grieve and lament, that the sacred truth of God needs assistance on account of the defect of the flesh, but since we cannot remove this defect, anyone who according to his capacity shall believe the Word, will immediately render full obedience to God. Let us, therefore, learn to embrace the signs along with the Word, since it is not in the power of man to separate them."[2]

Thus Calvin can speak in the strongest terms about the necessity of being baptised. "It is true that, by neglecting Baptism, we are excluded from salvation; and in this sense I acknowledge that it is necessary; but it is absurd to speak of salvation as being confined to the sign."[3] The fact that any man would neglect the sign of Baptism is itself a sign that he is far from being united to Christ. Calvin looks on it as a most serious sin for a Christian parent to deny to a child the sign of Baptism. "Whoever, having neglected Baptism, feigns himself to be contented with the bare promise, tramples, as much as in him lies, upon the blood of Christ, or at least does not suffer it to flow for the washing of His own children. Therefore, just punishment follows the contempt of the sign, in the privation of grace; because, by an impious severance of sign and Word, the covenant

---

[1]Comm. on Mark 16 : 16, C.R. 45 : 824.

[2]Comm. on Isa. 7 : 12, C.R. 36 : 152.

[3]Comm. on John 3 : 5, C.R. 47 : 55. *Verum quidem est, baptismi neglectu arceri nos a salute. . . .*

of God is violated."[1] What Calvin says about the necessity of
Baptism can equally be transferred to his views on the Lord's
Supper. Referring to the latter sacrament, he can write, "It is a
perilous thing to have no certainty on an ordinance the understanding of which is so requisite for our salvation."[2] To reject
the sacraments is therefore to reject the Word. "Fanatics of the
present day disregard Baptism and the Lord's Supper and consider them childish elements. They can not do so without at
the same time neglecting the whole Gospel; for we must not
separate those things which the Lord has commanded us to
join."[3]

When it comes to discussing the practical utility of sacraments
Calvin has much to say. There is "nothing more useful" in the
Church than the Lord's Supper, and this is the reason why from
the beginning the devil has sought to contaminate its observance
by errors and superstitions.[4] Indeed, Calvin is willing to transfer
to the sacraments Paul's title for the Gospel, and to call them the
power of God unto salvation to everyone that believeth.[5] He refers
particularly to three aspects of their usefulness. Firstly, they
assist spiritual growth by uniting us more fully to Christ the
more they are used by faith. "In so far as we are assisted by
their instrumentality in cherishing, and confirming, and increas-
ing, the true knowledge of Christ so as both to possess Him more
fully, and enjoy Him in all His richness, so far are they effectual
in regard to us. This is the case when that which is offered is
received by us in true faith."[6] In the Supper our communion
with Christ is "confirmed and increased; for, although Christ is
exhibited to us both in Baptism and in the Gospel, we do not,
however, receive Him entire but in part only."[7] Secondly, they

[1]Comm. on Gen. 17 : 14, C.R. 23 : 244. . . . *Ita signi contemptum sequitur
iusta poena, gratiae privatio, quia impio signi et verbi divortio, vel potius laceratione
violatur Dei foedus.*
[2]O.S. 1 : 503. *C'est une chose fort perileuse que de n'avoir nulle certitude de ce
mystere, duquel l'intelligence est tant requise à nostre salut.*
[3]Comm. on Isa. 7 : 12, C.R. 36 : 152.
[4]O.S. 1 : 517. *Nostre Seigneur n'avoit rien laissé plus utile à son Esglise que
ce saint Sacrement.*
[5]C.R. 9 : 182.
[6]Inst. 4 : 14 : 16. *Quantum igitur tum ad veram Christi notitiam in nobis
fovendam, confirmandam, augendam, tum ad eum plenius possidendum, fruendasque
eius divitias, illorum ministerio adiuvamur, tantum apud nos efficaciae habent : id
autem ubi quod illic offertur, vera fide suscipimus.* Cf. Inst. 4 : 17 : 33; C.R. 9: 114.
[7]C.R. 6 : 126. . . . *Eum tamen non recipimus totum sed ex parte tantum.*

confirm and increase the faith of believers, which, once engendered, is so continually beset by temptation to doubt and by manifold difficulties that it requires to be continually supported and continually purged from unbelief.[1] Those who possess Christ by faith must persevere in faith so that Christ may be a perpetual possession.[2] The sacraments assist in such perfecting and perseverence of faith, and, in so doing, again assist growth in Christ. "Faith is not without Christ; but inasmuch as faith is confirmed and increased by the sacraments, the gifts of God are confirmed in us, and thus Christ in a manner grows in us, and we in Him."[3] Thirdly, the sacraments are a spur to practical Christian living. The sacraments bring home to us so vividly the reality and intimacy of our union with the exalted Christ as to lead to practical conduct befitting those who enjoy such high privileges. "There cannot be a spur which can pierce us more to the quick than when He makes us, so to speak, see with the eye, touch with the hand, and distinctly perceive the inestimable blessing of feeding on His own substance."[4] The usefulness of Baptism in this connection has already been dealt with.[5]

In speaking of the Lord's Supper Calvin dwells especially on its power as an incentive to the cultivation of unity and brotherly love. In both sacraments it is true that the common use of the same visible signs helps to unite us and to bring us up "in one faith and in the confession of one faith",[6] but the Lord's Supper is above all a feast of fellowship instituted "especially that we should cultivate charity and concord together as becomes members of the same body".[7] Christ intended the Supper "to be an exhortation than which no other could urge or animate us more

---

[1]Cf. Inst. 4 : 14 : 7 ff.

[2]Cf. comm. on Heb. 3 : 14, C.R. 55 : 43. *Verum si fide possidetur, in ea perstandum est, ut nobis perpetua maneat possessio.*

[3]C.R. 7 : 741.

[4]O.S. 1 : 510. *Or nous ne sçaurions avoir aiguillon pour nous prendre plus au vif, que quand il nous faict, par maniere de dire, voire à l'oeil, toucher à la main, et sentir evidemment un bien tant inestimable : c'est de nous repaistre de sa propre substance.*

[5]Cf. pp. 186 f.

[6]Inst. 4 : 14 : 19.

[7]O.S. 1 : 511. Cf. O.S. 1 : 413. *Car nul aiguillon ne pouvoit estre donne plus aspre ne plus picquant a esmouvoir et inciter entre nous une mutuelle charite que quand Christ se donnant a nous ne nous convie pas seulement per son exemple a ce que nous nous donnions et exposions mutuellement lun a lautre, mais daultant quil se faict commun a tous il nous faict aussi tous un en soy mesmes.* Cf. p. 215.

strongly both to purity and holiness of life and also to charity, peace and concord. For the Lord there communicated His body so that He may become altogether one with us and we with Him. Moreover, since He has only one body of which He makes us all partakers, we must necessarily, by this participation, all become one body. This unity is represented by the bread which is exhibited in the sacrament. As it is composed of many grains so mingled together that one cannot be distinguished from the other; so ought our minds to be cordially united as not to allow any dissension or division."[1]

3. The celebration of the sacraments in the Church

Since the sacraments are the institution not of man but of Christ, it is important that the form in which they are celebrated in the Church should be as closely related to the original form of institution as possible.

(i) The sacraments in their celebration should be *subordinated to the Word*. The sacraments should not be celebrated without a Word giving "a full explanation of the ordinance and clear statement of the promises".[2] There must be no "muttering and gesticulating like sorcerers" by ministers who "think to persuade Jesus Christ to come down into their hands".[3] If this Word is lacking, the "proper and principal substance of the Supper is wanting",[4] for in the celebration of the sacraments the people must be led to "look not to the bare signs but rather to the promise thereto annexed",[5] and no one must be allowed to "stand gazing on the elements".[6] Therefore a "voice must be distinctly heard throughout proclaiming that we must adhere to none but Christ alone",[7] and the visible ceremony must not be allowed so to obtrude on the consciousness of the participants that they

---

[1] Inst. 4 : 17 : 38.
[2] O.S. 1 : 524.
[3] O.S. 1 : 524. *Pourtant leur consecration n'est qu'une espece de sorcelerie, vue que à la maniere des sorciers, en murmurant et faisant beaucoup de signes, ilz pensent contraindre Jesus Christ de descendre entre leurs mains.*
[4] Ibid.
[5] C.R. 7 : 738.
[6] C.R. 7 : 739. *In elementis non obstupescendum.*
[7] Ibid.

become taken up with the dramatic and spectacular vividness of the ceremony taking place before their eyes rather than with the meaning of the simple action through which the Lord is seeking to speak to them.

Therefore it is preferable that before the celebration of the sacraments a sermon should be preached, for the Word should be "not as pronounced but as understood".[1] It is from the Word "when it is preached intelligibly" that the sacraments derive their virtue.[2] It is important therefore that the minister in the celebration of the sacrament should remember the subordinate position of the sign to the Word in God's self-revealing activity. "If the sign be not seasoned with the promise, being insipid in itself it will be of no avail. For what can a man of mortality and earth do by pouring water on the heads of those whom he baptises, if Christ does not pronounce from above that He washes their souls by His blood and renews them by His Spirit? What will the whole company of the faithful gain by tasting a little bread and wine, if the voice does not echo from heaven that the flesh of Christ is spiritual food, and His blood is truly drunk? We therefore truly conclude, that it is not at all by the material of water and bread and wine that we obtain possession of Christ and His spiritual gifts, but that we are conducted to Him by the promise, so that He makes Himself ours and, dwelling in us by faith, fulfils whatever is promised and offered us by the signs."[3]

(ii) The sacraments should be celebrated in *a simple and close adherence to the original form of institution.*

Calvin, in collaboration with others, published in 1542 forms of prayer for the Church in Geneva. Amongst these there is a section entitled "La maniere d'administre les Sacremens selon la coustume de l'eglise ancienne".[4] This title indicates that Calvin, in drawing up his order of service, had in mind the pattern set by the ancient liturgies, and it has been pointed out[5] that if this order for the Supper is taken in conjunction with the ordinary morning service which it was designed to follow, then

---

[1]Cf. O.S. 1 : 524. *La parolle, non pas d'autant qu'elle est prononcée, mais entendue.* (This is from Augustine Tract 80, in Ioan.)
[2]Ibid. Cf. Inst. 4 : 17 : 39.
[3]C.R. 9 : 21–2.
[4]C.R. 6 : 193 ff.
[5]Lecerf: *Etudes Calvinistes*, pp. 45 ff.

the whole form corresponds in general outline, and in many details, to the form always followed in the Church for the celebration of the mystery. The approach begins with invocation, confession of sin, singing of Psalm, prayer for illumination, sermon, prayer of intercession, closing with a prayer based on the Lord's Prayer. This is followed by a repetition of the Apostle's Creed, and a prayer of approach specially relevant to Communion. Then come the words of institution followed by solemn warnings against unworthy participation, and an exhortation to communicants to examine themselves and seek salvation in Christ alone, this part corresponding to the "Sancta sanctis". Then follows a paragraph beginning with an exhortation to the people to "raise their hearts and minds on high where Jesus Christ is, in the glory of His Father, and whence we look for Him at our redemption", certain doctrinal considerations being added to this end. This latter part corresponds to the "Sursum Corda". The distribution of the elements immediately follows. The post-communion takes the normal form of thanksgiving, dedication and blessing.

In the 1545 edition of this work there are indications that more Psalms magnifying the majesty of God were sung, and lessons read from the gospel, law and psalms at different points in the service. There is mention of "saincts oblations et offrandes" to testify the gratitude of the people, taken before the prayer of intercession. There is mention that the minister prepares the bread and wine on the table, and it is suggested that on giving the bread the minister should say, "Take, eat the body of Christ who has been delivered to death for you." The deacon repeats the corresponding words with reference to the cup. Moreover, in this later edition there is an even greater stress on the need for admonition and instruction during the service, but all with a view to stirring up the desire of the people for the gift offered and exciting them to gratitude. The Lord's Prayer itself is said instead of the paraphrase of it incorporated in the former edition.

In spite of the apparent care taken to preserve the ancient liturgical structure of the celebration, it seems that Calvin was more anxious to ensure a fitting emotional attitude and intelligent participation on the part of the worshippers than to follow any rigid Church tradition, and that he used the ancient form only because he felt it best served these ends. It is remarkable that the form of celebration suggested in the *Institutes* is extremely simple,[1] and gives no impression that the liturgical details are of much importance.

It will be noted that Calvin gives no prominent place to a prayer of thanksgiving before the distribution of the elements. The whole service is rather to be pervaded with gratitude and punctuated with frequent expressions of praise. Nor is the distribution to be carried out in silence. It is clear from the *Institutes* that a psalm is sung or something read "while the faithful, in order, communicate at the sacred feast, the minister breaking the bread and giving it to the people". Moreover, there is no consecration of the elements recommended. On this point he writes: "As to the opinion entertained by some, that . . . the bread was *consecrated* (*consecratum*) so as to become a symbol of the flesh of Christ, I do not find fault with it, provided that the word *consecrated* be understood aright and in a proper sense. . . . The bread which had been appointed for the nourishment of the body is chosen and sanctified by Christ for a different use, so as to begin to be spiritual food.[2] And this is the *conversion* (*conversio*) which is spoken of by the ancient doctors of the Church."[3] There are many details of ceremony about which Calvin declares himself quite indifferent. "In regard to the external form of the ordinance, whether or not believers are to take in their hands and divide among themselves, or each is to eat what is given him; whether they are to return the cup to the deacon or hand it to their neighbour; whether the bread is to be leavened or unleavened, and the wine red or white is of no consequence. These things are indifferent and left free to the Church, though it is certain that it was the custom in the ancient Church for all to receive into their hand."[4]

[1]Inst. 4 : 17 : 43.

[2]*Panem ergo, qui alendo corpori destinatus erat, eligit ac sanctificat Christus in alium usum, ut spiritualis cibus esse incipiat.*

[3]Comm. on Matt. 26 : 26 f., C.R. 45 : 706; cf. Inst. 4 : 17 : 14. In his serm. on 1 Cor. 10 : 15–18, C.R. 49 : 665–6, Calvin regrets the abuse of the word "consecration" and gives a fine exposition of its true meaning. It is implied here that the consecration of the bread, wine, and water is part of the normal practice of the Church.

[4]Inst. 4 : 17 : 43. In his serm. on 1 Cor. 11 : 2–3, Calvin again refers to this diversity, and admits wide liberty on matters such as the position of the table. He urges that for the sake of love, there should be no change in local

Calvin claims that such a form of celebration is a return to a simple following of the "pure institution of Jesus Christ",[1] as contrasted with the "horrible abuses" and "adulterations" with "pomp, ceremony and gesticulations" prevalent throughout the religious world of His day.[2] He pleads for the "least possible admixture of human invention"[3] in the celebration. Especially does he condemn any tendency to give adoration to the elements or to make processions with the host since "the promises of the Lord extend only to the uses which He has authorised".[4] When Christ instituted the Supper He gave the command to eat the bread, and made no mention of adoring it. We must not divorce the words *This is my body* from the command *Take and eat.*[5] The practice of the Apostolic Church was to communicate "not in adoration but in the breaking of the bread".[6] They "sat down took, and ate".[7] "To prostrate ourselves before the bread of the Supper, and worship Jesus Christ as if He were contained in it, is to make an idol of it rather than a sacrament."[8]

With regard to the form of administration of Baptism Calvin takes up the same attitude. We are to "lay aside all theatrical pomp which dazzles the eyes of the simple, and dulls the minds, and when anyone is to be baptised to bring him forward and to present him to God, the whole Church looking on as witnesses, and praying over him; to recite the confession of faith, in which the chatecumen has been instructed, explain the promises which are given in Baptism, then baptise in the name of the Father, Son, and the Holy Spirit and conclude with prayers and thanksgiving. In this way nothing which is appropriate would be omitted, and the one ceremony, which proceeded from its divine

---

tradition where use and wont is not repugnant to the Word of God. He urges sobriety and humility, uttering a warning against the impetuosity of the human spirit which is ever ready to forge fantastic novelties, so that there is no end to changes once they have begun. (C.R. 49 : 711–3, cf. Inst. 4 : 10 : 30.)

[1] C.R. 6 : 202.

[2] Inst. 4 : 18 : 20.

[3] Ibid.

[4] O.S. 1 : 526. *Les promesses de nostre Seigneur ne s'estendent pas oultre l'usaige qu'il nous a laissé.*

[5] Inst. 4 : 17 : 37.

[6] Inst. 4 : 17 : 35. *Non in adoratione sed in fractione panis.*

[7] Ibid.

[8] O.S. 1 : 522. *C'est en faire un ydole au lieu d'un Sacrement.*

Author, would shine forth most brightly, not being buried or polluted by extraneous observances."[1]

About the question of whether sprinkling can be regarded as a satisfactory substitute for immersion and as a true representation of the grace signified in Baptism Calvin is not greatly troubled. He acknowledges that the original mode of Baptism was "by plunging the whole body beneath the water".[2] But he asserts that "the Church did grant liberty to herself, since the beginning, to change the rites somewhat"[3] in this respect. He asserts his opinion that "whether the person baptised is to be wholly immersed, and whether once or thrice, or whether he is to be sprinkled with water, is not of the least consequence".[4] He urges us on this point not to be "too fastidious"[5] or to divide and "trouble the Church with brawls" over a matter which to him is of no great weight,[6] and which should be determined "according to the diversity of climates".[7] A student of Calvin is bound to doubt whether his carelessness on this matter is consistent with his extreme concern on other like matters, and whether the general substitution of sprinkling for immersion is really adequate to signify the spiritual grace which Calvin in his fine exposition of the meaning of the rite defines as being attached to this sign of death and resurrection. It is of the utmost significance that Calvin makes no attempt to justify the substitution of sprinkling for immersion but merely asserts that it is an unimportant matter.

(iii) *The significance of the sacraments must not be obscured by the introduction of other ceremonies*

Calvin will not allow the introduction into the ritual of the Church of any visible aids to worship or ceremonies other than those that are essential to decency and order in the simple cele-

---

[1]Inst. 4 : 15 : 19. . . . *Sic nihil omitteretur quod ad rem faceret, et una illa ceremonia, quae a Deo auctore profecta est, nullis exoticis sordibus obruta, clarissime effulgeret.*

[2]Comm. on John 3 : 22, C.R. 47 : 69; cf. on Acts 8 : 38.

[3]Comm. on Acts 8 : 38, C.R. 48 : 198. *Quare ab initio libere sibi permisit ecclesia, extra hanc substantiam, ritus habere paululum dissimiles.*

[4]Inst. 4 : 15 : 19. *Caeterum mergaturne totus qui tingitur, idque ter an semel, an infusa tantum aqua aspergatur, minimum refert.*

[5]*Nimium morosi.*

[6]Comm. on Acts 8 : 38, C.R. 48 : 197.

[7]Inst. 4 : 15 : 19.

bration of the sacraments and the straightforward preaching of the Word. It is true that human nature needs to be appealed to in worship through visible rites as well as through the spoken word. We need ritual worship. But, Calvin argues, God has amply provided for our need of visible ritual in the institution of the sacraments, and it would be presumption and ingratitude to seek to improve on what God has instituted. Even with the best intentions, no one dare devise new forms of Church ritual. If the preacher is faithfully expounding the Word of God, and the sacraments are rightly and frequently being administered, no man should need more by which to enable him to grasp Christ, and to be enabled to do that is to be enabled to worship rightly.[1]

There were those in Calvin's day who urged that such simple forms of worship were inadequate and that the Church must appeal to the mind of the common man by means of pictures and images, colour and ceremony. Calvin held strongly, however, that if the ordinary worship of the Church, centring on the preaching of the Word and the sacraments, lost its hold over the "man in the street" the cause for such decline in worship must lie not in the wise institution of such simple forms of worship by God but in the sheer human incompetence of the preacher in the pulpit, and that the restoration of true worship must depend on the restoration of true preaching of the Word and of the pure sacrament. "Let those who would discharge aright the ministry of the Gospel learn not merely to speak or to declaim, but to penetrate the consciences of men, and make them see Christ crucified, and feel the shedding of His blood. When the Church has painters such as these, she no longer needs the dead images of wood and stone, she no longer requires pictures; both of which unquestionably were first admitted to Christian temples when the pastors had become dumb and been converted into mere idols, or when they uttered a few words from a pulpit in such a cold and careless manner that the power and efficacy of

[1]Cf. serm. on Deut. 4 : 15–20. *Or s'il est question d'images visibles, nostre Seigneur nous en a donné tant qu'il cognoist nous estre propre. Quand nous avons le Baptesme, ne voila point une image visible de ce qui est spirituel : c'est assavoir du lavement que nous avons par le sang de nostre Seigneur Jesus Christ, quand nous sommes renouvellez par son sainct Esprit. En la Cene, n'avons nous pas un mistere de ce secret celeste qui nous est là monstré? Mais quoy qu'il en soit, si ne nous faut il point faire image quelconque de l'essence de Dieu. Et pourquoy? Car cela ne nous est point utile.* C.R. 26 : 154.

the ministry were utterly extinguished."[1] "Paul testifies that in the true preaching Christ is *evidently set forth*, and as it were *crucified before our eyes*. To what purpose, then, was the erection of so many crosses of wood and stone, silver and gold, everywhere in the temples, if it had been fully and faithfully inculcated that Christ died that He might bear our curse on the cross? . . . From this simple declaration they might learn more than from a thousand crosses of wood and stone."[2]

It is to be remembered in this connection that under the dispensation of the New Covenant God has given us much simpler forms through which to deal with Himself. Through the very simplicity of those forms, Jesus Christ shines far more clearly than He did under the more complicated, though far more visibly fascinating, forms of the Old Covenant. We must not take the retrograde step of a return to a more involved worship which could only have the effect of obscuring Jesus Christ. "Since Jesus Christ has been manifested in the flesh, doctrine having been much more clearly delivered, ceremonies (figures) have diminished."[3] "We may justly say that the worship of the law was spiritual in its substance, but in respect of its form, it was somewhat earthly and carnal; for the whole of that economy, the reality of which is now fully manifested, consisted of shadows. . . . Whereas now *the vail of the temple has been rent*, nothing is hidden or obscure. There are indeed among us at the present day, some outward exercises of godliness, which our weakness renders necessary, but such is the moderation and sobriety of them that they do not obscure the plain truth of Christ."[4]

If the sacraments, as seals of the Word, are to shine out brightly in their simple purity,[5] then they must be given an exclusive position in the life of the Church, and no extra ceremonies must be invented to take a place alongside them. These two sacraments are the image by which it has pleased God to be represented to His people. We must worship God only in the image of His own choosing. They are the institution of the Lord. It is not for man to seek to improve on what God has ordained. They are

[1]Comm. on Gal. 3 : 1, C.R. 50 : 202–3.
[2]Inst. 1 : 11 : 7.
[3]O.S. 1 : 525.
[4]Comm. on John 4 : 23, C.R. 47 : 89.
[5]Cf. comm. on Acts 8 : 38, C.R. 48 : 198; Inst. 4 : 15 : 19.

the signs and seals of the New Covenant which is a covenant of grace, and man, as a recipient of the grace of God, cannot take the initiative against God. They are the signs of God's presence and men cannot bring God down into their midst by setting up new forms of ritual, however emotionally appealing to the observer. They are the mirror in which we alone can see (though darkly) the face of God, therefore "it becomes us steadily to fix our eyes on this view that it may not be with us as with the Papists, who, by means of the wildest inventions, wickedly transform God into whatever shapes please their fancy, or their brains have conceived".[1] They are the "helps by which God raises us up to His presence, descending from His inconceivable glory to us, and furnishing us on earth with a vision of His heavenly glory";[2] there is no other means by which we can be so raised to heaven. Therefore men have been deprived not only of "the power of making new sacraments in the Church of God"[3] but also of adding unauthorised ceremonies to the sacraments. "For true religion begins with teachableness; when we submit to God and to His Word, it is really to enter on the work of worshipping Him aright. But when the heavenly truth is despised, though men may toil much in outward rites, yet their impiety discovers itself by their contumacy, inasmuch as they suffer not themselves to be ruled by God's authority."[4]

In Calvin's view, nothing could be more dangerous to the spiritual life of the Church than to open the door for the introduction of new ceremonies, however carefully calculated to appeal to the worshipper. He admits a certain amount of necessary ritual in connection with the sacrament. "I mean not to condemn the ceremonies which are subservient to decency and public order, and increase the reverence for the sacrament, provided they are sober and suitable,"[5] but to open the door too widely here is to stand before "an abyss without end or limit"[6] which

---

[1]Comm. on Ps. 27 : 8, C.R. 31 : 676. . . . *Qui Deum erraticis suis figmentis impie transformant, dum ei pro libidine affingunt quascunque in suo cerebro pinxerunt imagines.*

[2]Ibid.

[3]Inst. 4 : 18 : 20.

[4]Comm. on Zeph. 3 : 2, C.R. 44 : 47.

[5]O.S. 1 : 525. *Je n'entens pas de reprouver les ceremonies, lesquels servent à l'honnesteté et ordre publique, et augmentent la reverence du Sacrement, moyennant qu'elles feussent sobres et convenables.*

[6]O.S. 1 : 525. *Abism sans fin et mesure.*

cannot be tolerated. On Jesus' words to the woman at Samaria, *You worship what you know not, we worship what we know*, Calvin comments, "This is a sentence worthy of being remembered, and teaches us that we ought not to attempt anything in religion rashly or at random, because unless there be knowledge, it is not God we worship but a phantom or an idol. All good intentions, as they are called, are struck by this sentence as by a thunderbolt; for we learn from it that men can do nothing but err, where they are guided by their own opinion without the Word or command of God."[1] Later on in the same commentary, remarking on the folly of those who wished to make Jesus a King, he says, "Hence let us learn how dangerous it is in the things of God to neglect His Word, and to contrive anything of our own opinion; for there is nothing which the foolish subtlety of our understanding does not corrupt. . . . Modes of worship regulated according to our fancy, and honours rashly contrived by men, have no other advantage than this that they rob God of His true honour, and pour upon Him nothing but reproach."[2]

To introduce such unnecessary modes of worship is to disfigure the true image by which God has revealed Himself so that we may worship Him. It is to alienate Christ from His Church and to violate the sanctuary of God. "All who oppress the Church with an excessive multitude of ceremonies do what is in their power to deprive the Church of the presence of Christ. I do not stop to examine the vain excuses which they plead, that many persons in the present day have as much need of these aids as the Jews had in ancient times. It is always our duty to enquire by what order the Lord wished His Church to be governed, for He alone knows thoroughly what is expedient for us."[3] "We must take heed, lest we, while seeking to adapt our own inventions to Christ, transfigure Him . . . so that He should not be at

[1]Comm. on John 4 : 22, C.R. 47 : 87. *Memorabilis sententia, qua docemur nihil in religione temere vel fortuito esse tentandum, quia, nisi assit scientia, non iam Deus sed phantasma vel spectrum colitur. Itaque hoc fulmine concidunt bonae omnes intentiones quas vocant : habemus enim, homines nihil posse quam errare, ubi sua eos reget opinio sine verba aut mandata Dei.*

[2]Comm. on John 6 : 15, C.R. 47 : 134–5. Cf. serm. on Deut. 4 : 15–20, C.R. 26 : 148. *Moyse monstre que nous ne devons pas anticiper pour concevoir ce que bon nous semblera : mais qu'il nous faut attendre que Dieu se manifeste. Voila pour un item. Car si les hommes veulent ici lascher la bride à leur raison charnelle, ils se ruineront, ils se rompront le col en se trop hastant.*

[3]Comm. on John 4 : 23, C.R. 47 : 89.

all like Himself."[1] "When I consider the proper end for which Churches are erected, it appears to me more unbecoming their sacredness than I can tell, to admit any other images than those living symbols which the Lord has consecrated by His own Word: I mean Baptism and the Lord's Supper, with the other ceremonies. By these our eyes ought to be more steadily fixed, and more vividly impressed, than to require the aid of any images which the wit of man may devise."[2]

(iv) *The Lord's Supper to be celebrated frequently*

Since the sacraments are to be given such an exclusive place in the life of the Church, it follows that they are to be celebrated with such frequency as will befit their importance, and justify the exclusion of all other ceremonies from a central place in the Church. The visible centre of the Church's worship must not be left as a blank space for long periods of the year. Calvin, accordingly, declares himself in favour of weekly communion. "All this mass of ceremonies being abandoned, the sacrament might be celebrated in the most becoming manner, if it were dispensed to the Church very frequently, at least once a week."[3] "It was not instituted to be received once a year and that perfunctorily (as is now commonly the custom)."[4] He, indeed, goes the length of saying that "we ought always to provide that no meeting of the Church is held without the Word, prayer, the dispensation of the Supper, and alms";[5] and he calls the custom of communication once a year "an invention of the devil".[6] "The practice of all well ordered Churches should be to celebrate the Supper frequently, so far as the capacity of the people will admit."[7]

It may be noted that Calvin in practice was forced to adapt himself to the capacity of the people more than he could have

[1]Comm. on Heb. 8 : 5, C.R. 55 : 99. *Cavendum est, ne dum volumus figmenta nostra Christo aptare, ipsum . . . transfiguremus ; ita ut iam non sit sui similis.*
[2]Inst. 1 : 11 : 13.
[3]Inst. 4 : 16 : 43.
[4]Inst. 4 : 16 : 44.
[5]Ibid.
[6]Inst. 4 : 16 : 45.
[7]O.S. 1 : 515. *Ceste coustume doibt estre en toutes Eglises bien ordonnées, de celebrer souvent la Cene tant que la capacité du peuple le peut porter.*

wished. In the "Articles on Church Organisation and Worship at Geneva" of 1537, which were drafted by him for the Council, he sets forth his view that the Holy Supper should be celebrated at least every Sunday, having regard to the comfort it can minister and the spiritual fruitfulness which is engendered in every way in the Church by its frequent use.[1] But, he concedes, "since the infirmity of the people is still such that there is danger that this holy and excellent mystery might be brought into contempt if it were celebrated too often . . . it has seemed good to us that the Holy Supper should be celebrated once a month".[2] Later on, in 1541, after his return to Geneva, he further gave in to the weakness of human nature and agreed to a celebration four times a year, viz. Christmas, Easter, Pentecost and the first Sunday of September.[3]

[1]O.S. 1 : 370.
[2]O.S. 1 : 371.
[3]C.R. 10 : 25.